Avenues of Transformation

Avenues OF TRANSFORMATION

ILLINOIS'S PATH FROM TERRITORY TO STATE

James A. Edstrom

Southern Illinois University Press
Carbondale

Southern Illinois University Press
www.siupress.com

Printed in the United States of America

25 24 23 22 4 3 2 1

Cover illustration: John Melish map of Illinois 1818. *Map provided courtesy of the Map Library at the University of Illinois at Urbana-Champaign.*

LIBRARY OF CONGRESS CATALOGING-IN-PUBLICATION DATA

Names: Edstrom, James A., 1962– author.
Title: Avenues of transformation : Illinois's path from territory to state / James A. Edstrom.
Other titles: Illinois's path from territory to state
Identifiers: LCCN 2021059670 (print) | LCCN 2021059671 (ebook) | ISBN 9780809338764 (paperback) | ISBN 9780809338771 (ebook)
Subjects: LCSH: Illinois—History—19th century. | Statehood (American politics) | Cook, Daniel Pope, 1795–1827. | Pope, Nathaniel, 1784–1850. | Kane, Elias Kent, 1794–1835.
Classification: LCC F545 .E245 2022 (print) | LCC F545 (ebook) | DDC 977.3/03—dc23/eng/20211208
LC record available at https://lccn.loc.gov/2021059670
LC ebook record available at https://lccn.loc.gov/2021059671

Printed on recycled paper ♻

SIU
Southern Illinois University System

CONTENTS

ACKNOWLEDGMENTS

The life of a professional librarian is punctuated by a thousand queries great and small, from "Where's the restroom?" to "Are carpet beetles edible?" Each represents a discrete learning opportunity, but—for myself—none has been more momentous than a phone call I received in the fall of 1987 when I was director of the Champaign County Historical Archives at the Urbana Free Library in Urbana, Illinois. "Is it true," the patron asked, "that the northern boundary of Illinois was originally supposed to be located at the southern tip of Lake Michigan?" I answered promptly—as I always do—"Gee, I don't know. Let me look it up and I'll get back to you."*

Thus began the journey that led to this book. That semester I was beginning my second master's degree at the University of Illinois at Urbana-Champaign with a course on Illinois history. I devoted an entire research paper to the subject of Illinois statehood, ultimately transforming it into my master's thesis under the wise guidance of Dr. Robert M. McColley, who was the first to suggest that I write a book. I said I'd think about it. I just never expected I'd take thirty years to do it.

During that time I have received generous advice and assistance from friends, family, and countless scholars and research institutions. I am grateful to Dr. McColley for pointing me in the right direction all those years ago, and to the late Dr. Robert M. Sutton and the late Dr. J. Alden Nichols from the University of Illinois at Urbana-Champaign for many years of sound advice and thorough mentoring. Dr. Ann Durkin Keating from North Central College in Naperville, Illinois, read my early drafts and provided invaluable feedback, as did my colleague Professor David Richmond in the Harper College History Department. Cheryl Schnirring, Debbie Hamm, Michelle Miller, and Megan Klintworth at the Abraham Lincoln Presidential Library in Springfield were instrumental in providing me with access to numerous images and manuscript

* In case you're wondering—the answer is "yes." But keep reading anyway.

documents. John Hoffman of the Illinois Historical Survey at the University of Illinois at Urbana-Champaign was a helpful source of research advice. Jenny Marie Johnson of the university's Map & Geography Library provided me with valuable input on historical maps. The staff of the Illinois State Archives in Springfield and the Legislative Research Center of the National Archives in Washington, D.C., guided me to many manuscript collections that were integral to my research. Tony Pawlyn of the National Maritime Museum Cornwall and Angela Broome of the Royal Institution of Cornwall in Falmouth provided me with tremendously useful background information on transatlantic shipping in the early nineteenth century. And I want to particularly thank the Chicago History Museum, the Massachusetts Historical Society, and the New York Historical Society for their kind permission to quote from documents in their collections.

I am also grateful to numerous friends and family for their input and support. Many of them read my manuscript and provided useful insights from a layperson's perspective, including Carl Kadie, Nanci Vaeth, my brothers Tom and Jeff, and the late Nancy J. (Vick) Edstrom. My fellow Harper College Library faculty and my dean, Njambi Kamoche, were a never-ending source of encouragement. And special thanks to my children, Natalie, Amanda, Nick, and Drew for their love and tolerance (not necessarily in that order) during the writing of this book. Finally, I am thankful to the anonymous reviewers—known but to God and Southern Illinois University Press—who provided constructive criticism and sound advice for improving my narrative. Rosy Fitzgerald, intern and editorial assistant at the press, contributed mightily to ensuring the book's successful production. And most of all—I am grateful to my editor, Jennifer Egan, who patiently guided me through the editing process to produce my final manuscript. Her editorial voice resounds throughout every page of this book.

This book is dedicated to my parents, Helen M. (Klotnia) Edstrom and Eric U. Edstrom Jr., who taught me that learning is a journey of discovery for the teacher and the student alike.

(P.S. Sorry that law school didn't work out. Everything's cool now. I promise.)

Avenues of Transformation

PROLOGUE: TWO CEMETERIES

Six miles northwest of Chester, Illinois, not far from St. Louis, a series of green bluffs overlooks the Mississippi River to the west. Atop these bluffs, shallow mounds of earth mark the rough outlines of what was once Fort Gage (also known as Fort Kaskaskia), erected in 1734. Only a few historical markers placed by the Illinois Historic Preservation Agency remain to testify that this site was once part of a line of French colonial military fortifications in Illinois stretching from Fort Massac near modern-day Cairo to Fort de Chartres near Prairie du Rocher.

Melancholy and isolation settle uneasily on the place, a mood underscored by the presence of the Garrison Hill Cemetery, one of the last vestiges of old Kaskaskia, the first capital of Illinois. Neat rows of crosses and headstones mark the final resting place of some three thousand pioneers. In life Bakers and Baronowskys, Colberts and DeRousses, Heckmans, Maxwells, and Morrisons once mingled and built a community together; now they molder away within a few inches of each other. Here lie hardy farmers such as George Colbert and Antoine LaBrier, the cooper Owen Cullen, and the miller Daniel Reily.[1] The state's first lieutenant governor—dark-eyed, elegant, kind-hearted Pierre Menard—is likewise buried here. Governor John Reynolds wrote of him: "The 'milk of human kindness' never reigned more triumphant in any heart than it did in his."[2]

For many years these departed pioneers lay at rest within strolling distance of their living haunts. But time and tide, geography and circumstance conspired to alter the landscape of the living and the dead alike. Kaskaskia—the first capital of the Illinois Country and a major social, commercial, political, and cultural center of early French and American settlement in the Midwest—is today largely forgotten, if not altogether deserted. Over much of the nineteenth century Illinois's spheres of political and commercial influence gravitated to successive state capitals in Vandalia and Springfield and to industrial and transportation centers such as Alton, East St. Louis, Galena, Galesburg,

Bloomington, Jacksonville, De Kalb, Rockford, and—looming above all else—Chicago. In the face of such geographic and demographic crosscurrents, Kaskaskia's population dwindled to only fourteen inhabitants by the time of the 2010 federal census.[3]

But the town's decline is not only the end result of a Prairie State awash in waves of settlement primarily to the north and to the east. Ultimately Kaskaskia's geography was its destiny. Illinois's first capital had been erected on a peninsula that jutted out between the Mississippi and Kaskaskia (or Okaw[4]) Rivers, which enabled watercraft to approach the town at any stage of the river and remain safely there throughout the winter. The Mississippi, however, is given to sudden changes in its course. Disastrous floods in 1725, 1785, and 1844 taught the people of Kaskaskia that they were vulnerable to its whims. "[W]e are left to wonder," wrote historian J. H. Burnham in 1914, "why the town site was continued at that particular location."[5] By 1881, the narrow spit of land connecting Kaskaskia to mainland Illinois—and separating the two rivers that surrounded the town—was no more than four hundred feet wide.[6] Thus it was little surprise when on 18 April of that year a final catastrophic flood breached this last barrier and the Mississippi River surged into the channel of the quieter, more complacent Okaw.[7] Locals stood awestruck as they witnessed the flood's raging fury:

> People would stand as near as they dared to the rushing stream. Pretty soon some one would notice the ground was cracking and opening behind the spectators, and then there would be a rush back to ground that appeared to be safe, which sooner or later would also crumble and drop into the fast widening channel.[8]

Legend held that this deluge marked the fulfillment of a centuries-old curse by a French priest set adrift upon the Mississippi in an open boat—"without oars or food, compass or guide"—by the too-worldly degenerates of Kaskaskia, annoyed by his vigorous efforts to ignite their consciences and revive their flagging morality. Long after he had disappeared from view, his tormentors could hear him calling upon the Lord to send the river cascading through their streets and engulfing their homes and fields. Afterward some came to believe that their community's watery destruction marked the terrible vengeance of their father confessor and spiritual leader.[9]

In the decades after the flood of 1881 the Mississippi daintily nibbled away at the eastern edge of what had become Kaskaskia Island—now the only part of Illinois west of the great river—endangering the living and disturbing the repose of the dead. In 1891 the Illinois state legislature authorized the removal of the pioneers' graves to a more secure resting place atop the bluffs of Fort Kaskaskia where they lie today. An obelisk erected by the state nearby reads: "Those who sleep here were first buried at Kaskaskia and afterwards removed to this cemetery. They were the early pioneers of the great Mississippi valley. They planted free institutions in a wilderness and were the founders of a great commonwealth."[10]

Only about thirty yards separate this memorial atop the bluff from the Father of Waters below. It is difficult to fathom that this place was once a thriving and prosperous agricultural community. John Reynolds observed many years later: "In olden times, Kaskaskia was to Illinois what Paris is at this day to France. Both were at their respective days the great emporiums of fashion, gaiety, and I must say happiness, also." It was a stark contrast to Reynolds's later recollection of his first glimpse of Kaskaskia as a young boy in 1800, when he marveled at its common fields, the "numerous camps and lodges of the Kaskaskia Indians," and the village's ancient cathedral housing "the first church bell I ever saw."[11]

At the time of Reynolds's arrival, the Illinois Country was only beginning to emerge from an extended era of uneven and indifferent governance dating back nearly forty years—that is to say, to 1763, when the French surrendered Illinois to the British in the aftermath of the French and Indian War, ending nearly a century of French colonization in the Mississippi Valley. Over the next fifteen years—in the face of a mass exodus across the Mississippi by French Illinoisans fearful of British rule and the possibility that they might have to relinquish their enslaved persons[12]—Parliament attempted to provide some sense of continuity by recognizing French law and the Catholic religion via the Quebec Act of 1774.

By and large, however, London pursued what amounted to a policy of benign neglect connected to a reluctance to encourage settlement of the area. The ongoing arrival of American settlers—primarily Protestants—inevitably led to cultural clashes with the older French Catholic settlers, and the failure of both Great Britain and Virginia—which assumed control of the Illinois Country in 1778—to provide effective governance only exacerbated the problem.[13] By the time Great Britain formally ceded the region to the United States (1783), Virginia had already offered to transfer it to the Continental Congress. That cession became reality in 1784, and three years later Congress passed the Northwest Ordinance to establish the rule of law in what would later become

Illinois, Indiana, Ohio, Michigan, and Wisconsin. The people of Illinois subsequently endured three more governmental transitions: the Northwest Territory, Indiana Territory (1800), and Illinois Territory (1809).

In spite of these rapid changes, Illinois settlers were nonetheless drawn by the enormously rich soil of the area, especially a wide strip of land running along both banks of the Mississippi and known as the "American Bottom." Voyageurs, fur traders, priests, Native Americans, hunters, farmers, African Americans, soldiers, politicians, speculators, rogues, ruffians, dreamers, and *coureurs des bois* lived, intermarried, prospered, fought, and died here. "They were rough in personal appearance and unrefined," wrote the Reverend John Mason Peck, an early Illinois historian who arrived in 1817, "yet kind, social, and generous."[14] In the winter they celebrated the pre-Lenten French Catholic "carnival." "Old and young engaged in its peculiar duties," remembered William H. Brown, who came to Kaskaskia in 1818, "and the joyous party, and the giddy dance, followed in such quick succession, that almost the whole time was devoted to amusements."[15] Whenever a widow or a widower remarried, the community marked the occasion with a "charivari," in which friends and neighbors of the happy couple would march late at night in noisy procession to the home of the newlyweds. "Upon such occasions," Brown remarked. "the serenading company was regaled with whiskey-punch, and the time fixed when the newly-married gentleman would give a ball, free, as upon other occasions, to the whole village. But woe to the stubborn bridegroom who faileth to comply with this custom!"[16]

For nearly a century and a half since the 1881 deluge, some vestige of old Kaskaskia has grimly hung on for dear life, a shadow of its former self that was further devastated by severe flooding in 1993. The cathedral is gone, replaced by a mid-nineteenth-century edifice. Only the church bell remains—housed now in a special shrine maintained by the State of Illinois—a bell that was forged in France in 1741 and presented as a gift to the local French *habitants* by King Louis XV. This same bell was rung by George Rogers Clark on 4 July 1778 to celebrate his successful—albeit bloodless—victory over the British in Kaskaskia (hence its nickname "Liberty Bell of the West").

There is a striking similarity between the eerie isolation of modern-day Kaskaskia Island and that of the final resting place of its founders sleeping on the hill across the Mississippi. Here is a rich vein of the life and folklore of early Illinois that could have been mined by Vachel Lindsay or Edgar Lee Masters to give voice to the departed pioneers and to place metaphorical flesh, muscle, and sinew on their dry bones. They are the physical, spiritual, and political ancestors of the people of modern-day Illinois. Like Masters's Abraham Lincoln and Ann Rutledge, the Prairie State and its ancient capital are forever wedded "not through union, But through separation."[17]

Nevertheless, somehow the town abides as a fragile connection to Illinois's antediluvian colonial past. Out of such humble origins rose a state that prided itself on a fertile agriculture, a prosperous industrial base, and an infrastructure that is the beating heart of a national transportation network. It all began in Kaskaskia.

Not all of the denizens of the old capital's original cemetery were moved to Garrison Hill. Now and then—especially after a period of high water—a skull or femur or other bone fragments will wash ashore from the forgotten churchyard to startle sporadic beachcombers.[18] And Kaskaskia reemerges from hibernation at other more predictable intervals, as when Illinois marks a historic milestone such as its 2018 bicentennial. In such moments the village's majestic loneliness evokes a time when that separation from the world was both a curse and a blessing, when its denizens bemoaned a distant, indifferent, unresponsive government far to the east while simultaneously decrying that same regime as a blooming tyrant bent upon quashing their full enjoyment of American citizenship. It offers the opportunity to imagine the world of 1818 in which leaders such as Daniel Pope Cook, Nathaniel Pope, and Elias Kent Kane brought forth a new state into the Union and diminished the psychological distance between a village at the confluence of the Mississippi and Okaw Rivers and the nation's capital on the Potomac.

INTRODUCTION

In mid-April 1818, having shepherded an act through Congress to begin the process of Illinois's admission to the Union, territorial delegate Nathaniel Pope was feeling both reflective and triumphant. The legislative ordeal had been rigorous, he told his constituents, but the territory had emerged largely unscathed and perhaps even better off. His congressional colleagues who advocated on Illinois's behalf, he wrote, "proved that the United States would gain rather than lose. It passed by a great majority. . . . We may say with truth, that we will enter upon a state government with better prospects than any state ever did. . . . Our avenues for navigation are towards the east and the west, the north and the south."[1]

There is nothing novel or surprising in the spectacle of an elected official trumpeting a legislative success for the voters back home. Nevertheless, the boisterous heart of Nathaniel Pope's rhetoric—and the geographic contours of what would become the Prairie State—encompassed a substantial truth: Illinois was uniquely positioned to exert a strengthening influence on national unity. Making this a reality had been the singular focus of Nathaniel Pope's effort from the moment he received a summons to work for Illinois's admission to the Union from the territorial legislature in January 1818. And the key was the placement of its borders—most particularly, its northern boundary, which had been extended some sixty-one miles beyond its original location at the southern tip of Lake Michigan. The importance of gaining this additional territory, Pope observed, was "obvious to every man who looks to the prospective weight and influence of the state of Illinois."[2] Acquiring Chicago was a crucial step in Illinois becoming the central linchpin of the nation's infrastructure. Now Illinois would connect East and West along an all-water pathway running from the Atlantic Ocean through the Hudson River and the Erie Canal. Within thirty years following admission, Illinois's stature as the nation's internal maritime transportation hub extended over the Great Lakes through the Chicago River and the Illinois and Michigan Canal to the Illinois

River, the Mississippi, and ultimately all the way to the Gulf of Mexico. Illinois would thus be intertwined with the entire continent, and in the process, Pope told his congressional colleagues, it "would afford additional security to the perpetuity of the Union."[3]

The story of Illinois's admission to the Union is of a piece with two of the most arresting qualities of the Prairie State: the richness of its historical narrative and the manner in which it reflects our larger national history. Like other signal events in the annals of the state—George Rogers Clark's conquest of Kaskaskia, the Battle of Fort Dearborn, the Black Hawk War, the establishment of New Philadelphia by African American entrepreneur "Free Frank" McWhorter, the Lincoln-Douglas debates, the Haymarket incident, and the Pullman Strike—the dramatic arc of Illinois's admission to the Union encompasses a variety of compelling themes, such as race, class consciousness, relations with Native Americans, the exploitation of natural resources, and above all, political conflict.

In framing this tale, the historian can choose from a number of options. One might focus upon the rich vein of individual biography; articles devoted to contemporary figures such as Daniel Pope Cook, Nathaniel Pope, Ninian Edwards, Elias Kent Kane, and Jesse B. Thomas have appeared at frequent intervals over the course of the last century in the pages of the *Journal of the Illinois State Historical Society*. Only Edwards and Thomas have been the subject of book-length biographies, although that of the former was authored by his son and thus fell short of the standards of true historical objectivity. Another scholar might incorporate the chronicle of admission into a larger state history, as was the case with Theodore Calvin Pease's *The Frontier State 1818–1848* in 1919, Clarence Alvord's *The Illinois Country, 1673–1818* in 1922, Robert Howard's *Illinois: A History of the Prairie State* in 1972, James E. Davis's *Frontier Illinois* in 1998, and Roger Biles's *Illinois: A History of the Land and Its People* in 2005. In all of these works the road to statehood is discussed as part of a larger storyline. The sole exception to this pattern in the historiography of Illinois's admission is Solon Buck's masterful *Illinois in 1818*. First published in 1917, this work strove to explore "the social, economic, and political life of Illinois at the close of the territorial period, and . . . to tell the story of the transition from colonial dependence to the full dignity of a state in the union."[4] Indeed, *Illinois in 1818* devoted a greater amount of time and effort to the admission story—nearly a third of its length—than any other comparable work. Ultimately, however, it treated that particular history as a distinct *process* rather than as a significant event in and of itself.

It is the purpose of the present work to narrate the complete story of admission—in all its complexity—by placing particular emphasis upon three individuals who played outsize roles in advancing the cause of statehood. There was the ambitious Daniel Pope Cook, who in the fall of 1817 orchestrated a public relations campaign advocating statehood that culminated in a legislative memorial to Congress praying for that transition. There was the wily Nathaniel Pope, Illinois's congressional delegate who ably guided the formulation and passage of an enabling act by the U.S. Congress in the spring of 1818 authorizing the first stages of the statehood process. And then there was Elias Kent Kane, the brilliant and precocious young lawyer who was a leading actor in shaping Illinois's future instruments of governance at its first constitutional convention in the summer of 1818.

This is not to suggest that the admission narrative can be easily reduced to the biographies of its leadership. That story was decisively influenced by historical forces large and small, by numerous and largely unnamed individuals representing a myriad of ethnic, racial, and social backgrounds, by geographic and environmental realities, and by economic and political disquiet. The significance of Cook, Pope, and Kane ultimately lies in their status as avatars of the larger effort to transform Illinois from territory to state in 1817 and 1818.

But the most striking feature of the state's admission to the Union is connected to two important realities. One lies in Illinois's location in the heart of what was then the western frontier, amplifying its remoteness from the centers of power in the nation's capital. The difficulty of providing the territory with a stable, coherent governmental structure had long bedeviled not only the federal government but also the successive regimes—France, Britain, Virginia—that had preceded it. For their part, settlers lamented the distance that constrained their ability to participate in American democracy even as they resented the national government's ability to reach across half a continent to intrude into their lives. From the perspective of Washington, D.C., that same remoteness underscored the tenuous grip of the United States on the Old Northwest that was exacerbated by the continuing influence of foreign interests—France, Britain, Spain—in the region. And no one understood this reality better than western settlers. They recognized that the presence of these European powers gave them other options besides connection with the American Union. It gave them a certain amount of leverage in reaching agreement with the federal government regarding a second important reality: the ongoing presence of slavery in Illinois Territory and elsewhere in the Old Northwest.

In the years before the War of 1812, there was a consensus that although the federal government had the constitutional power "to prohibit slavery in the federal territories," it was still an open question "whether the government possessed the real, effective power needed to implement meaningful restrictions

. . . and whether restricting slavery would weaken the prospects for a lasting American Union in the West." This had significant implications, wrote historian John Craig Hammond:

> Whenever the possibility of restricting slavery in a territory had been raised, white Westerners and American officials in the West warned that disunion might follow. Indeed, Western farmers, slaveholders, merchants, and speculators made clear their preference for living under European powers who would protect slavery, rather than under an American empire whose commitment to Western slavery seemed questionable.[5]

The conclusion of the war, Hammond added, marked the end of "European designs for a mid-continent empire" and "solidified Western loyalties and consolidated the place of the West in the American Union."[6] Whatever leverage that white pro-slavery Illinois settlers had possessed was gone.

And this placed Illinois in a unique position. The two new states preceding Illinois were admitted to the Union after the conclusion of the war, but in neither of those instances was there ambiguity as to the legality of slavery within their borders. Indiana (1816) entered the Union as a free state with a constitution that was in complete accord with Article VI of the Northwest Ordinance that prohibited the institution. Mississippi (1817) was not subject to any such restriction; indeed, enslaved persons accounted for some 42 percent of its territorial population. Neither state needed to exert special leverage to resolve the issue.

But Illinois was a different story. Many of its white settlers were strongly inclined to tolerate this morally repugnant institution, but the Northwest Ordinance proved to be a formidable obstacle to these interests. And the disappearance of European powers from the landscape only strengthened the federal government's ability to hold Illinois to the standards of Article VI. In this context, Illinois was the first state to gain admission to the Union under such a marked asymmetry of power.

And this reality highlights other ways in which Illinois's admission narrative was distinct from those of other states. Its uniquely interlocking connection with every region—North, South, East, and West—via the state's natural infrastructure, reinforced by its fertile agriculture and—in time—its vigorous industrial base enabled Illinois to amplify the larger growth and development of the nation as a whole. Its admission illuminated the essential nature of the relationship between a territory and the national government and highlighted nascent sectional conflicts. It presented troubling reminders that the moral stain of slavery was by no means fully restricted to the South. And it provided an occasion to contemplate the meaning of national unity and how the bonds of the Union might be perpetuated. During the eventful months of 1817 and 1818, the themes that have defined the Prairie State consistently throughout its history—patronage, race, infrastructure, and political intrigue—marked Illinois's unique transformation from territory to state.

PART I

The Long Voyage of Daniel Pope Cook

I

TWENTY GALLONS OF WHISKEY

In the gathering twilight of 18 November 1817, a solitary figure stepped a trifle unsteadily onto the dock at Kaskaskia, Illinois.[1] Daniel Pope Cook was a distinctly handsome fellow some twenty-four years of age and slight of frame, his countenance punctuated by a thin nose and an air of quiet abstraction. Frail and tubercular, he was returning after an absence of nearly a year that had begun as a quest to restore his health and his sense of direction. Having completed a journey covering two continents, ninety-two hundred miles and a world of ambition, Cook was returning home recovered in resolution if not in constitution. Within days of his homecoming, he would embark upon an effort to midwife a new state into the Union, altering the social, economic, and political landscape of the United States and in the process launching his own political career.

At its heart the story of the Illinois Country—certainly from the time of its incorporation into the Northwest Territory in 1787—is a narrative of the region's vaguely defined relationship to the United States. The Northwest Ordinance had declared that Illinois "shall forever remain a part of this confederacy of the United States of America, subject to the Articles of Confederation" and to any of its successor documents, as well as "to all the acts and ordinances of the United States in Congress assembled." The people of the territory were responsible for a share of the national debt and subject to federal taxation. The establishment of more representative government—so-called "second stage" status, with the right to an elected assembly—had to wait until the territory reached a population of five thousand male inhabitants "of full age in the district." Even at that point, only white male residents who were citizens of the United States and owned fifty acres of land would be eligible to vote.[2] Suffrage was expanded when Congress promoted Illinois to that second stage in 1812, but political power remained largely in the hands of a few individuals appointed by the president or by the territorial governor. It was an asymmetrical relationship, to be sure. The true status of Illinois and its inhabitants, however, remained ambiguous. Were they the mere denizens of a colony or full citizens of the United States? To what extent could they exert leverage against the national government to attain control over their own environment and their own lives? The political career of Daniel Pope Cook was an embodiment of these pressing questions. And his return to Kaskaskia proved to be the moment when he served as the engine by which Illinois transformed itself from a state of uncertainty to a state within the Union.

To understand this pivotal moment, we must go back nearly three decades before to Scott County, Kentucky, which stands today just south of the Ohio River at the border confluence of the Bluegrass State with Indiana and Ohio. In 1790—two years before the admission of the state and the formal establishment of the county—two of the region's first pioneers, Thomas Herndon and Cornelius Duvall, settled on McConnell's Run in a region known then and now as "Stamping Ground." Close to this place was a series of salt springs that drew early settlers; salt was a valuable commodity and its manufacture a lucrative enterprise on the frontier. In those early days herds of buffalo were attracted to the brackish water and would "'stamp' the ground as they stood under the shade of the trees."[3] Thus they left their mark on the open vistas of Scott County in the name of the region and the village.

Despite its impending statehood, Kentucky was still substantially in the vanguard of the untamed western frontier of the United States. In its final census as a territory in 1790, Kentucky encompassed 73,677 souls, of whom 12,430 were enslaved persons (or nearly 17 percent). Woodford County, from which Scott County was formed in 1792, was home to 9,210 Kentuckians, of whom 2,220 were enslaved persons (24 percent). By 1800 Scott County boasted a population of 8,007, including 1,910 enslaved persons (nearly 24 percent); by 1810 the latter amounted to 3,732 out of a total county population of 12,419 (30 percent, one of the highest such proportions in the state).[4] They made their homes in a gently sloping landscape topped with rich soil that crumbled easily and provided a hospitable home for trees, including oak, ash, poplar, walnut, maple, and elm.[5] Those who settled here saw their patient efforts rewarded with a bountiful agriculture teeming in hemp and tobacco.

Daniel Pope Cook came into the world on this frontier in 1793; the exact date is unknown.[6] The second son of John Dillard Cook, a "thrifty farmer" born in Lincolnshire, England, around 1753, and Mary Jane Mothershead (known as Jane), young Daniel was by all accounts a sickly child.[7] In his *Pioneer History of Illinois*, former Illinois governor John Reynolds speculated that Cook's delicate constitution "was one reason, together with the circumscribed means of his father, that his education in his youth was not much attended to."[8] At all events the schooling of a frontier farmer's children was subject to the interruptions occasioned by the need for their labor at home. Young Cook's education came in fits and starts in the common schools of the region; nonetheless, he was by nature and inclination a thoughtful and inquisitive student; "[H]e acquired information," wrote Reynolds, "as if by intuition. His mind was rapid as well as deep in its researches."[9]

The pioneer community that nurtured Daniel Pope Cook was close-knit, drawing strength from family—Jane Cook's brother Nathaniel Mothershead and his wife Ruth lived nearby—and faith. Indeed, Scott County and its surrounding region was at the very center of an early nineteenth-century religious revival that came to be known as the "Second Great Awakening." It rejected rationalism and emphasized the spiritual and the emotional; its adherents witnessed the pervasive presence of God in their everyday lives. One of the most important events associated with the Second Great Awakening was a weeklong revival meeting that took place in August 1801 in Cane Ridge, Kentucky—only about thirty-five miles from Stamping Ground—and attracted between ten and twenty-five thousand worshipers "at a time," wrote historian Sydney E. Ahlstrom, "when nearby Lexington, the state's largest city, barely exceeded two thousand."[10]

One concrete consequence of the Second Great Awakening was the proliferation of local Baptist, Methodist, and Presbyterian churches across the western frontier. Among these was McConnell's Run Church, a Baptist congregation founded in September 1795 and counting the Cooks and the Mothersheads among its thirty-five charter members.[11] As time passed they discovered that if the eyes of the Lord are in every place, beholding the evil and the good, the same could be true of their fellow congregants as well. Even the holiest of sanctuaries could serve as a breeding ground for the transformation of minor differences and petty personal conflicts into wider discord and even the breakup of an entire community. In 1804 a committee of seven men was required to successfully dissuade Nathaniel Mothershead from "braking [*sic*] off violently as a member of this church." Ultimately Nathaniel saw the error of his ways and "agreed to continue his membership."[12]

Soon thereafter Daniel's father John Cook embroiled the entire church community in a dispute that illustrated the fine lines that sometimes existed between the worldly and the spiritual in frontier society. The row originated in the question of how much Cook should pay Lewis Denny, a fellow member of the church, for twenty gallons of whiskey. At its business meeting in January 1806, the church ruled that "Forty Shillings (about ten dollars)" would be the proper price, essentially siding with Denny. The unseemly interference of his spiritual community in the matter of spirits was too much for John Cook, and he consequently refused to attend services for months, bringing the wrath of the church down upon himself to the extent that at the May meeting he was "Admonished and Reproved" for his absences.

At the June business meeting Cook brought forward a complaint against Lewis Denny "for deviating from that line of rectitude becoming his profession in Several Instances, and in some of which tend to lead the Church into Error." To Cook's chagrin the church voted to clear Denny of the charges. Denny in turn charged Cook with alleging that he (Denny) was a man of neither honor nor character, lacking in honesty and capacity for truth telling. The church ultimately split the difference by voting that Cook be both "admonished and acquitted of these charges."[13]

After an eighteen-month interval of relative calm the conflict resumed in the wake of a 45–6 vote in favor of retaining the church pastor, Jacob Creath, for another year. John Cook led the minority faction, bitterly opposing those favoring Creath's retention, who were championed by Lewis Denny. A charge was brought against Cook "accusing him of being contentious, self-willed and heady because of his threats and opposition to the decisions of the church during the past two years," and in July 1808 he "was excluded from the church for his disorderly and refractory conduct." He was later restored to membership and then excluded once more in 1814 for accusing the church of keeping false records and for referring to its pastor as a "hireling."[14]

In some respects this incident foreshadowed the larger political environment that young Daniel Pope Cook was to encounter in his adopted home of Illinois. Although a fine, deeply felt religious sentiment served to bind his family and their neighbors together in a close-knit community, such proximity could be a double-edged sword. He witnessed the consequences of a conflict between idealism and political factionalism, and young Daniel must have watched wide-eyed as his elders allowed their petty daily conflicts to spiral into wider controversies going well beyond the realm of the spiritual.

A Fear of Servile Rebellion

One potential source of conflict was slavery, which Kentucky had permitted from the very beginning. In 1792 the legislature of Virginia had demanded that Kentucky's constitution confirm the institution's legality as a condition for separation from the Old Dominion. Nevertheless, even at that early date there were those who opposed such toleration. One member of the Kentucky convention, the Reverend David Rice, opposed slavery on moral grounds as infringing upon natural rights. His arguments fell on deaf ears, as most of his colleagues were themselves slaveholders.[15] Many if not all of them had a benign view of the institution; in after years Kentuckians comforted themselves with the myth that slavery in their state was milder than elsewhere. After all, they argued, had not whites and Blacks fought marauding Indians side by side to carve out new settlements on the frontier? Had they not in the process created a genteel civilization that benefited both races?[16]

Slavery was consequently part and parcel of the world in which Daniel Pope Cook grew and matured, not least because his father and his uncle were both substantial slaveholders. John Cook was recorded as owning ten enslaved persons in 1810 and nine in 1820, while Nathaniel Mothershead held ten and seven respectively in those same census years.[17] It is fascinating to note that some of those enslaved by the Cooks and the Mothersheads were fellow members of the McConnell's Run Baptist Church. For example, Jane and Lucy, who were owned by John Cook, joined the congregation in July and September 1796 respectively, and Molly, who was owned by Nathaniel Mothershead, joined in February 1801.[18] The balance of the week these three were salable property, but on the Sabbath they worshipped side by side with the Cooks and the Mothersheads and told themselves that in the presence of the Lord, at least, they were on an equal footing. It must have been an uneasy and uncomfortable association, and if Daniel Pope Cook's later writings are any guide, it ultimately rendered him ambivalent about slavery in Illinois. In a column in the Kaskaskia *Western Intelligencer* in 1818, he meditated upon the question of which condition—slave or free—rendered a state "the *safest*, the *happiest*, the *wealthiest*, and the most *beautiful*." He appealed "to the man whose mid-night hours have been disturbed with the thoughts of house breaking, house burning, and thefts of every kind, committed by his own, or the refugee slaves of others" and "to the man, who in southern luxury has laid with his gun by his bed, fearing a general and even a domestic servile rebellion."[19]

His comments along these lines are striking in light of slaveholding patterns in Scott County as recorded by the U.S. Census in 1810 (the year before Cook departed westward). Not all of the schedules from that enumeration have survived, but those that remain document 2,780 individuals owned by 507 slaveholding households. In these same households there were just 3,438 whites, or 1.24 whites to each enslaved person. (There were also 41 "other free persons" listed with no reference to their race. The largest number of households—327 of the 507—were those owning 1 to 5 enslaved persons.[20]) If they flattered themselves that they had conjured up a civilization out of a wild frontier side by side with their bondspersons—if they considered that achievement to be the result of a partnership—it was not much of a stretch to suppose that their chattels could channel their newfound powers into an uprising against their masters. Kentuckians were uncomfortably well aware of two slave rebellions that had recently misfired in neighboring Virginia in 1800 and 1801–2—the so-called "Gabriel's Rebellion" and the "Easter Plot," both of which were betrayed by participants before they could go into action. Dozens of enslaved persons—some of them innocent of any involvement—met their fate at the end of a hangman's noose as a result.[21] The most striking consequences, however, were to be found in the reaction of that state's white majority. After briefly considering the possibility of outlawing slavery, the Virginia legislature instead placed a series of onerous restrictions upon the lives of the state's Black population, both enslaved and free persons alike. These included extended curfews (and harsh penalties for violators), severe limitations upon gatherings of enslaved persons, bans upon their literacy, encroachments upon hiring out bondspersons, and a requirement that emancipated African Americans leave the state within twelve months or risk being sold back into bondage.[22] All of these provisions foreshadowed similar measures enacted afterward in Illinois, both as a territory and as a state.

The Fortune-Seeker

The exact circumstances of Daniel Pope Cook's removal to Illinois are unknown. It is best understood in the larger context of the westward movement of settlers from the older states in search of a better life. Although Illinois migrants originated from every section of the country, the larger portion came from the South—the Carolinas, Tennessee, Virginia, Maryland, and especially—like Cook himself—from Kentucky. This reality had everything to do with proximity, opportunity, and convenience, of course, and the emigrants' primary transportation avenue was the Ohio River by way of Shawneetown in southeastern Illinois.

They came westward for a complex variety of reasons and motivations. Along these lines historian Theodore Calvin Pease described the settlers as falling into several categories. The squatter—the first arrival after the original *voyageurs* and trappers—would stop "a year or five years in a place to build a cabin and clear a few acres of corn for his family to supplement the spoils of his rifle, until he sold his improvements to a more permanent settler and moved on." He did not own the land thus improved. His successor was the farmer, "who did not settle on any land save what he owned or expected to be able to buy. Primitive in his first living arrangements on the frontier, he kept in his mind the ideal of approximating as soon as possible the comforts of his old home back East."

The third category—and the one most closely (if imperfectly) matching Daniel Pope Cook's situation—was the "fortune-seeker," whom Pease deemed as "[r]ising above [the farmer] in gentility of birth and breeding, in good social position, and in education."[23] Nearly sixty years later his brother-in-law Ninian Wirt Edwards reported that Cook was initially sent by his parents to work in a Kentucky "mercantile establishment" for a short time. This situation being "too limited for his high aspirations," Cook commenced to study law under the watchful tutelage of John Pope, who was at that time a U.S. senator from Kentucky.[24] Born in 1770, Pope was a leading figure in Kentucky politics who had been elevated to the Senate in 1807. He had built a flourishing legal career despite losing his right arm in a cornstalk mill accident at an early age.[25] In Pope Cook found not only an opportunity to expand his education but also to develop his first important political contacts, both in Kentucky and—more importantly—in Illinois. For Pope was both the older brother of Nathaniel Pope, secretary of Illinois Territory, and the first cousin of that territory's governor, Ninian Edwards, who later became Cook's father-in-law.[26]

As it happened, Cook's initial destination was not Kaskaskia but rather just across the Mississippi River in Ste. Genevieve, Missouri. John Reynolds wrote long afterward that upon his arrival in 1811 Cook was employed as a clerk in a store owned by William Shannon.[27] John Mason Peck, a prolific historian of the Old Northwest and founder of Rock Spring Seminary (later Shurtleff College in Alton, Illinois), confirmed the 1811 arrival date in his oration at Cook's funeral in 1827. Reynolds and Peck were likewise in agreement that Cook continued to study law in Kaskaskia under the guidance of Nathaniel Pope, which Peck dated as beginning in 1813.[28]

Cook's status as a "fortune-seeking" emigrant is in accord with the support of his mentor, John Pope. A sharp judge of character and talent, Pope surmised that Illinois Territory was an appropriate venue for a young man of ambition, and Pope's brother Nathaniel and his cousin Ninian Edwards could provide substantial training and political opportunities. Furthermore, Cook's older brother—also named Nathaniel—had settled in the Ste. Genevieve district in 1800.[29] To be sure, Illinois had been its own separate territory for only two years, with a relatively modest population of 12,282 per the federal census of 1810.[30] At all events, in 1811 Illinois seemed a congenial field for his political prospects in comforting proximity to family.

In some respects Ste. Genevieve and Kaskaskia functioned in the early years of the nineteenth century as twin communities that anchored the commerce and politics of what was then the western frontier. They were part of what historian Stephen Aron called "the American confluence," encompassing "the lands adjacent to the conjunction not only of the Missouri and Mississippi rivers, but also of the Ohio River with the Mississippi." The intersection of these natural transportation routes had "[f]or thousands of years . . . facilitated the movement of peoples and objects to and through the center of the confluence region."[31] For its part, Kaskaskia was already more than a century old, having been originally settled in 1703 by a band of Kaskaskia and Tamaroa Indians guided both spiritually and temporally by Father Pierre-Gabriel Marest. With the arrival of French traders and their Native American wives, the settlement gradually coalesced into a thriving village. Ste. Genevieve owed much of its rise to migration by inhabitants of Kaskaskia who were fearful of British rule in the aftermath of the French and Indian War. The rise of the younger town—whose full name "Ste. Genevieve des Cascaskias" "attested to its satellite status," as Aron remarked—has been variously dated as taking place in 1732, 1735, the 1740s, "or even as late as 1751."[32]

A Fitting Pathway

The Kaskaskia and Ste. Genevieve encountered by Daniel Pope Cook in 1811 were becoming increasingly distinct communities. Some Illinois settlers of French lineage had fled across the Mississippi in fearful anticipation that American territorial government would require that they relinquish ownership of their enslaved human property, given that Article VI of the Northwest Ordinance decreed that "[t]here shall be neither slavery nor involuntary servitude in the said territory, otherwise than in the punishment of crimes, whereof the party shall have been duly convicted."[33] Nevertheless, the French influence in Kaskaskia had not disappeared altogether, embodied as it was in the ongoing presence of prominent citizens like Pierre Menard and visibly on the landscape in the long-lot property lines of early French land grants.[34] Relics of the French regime were likewise plainly evident in the local domestic architecture. Houses, wrote historian David Buisseret, "were built using wooden uprights (sometimes sunk into the ground) to form a frame around a limestone chimney; an encircling covered verandah [*sic*] gave protection against the summer heat. Mud and clay formed the walls between the timbers, and these walls were normally plastered both inside and out, which gave them a tidy appearance."[35]

For a young man of talent and high aspirations, Kaskaskia served as a fitting pathway into a position of influence and prosperity. But first Daniel Pope Cook was confronted with the dynamic forces that governed territorial politics: land, the distribution of power, and slavery. Their roots can be traced back to Illinois's early status as part of the Northwest Territory and, indeed, to the provisions of the Northwest Ordinance of 1787 itself.

2

THE UTMOST GOOD FAITH

In some ways the word *territory* fails to fully describe Illinois's true status in the years before statehood. Perhaps *colony* comes closer to the mark, emphasizing Illinois's subordinate role to the larger American nation as a source of raw materials, a place for settlement at a time when new land was becoming less available in the East, and a market for goods from the more developed areas of the country. There were opportunities in abundance for men of ambition, whether in the form of land, business prospects, or political patronage. It was an environment filled in equal amounts with risk and reward for young Daniel Pope Cook.

Issues related to control and ownership of land exerted an enormous influence over relationships between those who occupied those lands, especially as between Americans and Native Americans. Historian Jacob Lee observed that "Americans built their empire atop the remnants of French, British, and Spanish colonies on a continent still largely dominated by Native peoples."[1] This was especially true of the Illinois Country. The Revolutionary War had been fought in part over the right of settlers to move westward freely and secure land. Britain had issued the Proclamation of 1763 prohibiting settlement west of the Appalachians as a way of minimizing conflict with the Native American tribes of the interior. Thus, after the British ceded the Northwest Territory to the United States at the end of the conflict, the Americans were confronted with the same problem. Establishing the new nation's dominion over the region was one thing; securing it was a completely separate issue that they sought to resolve by establishing a legal basis for gaining land cessions from the western tribes.[2] In the context of Illinois, that relevant authority was found in the Northwest Ordinance, which required the extinguishment of Indian title to lands before counties and townships could be laid out. "The utmost good faith," it declared, "shall always be observed towards the Indians; their lands and property shall never be taken from them without their consent."[3]

If the American settlers and their national and territorial governments were ambivalent as to the means by which they appropriated Native American lands, there was no mistaking their long-term intentions to accomplish that purpose. The 1795 Treaty of Greenville, negotiated in the wake of General "Mad Anthony" Wayne's victory over a coalition of Miami, Ojibwa, Ottawa, and other Native American forces at the Battle of Fallen Timbers, is a striking example. That agreement granted the Americans most of the future state of Ohio and strategic tracts of territory at the future site of Chicago and at the mouth of the Illinois River. The Native Americans of the region were furthermore required to allow the people of the United States to move freely through their lands "by land and by water." In return, the twelve tribes that signed the treaty received goods in the amount of $20,000 upon signing and a total of $9,500 to be divided among them annually.[4]

The purpose was twofold: to establish peace with these indigenous peoples and to acquire vast new tracts of territory. That success was diminished, however, by the dubious claims of some of the signatories. Historian Robert M. Owens deemed the Potawatomi as having "few if any claims to the lands ceded, yet [they] signed anyway to receive their gifts. The huge cession forced others, especially Shawnees and Delawares, west into what would become Indiana Territory, further complicating land ownership questions."[5]

To be sure, the Americans had additional considerations. President Thomas Jefferson worried about French designs on the Mississippi Valley in the wake of the Napoleonic Wars. American ownership of the Northwest Territory had not impeded French, British, and Spanish interests in the heart of North America. The rivers of the region—the Mississippi, the Illinois, the Wabash, and the Ohio—remained vital channels for their trade and communication.[6] It was thus by no means a foregone conclusion that Illinois and the other western territories would retain their loyalties and connections to the United States.

But it was the Native Americans—more closely tied to the Illinois Country than anyone else—who represented the most significant challenge. This was the context in which Thomas Jefferson advocated the aggressive acquisition of their lands by making them dependent upon the federal government. If they were to become small farmers, he told William Henry Harrison in 1803, they would eventually prove willing to relinquish stewardship of "their extensive forests" and to barter those natural resources as part of their livelihood. To encourage this, Jefferson declared, "we shall push our trading houses, and be glad to see the good and influential individuals among them run in debt, because we observe that when these debts get beyond what the individuals can pay, they become willing to lop them off by a cession of lands."[7] Over time Harrison was instrumental in negotiating eighteen separate Indian treaties between 1795 and 1833, resulting in the acquisition of nearly ninety million acres. He was not, as historian James E. Davis observed, "excessively fastidious about whether signing Indians had authority to sign."[8] And it proved to be an effective strategy in Illinois; by 1815 it was estimated that there were no more than 13,260 Native Americans living in the region.[9]

The clearing of Native American title to lands in Illinois and elsewhere in the Old Northwest did not completely resolve the issue of land ownership, however. The process for settlers to acquire land was complex and burdensome. An act of Congress in 1796 set land prices at two dollars per acre, with a minimum purchase of 640 acres on only a year's credit, which "placed the land," wrote Theodore Calvin Pease, "beyond the reach of the average frontier farmer."[10] Daniel Pope Cook was one of those who sought to acquire public land in this fashion. Between 1816 and 1821 he purchased nearly 3,400 acres in the counties of Randolph, St. Clair, Washington, and Fayette at a total cost of close to $4,300,[11] an amount roughly equivalent to $85,000 today. That was a substantial investment for a young man of modest means, and it may explain in part Cook's long-running and at times almost desperate effort to secure a dependable source of income.

The United States also faced the problem of determining the legitimacy of ancient land grants previously made to settlers by the French government more than a century earlier. Some grew weary of waiting and sold out to speculators like John Edgar and William Morrison, further complicating a situation that was already rife with fraud and corruption. Not until 1810, when Congress received the report of a special commission outlining these issues, was it possible for the federal government to enable "the survey of townships and the sale of quarter-sections at the land offices of Shawneetown and Kaskaskia."[12]

Simplifying the means by which pioneers obtained clear title to the lands on which they settled was directly connected to issues of governance. Under the Northwest Ordinance, a territory was entitled to an elected general assembly once its population totaled "five thousand free male inhabitants, of full age in the district." Eligible voters included those who owned fifty acres of land, were citizens of one of the states, and were residents within the territory. When Illinois was separated from Indiana in 1809, Congress removed the population requirement but retained the land ownership standard. This meant that the ability of the vast majority of the male population to exert influence in public affairs was severely restricted. Consequently, when Congress elevated Illinois to the second stage of territorial government in 1812, they "extended the right of suffrage to any white male person 21 years old, who had paid a territorial tax and resided one year in the territory next preceding any election"[13]—conditions that Daniel Pope Cook had met by the end of 1815.

Insults and Retorts

Surveying, determination of land ownership, the conditions under which land was to be sold, exchanged, and settled—all of these were ultimately political issues that could be facilitated, or hindered, depending upon who exerted the levers of power. The roots of this reality lay in sections 3–4 of the Northwest Ordinance, which decreed that political power would be vested in a territorial governor, a secretary, and three judges to be appointed by Congress (and later by the president with congressional approval). The governor in turn was empowered to make appointments to subsidiary offices such as local magistrates, county sheriffs, and militia officers. Political influence was thus concentrated in the hands of one person, and consequently—as the central figure in an environment bedeviled by factionalism—he was bound to become the target of idle flatterers and raging malcontents alike. Indeed, as Theodore Calvin Pease observed, William Henry Harrison scarcely had time to assume office as governor of Indiana Territory in 1801 before a battle commenced between "Harrison and anti-Harrison parties," as "Edgar and the Morrisons, the speculating interests, ranged themselves against the governor" in Illinois.[14] It was entirely up to a would-be political careerist like Daniel Pope Cook to decide with which group he would be best advised to cast his lot.

Those who sided with Governor Harrison—opposing partition of the territory and supporting the land claims investigations of land commissioners Michael Jones and Elijah Backus—included Shadrach Bond, James Gilbreath, Nathaniel Pope, and Robert Robinson. Among Harrison's opponents were John Edgar, the brothers Robert and William Morrison, and John Rice Jones and his son Rice.[15] It was a ferocious rivalry. "Public insults and angry retorts," wrote historian James D. Rees, "were the common language of the day, as were the resulting affairs of honor."[16] The most noteworthy of these disputes commenced on 7 August 1808 when young Rice Jones, at that time a candidate for the Indiana territorial assembly, accused Shadrach Bond of having "been opposed to the interest of these counties in the legislature, (to wit St. Clair and Randolph,) that he held a commission of gov. Harrison, was his tool, and governed by unworthy motives." An insulted Bond challenged Jones to a duel that same evening, and they subsequently met on nearby Carpenter's Island, where, as Dr. James Dunlap reported in a letter to the Vincennes *Western Sun*,

Rice Jones disavowed any intention of calling Bond's private character into question.[17]

Rice Jones was infuriated by Dunlap's account of the fracas. The "meddling little doctor" had been Bond's second, and Jones charged Dunlap with accusing him of cowardice.[18] Dunlap in turn derided his antagonist as "*little Ricey Jones*; the puppet of the farce" who "observes that I do not understand the 'force of the English language;' perhaps I do not yet I perfectly understand the necessary force to be given to the Cowhide when properly applied to the back of a cowardly paltroon [*sic*]."[19] The war of words escalated; Elijah Backus and Robert Robinson weighed in publicly, the former belittling Jones as a "jackanapes" and the latter scolding him for making unfounded accusations of neglect in the Kaskaskia Board of Commissioners land office.[20] Jones's ally William Morrison attempted to calm the waters with "an impartial statement of facts," but to no avail.[21]

This very public squabble between Rice Jones and James Dunlap came to a sudden and violent conclusion in Kaskaskia on 7 December 1808. In a subsequent account in the *Western Sun*, "Spectator" related that Jones had "endeavoured to place the Doctor in the most rediculous [*sic*] point of view, as a physician; and to distroy [*sic*] his practice by which alone he supported a young and rising family." A chance encounter on the street led to harsh words; Dunlap threatened Jones with his cane, and after Jones brandished a small dagger, "the Doctor conceiving himself in danger had drawn his pistol and discharged."[22]

Dunlap almost immediately fled the territory, never to return. He was never indicted on any charges connected with the death of his antagonist, but his political alliance with Shadrach Bond—and therefore with Michael Jones, Elijah Backus, and the rest of the reviled pro-Harrison faction—gave the anti-Harrisonians the political opening they had been waiting for. The death of Rice Jones, observed historian Clarence Alvord, was directly connected by his allies to the actions of Michael Jones and Elijah Backus: "In conversation the members of the anti-Harrison group asserted their belief in the guilt of the accused and declared that the people were prepared to 'exterminate or drive out of the country' the 'murderous faction.'" Seven months later a grand jury indicted Michael Jones for inciting James Dunlap to murder Rice Jones. When the case came to trial in April 1810, the accused was exonerated, and he almost immediately sued John Edgar and William and Robert Morrison for defamation of character. Subsequently he obtained a judgment of two hundred dollars against William Morrison, dropped the case against his brother, and settled with Edgar for three hundred dollars and Edgar's public declaration of Jones's innocence.[23]

Rice Jones was dead, and Michael Jones was a free man, but the warfare between the pro- and anti-Harrison factions continued even as the Illinois Country morphed from Indiana's backwater to a territory in its own right. Other contentious issues were yet to arise, and new and important players were still in the future, but the ongoing battle over the distribution of power and patronage remained remarkably consistent. It was a battlefield tailor-made for an aspiring politician like Daniel Pope Cook.

Garnisheed Rights

Perhaps most fundamental to the territory's political disquiet was the presence of slavery within its borders. The Northwest Ordinance's prohibition against involuntary servitude notwithstanding, the practice nevertheless maintained a tenacious foothold in Illinois at the time of Daniel Pope Cook's arrival. It had a long and storied history in the region dating back long before European settlement. Slavery was a crucial component of the Illinois Indians' trading network. But far from being a mere labor system, wrote historian M. Scott Heerman, "it also served important political functions. By controlling captives of diverse nations, the Illinois Indians became important brokers in a long-distance trade in slaves." In the course of settling in the Illinois Country, instead of "constructing a colonial slave economy based on dominating enslaved Africans and displacing Native Americans, the French joined existing systems of Indian slave trading in their efforts to form native alliances." And their successful cultivation over time of the fertile American Bottom to produce bounteous wheat harvests ultimately provided a foundation for importing enslaved persons from West Africa by way of New Orleans.[24] In addition to devoting their uncompensated labor to the region's agriculture, they frequently served as waiters in taverns, as wagon drivers, and as household servants.[25] And when Americans began settling in significant numbers, the fact that the largest portion hailed from Southern states—especially Kentucky and Tennessee—meant that those emigrants resented their inability to bring their property—their enslaved persons—with them. In 1880 Joseph Gillespie, a close friend of Abraham Lincoln's, told a story dating from the early statehood period of a native Southerner's response in the state legislature to a Yankee legislator who questioned the validity of indentures with enslaved persons. The Southerner declared that

> fittener men . . . mout have been found to defend the masters agin the sneaking ways of these infernal abolitioners; but, having rights on my side, I don't fear, sir. I will show that ar proposition is unconstitutionable,

> inlegal, and fornenst the compact. Don't every one know, or at least wise had ought to know, that the Congress that sot at Visann [Vincennes] garnisheed to the old French inhabitants the right to their [racial epithet], and hain't I got as much rights as any Frenchman in this State?[26]

Consequently, these slaveholding settlers contrived myriad ways to circumvent Article VI and otherwise protect the right to own other human beings. During a period from 1807—when Illinois was still part of Indiana Territory—through 1814, territorial legislators passed a series of laws enabling slaveholders to create the appearance that enslaved persons from states such as Kentucky and Tennessee were entering into voluntary contracts of servitude in Illinois.

Three of these statutes were passed on 17 September 1807. "An Act Concerning the Introduction of Negroes and Mulattoes into This Territory" legalized bringing those over the age of fifteen to Indiana and Illinois, required their registration, regulated terms of service, and punished efforts to escape. "An Act Concerning Servants" held "Negroes and Mulattoes" to their terms of service, required proper food and clothing, enabled the assignment of an enslaved person's contract to another master with the former's free consent, established punishment "by stripes" for servants deemed guilty of misbehavior, provided enslaved persons with means of redress for mistreatment, forbade "Negroes, mulattoes, or Indians" from buying any servant "other than of their own complexion" and from buying white servants, punished enslaved persons for traveling without permission, and criminalized anyone assisting them to escape. In 1808 this law was amended to prohibit the gathering of three or more enslaved persons for "dancing or revelling," punishable by up to thirty-nine stripes. And "An Act Regulating the Practices in the General Court, and Court of Common Pleas, and for Other Purposes" prohibited "Negroes, Mulattoes, and Indians" from being witnesses in court against anyone except others of their class. It likewise defined "mulattoes" as having at least one-quarter African ancestry. "An Act to Prevent the Migration of Free Negroes and Mulattoes into This Territory, and for Other Purposes" (passed 8 December 1813) prohibited the entry of free African Americans into Illinois and required the registration of all those then resident in the territory. "An Act Concerning Negroes and Mulattoes" (passed 22 December 1814), citing a dearth of free labor for building mills and manufacturing salt, provided for enslaved persons to come to Illinois and hire themselves for up to one year with their master's consent without any negative impact upon the latter's property rights.[27] The idea was that such individuals could voluntarily agree to such a contract. The reality, wrote historian Allison Mileo Gorsuch, was that they "faced a false choice. . . . Refusing to sign an indenture in Illinois Territory was a one-way ticket back to the slave markets of the South. Signing the contract was a compelled performance, not an act of free consent."[28]

Given the apparent clarity of Article VI—"There shall be neither slavery nor involuntary servitude in the said territory, otherwise than in the punishment of crimes"—these provisions were seemingly in direct contravention of the Northwest Ordinance. But the status of slavery within Illinois Territory was muddied from the very beginning, given that, as historian Robert M. Sutton emphasized, "The Virginia cession of 1783 guaranteed that French inhabitants of the Illinois villages . . . 'shall have their possessions and titles confirmed to them, and be protected in the enjoyment of their rights and liberties.'" There was a conflict, in other words, between the act of cession and Article VI that, Sutton argued, was never truly reconciled.

This contradiction was at the very heart of the interpretation of Article VI by the first governor of the Northwest Territory, Arthur St. Clair. That provision, he maintained, did not apply to those already held in bondage within the territory; it "was prospective in character, not retrospective," wrote Robert M. Sutton, "and should be interpreted as 'a prohibition to any future introduction of slaves.'"[29] It was a deliberate policy, inspired in part by a desire to discourage slaveholders from moving across the Mississippi River to Spanish Louisiana, where the institution was still tolerated.[30] And the presence of extensive salt springs along the Saline River in what is now Gallatin County in southeastern Illinois provided a rationale for the use of enslaved persons in manufacturing salt—as outlined in 1814's "Act Concerning Negroes and Mulattoes"—as opposed to scarce, free white labor. The result, wrote contemporary observer George Flower, was that "[f]or all practical purposes . . . [Illinois] was as much a slave-state as any of the states south of the Ohio River. To roll a barrel of salt once a year, or put salt into a salt-cellar, was sufficient excuse for any man to hire a slave, and raise a field of corn."[31]

Thus a conflict was building between the opponents and proponents of slavery in Illinois. Cook observed in July 1818 that many immigrants to the territory arrived in the expectation that the Northwest Ordinance intended for the region to become a free state. "[T]o defeat that expectation," he wrote, "would seem to be unfair. . . . [M]any who have settled here under that expectation, are so decidedly opposed to slavery that they would not possess them, *if they* were given them."[32] Cook may well have been thinking of himself; in spite (or perhaps because) of his own family's slaveholding in Kentucky, he apparently never purchased or hired any enslaved persons during the sixteen years he resided in Illinois.

Land ownership and speculation, the distribution of power, and the existence of slavery thus served as the foundations of Illinois Territory's lively political environment. Time and again settlers seized upon these issues in expressing frustration and dissatisfaction with their governance. In 1802, for example, they petitioned Indiana territorial governor William Henry Harrison to convene a general territorial convention with the ostensible purpose of repealing Article VI of the Northwest Ordinance. In response Harrison scheduled an election for 11 December of that year to select delegates.[33] Meeting later that month, the so-called Vincennes Convention issued a petition to Congress seeking a ten-year suspension of Article VI; the extinguishment of Indian land titles between the Illinois Country and the Ohio River; the right of preemption for all settlers on public lands; land grants to support schools and seminaries in both Illinois and Indiana settlements; four-hundred-acre land grants for individuals constructing roads and establishing "houses of Entertainment thereon for Five Years"; a grant to the territorial legislature of salt springs in Illinois's saline district; permission for French settlers who had received land grants before 1783 to locate their 400 acres in separate tracts; the extension of suffrage to all free male inhabitants ages twenty-one or older; and the provision of a salary to the territory's attorney general. The repeal or suspension of Article VI would continue to be the primary focus of petitions to Congress from the territory. On this occasion the convention argued that the prohibition had retarded population growth and had driven "many valuable Citizens possessing Slaves" across the Mississippi, "and the consequences of keeping that prohibition in force will be that of obliging the numerous Class of Citizens disposed to emigrate, to seek an Asylum in that country where they can be permitted to enjoy their property."[34]

The Indiana territorial legislature appealed to Congress to suspend Article VI on at least three additional separate occasions—in 1805, in 1806, and in 1807.[35] Congress's response was decidedly mixed. In March 1803 a special House committee initially deemed suspension as "inexpedient," although they were more favorably inclined on the questions of preemption and land grants to benefit schools and seminaries.[36] A second committee convened in February 1804 in the House supported suspension as well as extending suffrage, and they recommended that Congress adopt resolutions to those effects. Congress never acted upon this recommendation, nor did they take any action upon subsequent proposals in 1806. In November 1807 committees in both the House and the Senate, reacting in part to antislavery petitions from citizens in Clark County in the southeastern section of Indiana Territory, once again rejected the idea of suspension.[37]

Thus thwarted, settlers in the Illinois Country attempted a different approach: division of the territory. In February 1805 the Indiana territorial house of representatives reported that petitions were circulating advocating the attachment of the western counties along the Mississippi River to Louisiana on the basis of "the essential difference in the interests of the Western counties from the other parts of the Territory, and the distance of the Mississippi Country from, and the obstacles that exist in the communication with the seat of Government Vincennes."[38] Three years later a group of settlers submitted a petition to Congress through Representative Matthew Lyon of Kentucky[39] and signed by a number of anti-Harrisonians including John Edgar, William Morrison, and James Dunlap. Governor Harrison, they declared, was "guilty of a conduct unworthy of his Office and disgraceful to the Nation." They cited Harrison's signing of laws requiring that a list of confirmed land claims be delivered to the territorial auditor and laws requiring taxation of all claims that had not been finalized. They accused him of a conflict of interest stemming from Harrison's land speculations in spite of his status as superintendent of public land sales. Most notably, they accused him of violating Article VI by sanctioning indentured servitude in "a Law which may properly be entitled 'A Law for the Establishment of disguised slavery in opposition to the National Will.'" The petitioners concluded that in the absence of any other solution, "we cannot but humbly request of Congress that we may be erected into a seperate [*sic*] Colony and permitted to possess a Government of our own."[40] Congress, however, felt differently. Citing the looming end of the current session on 25 April and the lack of a clear necessity for establishing yet another territorial government, the U.S. House of Representatives concurred in the recommendations of a committee led by Matthew Lyon that division was inexpedient at that time.[41]

The partisans of division were not to be dissuaded, however. On 12 October 1808 the territorial house of representatives, acknowledging "great and increasing discontents" in the Illinois Country, approved a petition to Congress requesting that Indiana Territory be divided as "the only means now left of restoring harmony, terminating those discontents and quieting the minds of the people, so essential to the prosperity of an infant Country."[42] On 22 October the territorial legislature selected House Speaker Jesse B. Thomas as Indiana's new congressional delegate and therefore the individual who would be responsible for carrying the division measure forward.[43] Questions were almost immediately raised by "Veritas" in the *Western Sun*, who intimated that Thomas had made a deal—in writing—with John Rice Jones, Rice Jones, William Biggs, and John Messinger (the latter three being members of the territorial house of representatives representing the Illinois counties) to support division in return for their votes to elect him as delegate.[44]

Be that as it may, Jesse B. Thomas introduced a motion in the House of Representatives on 13 December 1808 "to inquire into the expediency of dividing the Indiana Territory." The House appointed Thomas and four other members to a committee for that purpose.[45] On 31 December they issued a report and a bill supporting division of Indiana Territory into two separate governments largely on the basis of the distance between the western settlements and Vincennes that made the administration of justice uneven and the governance of that region problematic. Division, they argued, would tend to "encourage and accelerate migration to each district"; the only objection—the cost of establishing a new territorial government—would be overcome by land sales.[46] The House discussed the bill as a Committee of the Whole two weeks later and passed it with amendments on 18 January. The Senate read the bill twice on 20 January and referred it to a special committee that included John Pope of Kentucky. Pope knew an opportunity for patronage when he saw one, an instinct borne out by the subsequent appointment of his brother Nathaniel as secretary of the new territory and his first cousin, Ninian Edwards, as governor. The committee reported the bill out to the Senate without amendments four days later, in which form it was ultimately passed on 31 January and signed by the president on 3 February.[47]

And so the new territory stood ready to assume its uncertain place within the satellites of the Union. No longer would the Illinois contingents of pro-Harrison and anti-Harrison factions jockey for advantage in Vincennes's political arenas. Now Kaskaskia could take its place as a partisan battlefield for fighting old conflicts and creating new ones. And now the stage was set—when the time was right—for the political apprenticeship of Daniel Pope Cook to begin.

3
TIES OF BLOOD

For all of the effort expended on separating Indiana and Illinois into their own territories, no one had any illusions that this would immediately resolve issues related to land, power, and slavery. It succeeded—if only temporarily—in opening a window of opportunity for the apportionment of the patronage jobs that became available with the creation of a new government. It was, in other words, a rehearsal for the campaign to bring Illinois into the Union nine years later.

Cook's association with Senator John Pope was all the introduction he needed to gain entry into the political circle surrounding Ninian Edwards, governor of Illinois Territory, for such factions were deeply rooted in local issues and personal loyalties.[1] And John Pope, as historian James Simeone observed, was Ninian Edwards's "political Godfather"; he firmly believed, Pope had told Edwards in 1809, that "[w]e must . . . identify ourselves with those allied to us by ties of blood and such others as we can rally around us by all honorable means."[2] Daniel Pope Cook had chosen the bloc that for better or worse controlled the lion's share of patronage, public contracts, and other governmental largesse.

A Political Maverick

Oddly enough, the man at the center of this faction had originally assumed his powerful position as part of an effort to *counteract* territorial political infighting. Described by Robert Howard as a "large and distinguished-looking man with courtly manners," Edwards was a native of Maryland who had been raised in Kentucky and educated at Dickinson College in Carlisle, Pennsylvania, and he subsequently studied both law and medicine. His son Ninian Wirt Edwards wrote tantalizingly of a dissolute youth misspent on "dissipation and gambling."[3] Forswearing this life of iniquity, Edwards channeled his energies instead into a vigorous legal and political career. In relatively short order he gained election to the Kentucky state legislature by the time he was twenty-one and amassed a large fortune from a lucrative legal practice in Kentucky and west Tennessee. He rose rapidly on the other side of the bench as well, serving as presiding judge of the General Court, circuit judge, fourth judge of the Court of Appeals, and chief justice of Kentucky—all before the age of thirty-two. His rapid rise gained him the political sponsorship of powerful figures such as Henry Clay as well as his cousin John Pope.[4]

Edwards's ability to develop such affiliations is impressive in light of his reputation as something of a political maverick. He had, after all, cast one of the few dissenting votes in the state legislature against the Virginia and Kentucky Resolutions that claimed the right of states to nullify actions of the federal government.[5] Although at core in sympathy with Federalist sentiments, Edwards nonetheless aligned himself politically with Republicans, casting his vote as an elector in 1804 for Thomas Jefferson,[6] a point that Senator Pope emphasized in successfully recommending Edwards to President James Madison for governor of Illinois Territory in April 1809. "Although not more than thirty-four years of age," Pope remarked, "few men better understand the human character or can penetrate with more quickness & certainty the designs of others."[7]

Ninian Edwards was going to need every spark of intuition he possessed in the unwieldy political environment of Illinois. His selection by President Madison was something of a double-edged sword; it bypassed the territory's native factions and interposed a leader lacking any stake in those struggles but who was simultaneously unfamiliar with its local problems and peculiarities.[8] He had been appointed as governor in the wake of a partition of Indiana Territory that came about not only because of land speculation and slavery but also because of settler resentment over their geographic remoteness from the seat of government at Vincennes.[9] This had been an ongoing issue over the entire course of European settlement, and it was amplified by the fact that between 1760 and 1809 Illinois had been ruled by six separate authorities: France, Great Britain, Virginia, the United States, the Northwest Territory, and Indiana Territory. Long intervals in which Illinois was utterly without any centralized authority inclined her settlers to fix upon the Northwest Ordinance of 1787 as their one eternal verity. Historian Michael Bakalis wrote that they viewed the ordinance as "more significant to their individual destinies than the Federal Constitution of 1787. When the frontiersmen in these wilderness communities engaged in a dialogue regarding their rights as individuals, they discussed . . . the Northwest Ordinance rather than the nature of the national frame of government."[10]

A Considerable Degree of Party Spirit

The ordinance's importance in the daily life of Illinois Territory emanated at least in part from its concentration of executive power. Section 3 established two executive offices—a governor and a secretary—who were to be appointed, at first by Congress and then (after 1789) by the president.[11] The governor was empowered to appoint all military officers below the rank of general officers, magistrates, and other civil officers in each county or township. He would retain those appointive powers—largely unlimited by any territorial assembly—for the duration of his office.[12] Thus the path to patronage, public contracts, power, and influence led ultimately to Governor Edwards. "Federal appointees," wrote James Simeone, "ruled pluralistically by distributing positions and honors to recognized leaders in the state's settlements and towns."[13] Every new county created meant the appointment of justices of the peace, sheriffs, coroners, and other public officials. It also gave rise to numerous disappointed office seekers, a rich new source of political opposition, and consequently a fertile field for the growth of factions.

This was the context in which Ninian Edwards prepared to assume the duties of his new office. On 11 May 1809 territorial secretary (and acting governor) Nathaniel Pope wrote Secretary of State Robert Smith that his ability to perform his duties was being called into question by "persons of influence"—specifically naming his political nemeses Robert Morrison and John Edgar—on the basis that Pope had not been properly sworn into office. Pope refrained from imputing their motives, but he worried that the whispering campaign was "calculated to embarrass me in the organization of the Government, & to weaken the confidence of the people in the Executive, in these times of danger."[14]

Little wonder, then, that newly minted Governor Edwards wrote on 28 June: "Soon after my arrival at this place I discovered very much to my regret that a considerable degree of party spirit divided the people of this Territory." He was committed, he declared, "[t]o guard against the consequences of it . . . to protect the equal rights of the good people over whom I am called by my country to preside—and inspire them with Confidence in the administration of public justice." In this spirit Edwards determined to remove James Gilbreath—who had sided with Pope as a member of the pro-Harrison faction—as sheriff of Randolph County owing to the latter's status as a "partizan." "[T]he man who fills it [the position]," he told Gilbreath, "should not only be free from all prejudice bias & partialities but should be entirely free from the suspicion of either." Consequently, he wrote, it was his intention to appoint Benjamin

Stephenson as his replacement.[15] He conveniently neglected to make reference to his own political and familial connections to Stephenson, who had become his close friend back in Logan County, Kentucky.[16]

The Legislative Mill

In this context, Daniel Pope Cook's decision to forgo the charming life of a mercantile clerk for the study of law under Nathaniel Pope—again, Senator Pope's brother and Governor Edwards's cousin—was a shrewd career move. Here was an opportunity to begin a legal career in close proximity to the man who was responsible for keeping, revising, and indexing the laws and records of the territory.[17] Here was a chance to ingratiate himself with the influential territorial leader with whom the governor (as Edwards himself expressed it) enjoyed "for upwards of seven years the most uninterrupted cordiality . . . which has enabled me to harmonize a population perfectly convulsed by party feuds."[18]

Cook had an early opportunity to observe these battles firsthand in the course of serving in his first public office as engraving and enrolling clerk to the territorial legislature beginning in December 1813.[19] In that capacity, Cook prepared and relayed all messages between the two houses—the territorial council and the house of representatives—and ensured that all legislation passed by each body was properly reconciled. In the process Cook had the opportunity to become familiar with the issues of greatest concern to Illinois frontiersmen and to witness the compromises and horse-trading so crucial to building legislative and political consensus. And certainly there was plenty of grist for the legislative mill. During the very first session Cook attended beginning in December 1813, the legislature passed measures allowing conscientious objectors to be exempted from militia duty; banning the sale of liquor or any other trade articles to Indians; and requiring that ballots be cast by voice vote to lessen the influence of "electioneering Zealots."[20]

But the law that must have been of particular interest to Cook—given his unease regarding slavery—was the 1813 measure "to prevent the Migration of Free Negroes and Mullattoes [*sic*] into This Territory and for Other Purposes." Under its provisions, any free African Americans caught migrating to Illinois would be required to leave within fifteen days; those already living in the territory were required to prove their free status by registering with the county clerk of the court of common pleas. The punishment for violating these provisions was to be no fewer than twenty-five and no more than thirty-nine stripes on the bare back. Free African Americans who aided those escaping bondage were subject to a yet harsher punishment: no fewer than thirty-nine and no more than fifty stripes.[21]

This was the first provision in the territorial code focusing upon free African Americans rather than those who were enslaved. To some extent it reflected, perhaps, a growing awareness of the ways in which Article VI of the Northwest Ordinance complicated issues of labor supply and race in Illinois. This complexity comes into sharper relief in light of the fact that at least two of the six members of the territorial legislature that enacted this provision into law were avowedly antislavery. Risdon Moore of St. Clair County was a recent arrival to Illinois, having removed from Georgia in 1812 partly on account of his distaste for slavery. It was said that he brought with him fifteen or eighteen enslaved persons, whom he allowed "to look out for themselves and use their own earnings" as soon as they came of age.[22]

James Lemen Sr.—also from St. Clair County—had migrated from Virginia to Illinois in 1786, according to John Mason Peck, to "enjoy, uninterrupted, the advantages of a country unembarrassed with slavery."[23] Lemen was a founder or cofounder of a number of antislavery Baptist churches in southern Illinois; his grandson Joseph Lemen claimed—falsely—that James Lemen Sr. had conspired with and been bankrolled by Thomas Jefferson specifically to maintain the antislavery character of the Old Northwest.[24] Lemen and Moore later vigorously opposed the legalization of slavery in the new state of Illinois, signing an 1818 petition urging that "no exertions of a fair character should be omitted to defeat the plan of those who either wish a temporary or unlimited slavery."[25]

The enactment of such a harsh measure by the territorial legislature counting such men among its members was a stark reminder that opposition to slavery by no means implied a willingness to consider free African Americans as the social and political equals of white settlers. If anything, it served to reinforce a fear that they represented an unsettling example for their enslaved brethren and thus constituted a threat—in the eyes of Cook and his allies—to the safety and well-being of Illinois Territory.

My Solicitation of Your Patronage

Meanwhile, Cook's legal studies continued, and his zeal for professional advancement was unabated. Catching the eye of Governor Edwards was key. Through his work with the legislature Cook became aware of a proposal in November 1814 to create a supreme court for the territory composed of the three territorial judges appointed by the president. Cook's focus was upon section 20 of the law, which provided for the appointment by the governor of two attorneys to prosecute all cases; one would have jurisdiction over a district encompassing Madison, St. Clair, and Randolph Counties, while the other would oversee the counties of Johnson, Gallatin, and Edwards. Each would be paid an annual salary of one hundred dollars.[26] In spite of his youth, inexperience, and the fact that he had not yet been licensed to practice law, Cook boldly solicited appointment to one of these sinecures. He wrote a letter on 30 November 1814 to Governor Edwards that serves as a fascinating declaration of the purposes that were to animate Cook throughout the course of his career and sets him apart as a prototype of future Illinois political professionals who sought to reconcile multiple—and frequently conflicting—impulses. "My solicitation of your patronage on this occasion," he wrote, "emenates [*sic*] from an anxiety to facilitate the acquisition of a practical knowledge of the law, to provide for my pecuniary exigencies, and to become useful to the public."[27]

This particular effort at political advancement ultimately proved unsuccessful. On 24 December 1814 Edwards appointed other more experienced hands to the offices: William Mears, who had been serving as the territory's attorney general since 1813, and Thomas C. Brown, a member of the territorial house of representatives from Gallatin County and a political ally of the governor.[28] Nevertheless, it was not the last time Cook would attempt to cultivate Governor Edwards or other men of influence.

Cook's tutelage as a law student under Nathaniel Pope ended with the acquisition of his law license and with the commencement of his professional practice in Edwardsville in 1815, but it was only the beginning of a lifelong political, and later familial, affiliation with Ninian Edwards, marrying the governor's daughter Julia in 1821.[29] Indeed, Edwards cemented the relationship between Cook and Pope through their designation on 11 January 1816 as a committee "to superintend the printing of the laws and journals of the present session of the legislature" for the princely sum of twenty-five dollars to be paid by the auditor of public accounts, who, as it happened, was to be Daniel Pope Cook, appointed to that position on 13 January 1816.[30] In this capacity—which he fulfilled for just over a year until he resigned in early 1817—Cook was responsible for keeping and auditing the territorial accounts as well as to make payments from public funds. He was also enjoined to publish notices relating to land tax liabilities and due dates "in some Newspaper for three weeks successively."[31]

Here was yet another happy circumstance for Daniel Pope Cook. Within three months—by the end of April 1816—Cook found himself a proprietor and editor of the territory's only newspaper, the Kaskaskia *Western Intelligencer*, which placed him in a position to benefit from government printing contracts.[32] The *Intelligencer* was a peculiar frontier amalgam of legal notices, breathless prospectuses for gestating hamlets waiting to rise from the prairie, belated accounts of intrigues in European royal courts, advertisements for escapees from slavery, and occasional genuine specimens of local news. Cook had purchased the newspaper (originally called the *Illinois Herald*) from Matthew Duncan, a Yale graduate and the older brother of future Illinois governor Joseph Duncan as well as a friend of Ninian Edwards from their days together back in Russellville, Kentucky, where Duncan edited the *Mirror*. Duncan's granddaughter Elizabeth Duncan Putnam reported that it was through Edwards that Duncan "secured the printing of the first edition of the Illinois Territorial Laws in 1813." He moved to Illinois to publish the *Illinois Herald* in hopes of continuing to gain government printing contracts.[33] Thus Cook was by no means the first printer seeking to gain commercial advantages from a personal association with Ninian Edwards. Nor, for that matter, was he to be the last. His fellow publisher on the *Western Intelligencer*, Robert Blackwell, was appointed to succeed Cook as auditor of public accounts on 5 April 1817. Blackwell was in turn succeeded by Elijah C. Berry, who by then had become Blackwell's copublisher at the *Intelligencer*.[34]

Cook's proprietorship of the *Western Intelligencer*, then, served the dual purposes of providing him with a source of income and keeping his own name in the public eye.[35] It enabled him as well to serve the interests of his patrons, Governor Edwards and Secretary Pope. This was made abundantly clear in an epistle from Cook to the governor dated 8 June 1816 concerning the prospective publication of a letter from Edwards to the U.S. secretary of war in the *Intelligencer*. Cook advised delaying publication until after the upcoming fall election in which Nathaniel Pope was a candidate for territorial delegate to Congress, citing the danger that "it might excite some party feeling that is at present entirely neutralized." He ended his remarks with a complimentary reference to Edwards's status with the general public. Noting that the governor's friend Joseph Oglesby spoke of campaigning for delegate against Pope on a platform devoted to appointing a new governor—a position calculated to draw support from Edwards's political enemies—Cook observed that this strategy was founded upon the assumption that the governor was "very unpopular, which in candor, I think, [is] a dam'd foolish one."[36]

In the space of a few paragraphs Cook strove to strengthen a political alliance by supporting Pope's run for public office and flattering Governor Edwards as a means for bolstering his own prospects. The *Intelligencer*, like many early Illinois newspapers, was to a large extent a political organ, in this case intended to advance the interests of the Edwards-Pope combine. Franklin William Scott, an early historian of Illinois newspapers, wrote: "Had there been no public printing and no politicians who felt the need of 'organs,' probably no early paper could have lived a year, for the subscribers were few and the advertisements yielded little income."[37]

A Gentleman of Every Necessary Qualification

Nathaniel Pope's resignation on 5 September 1816 as territorial secretary upon his election as territorial delegate to Congress provided the political opportunity that Daniel Pope Cook had been hoping for. In the interim—while awaiting President James Madison's choice for a permanent replacement—Cook stepped forward to act as temporary secretary. In this capacity he served from 22 September to 17 December 1816 and was paid $260.[38]

Given his close alliance with Edwards and Pope, Cook could have been forgiven for thinking that he was the logical heir apparent. It may be a measure of his confidence in assuming the office permanently (and guaranteeing a secure source of income) that in late September 1816 he arranged to purchase nearly 1,120 acres of land in the counties of St. Clair, Washington, and Randolph at a cost of just under $1,600 (almost $25,000 today).[39] He also worked to obtain letters of recommendation from old friends and political allies alike. Senator John Pope characterized Cook as "a man of real worth in politics a republican & friend to the administration."[40] Edward Hempstead, formerly Missouri Territory's congressional delegate, deemed Cook "a Gentleman of talents, information, respectability and Integrity, and whose political Sentiments are decidedly Republican." Benjamin Stephenson, Governor Edwards's ally and later a delegate to the state's first constitutional convention, wrote: "I feel no hesitation in recommending him as a Gentleman of every necessary qualification to discharge the duties of that office, or any other."[41] Perhaps fearing that he had damned Cook with faint praise, in a follow-up letter Stephenson added that Cook "is universally, admired for both his talents and his virtues—Since the date of the letter written by Mr. Hempstead and myself I have had an excellent opportunity of ascertaining the public sentiment in regard to Mr. Cook which convinces me that no man from any quarter would be more acceptable."[42] Additional testimonials came from Alexander McNair, William Clark (of Corps of Discovery fame), and Josias Randle.[43]

Noticeably silent in all this was Governor Edwards. In a striking passage from his second letter of 14 October 1816, Benjamin Stephenson emphasized that he had encouraged Edwards to recommend Cook for the office given the importance of close collaboration between the governor and the secretary. Edwards, Stephenson reported, had "a very high opinion of his [Cook's] talents and integrity and that he would vastly prefer him to any other candidate from this Territory—with some of whom if appointed he could expect nothing less than continual collision of the most unpleasant kind."[44]

Stephenson's judgment that the governor valued Cook's talents was not far off the mark; nevertheless, Edwards ultimately recommended another gentleman to succeed Pope as territorial secretary. That man was Joseph Philips, a native of Tennessee who had formerly served in the regular army and after statehood became Illinois's first chief justice and later ran unsuccessfully for governor in 1822.[45] On 25 September Edwards wrote to Philips that some of the candidates for Pope's old office—he named no names—would lead to "an end to the repose and tranquility which we have enjoyed, in a preeminent degree, for some years past," which Edwards attributed to the congenial relations between Pope and himself. "I therefore feel," he continued, "personally more interest in your success than any other man—but this very circumstance places me in that delicate situation, which alone, could restrain me from tendering you a recommendation to the President of the United States."[46]

Edwards was right to be wary. He had been particularly sensitive to charges of political favoritism since the election for territorial delegate in 1816, when he had supported Nathaniel Pope's candidacy. That position, observed Michael Bakalis, elicited "criticism centered around the question of whether there was a closed group within the territory which controlled political affairs and whether this group should be longer tolerated."[47] Russell Heacock, who styled himself as an opposing candidate, was blunt: "I do not think that, because a man is rich, he has the greater claim to any office, nor do I think a man the more entitled for having been loaded with territorial, or any other commissions, nor for that he has long been a public servant, unless he can shew that he has been a good one."[48] Cook had already anticipated and answered these concerns, rising to Pope's—and by implication, Edwards's—defense a week earlier. He deemed Pope as "unbiassed [*sic*] by party prejudices; for it is well known that he has always stood aloof from those party disputes, which have so frequently disturbed the reposed [*sic*] of the Territory."[49]

Thus Edwards's professed regard for Joseph Philips can be interpreted in a variety of ways. It may have been genuine, but given that Philips was very much a newcomer to Illinois—perhaps as recent as September 1816[50]—it is difficult at first glance to perceive the source of that regard. The picture, however, becomes clearer upon a closer examination of the most prominent men of the nine candidates whose names were put forward in consideration for the position. Robert Morrison of Randolph County, formerly one of the anti-Harrisonians and therefore a political opponent of Nathaniel Pope, was rather half-heartedly recommended on 19 November 1816 by William Lowry of Baltimore, who admitted that Morrison was his son-in-law and who candidly advised that if he was "not worthy of the office, he ought not to receive it."[51] His application was also supported by Guy Bryan, a business partner of Morrison's brother William, who was—as Bryan took pains to emphasize—"the present Contractor for the supply of Rations in that Territory."[52] Jephthah Hardin of Gallatin County came recommended courtesy of Jesse B. Thomas, William Sprigg, and John Caldwell. Hardin, described by historian Joseph E. Suppiger as an "anti-Edwards lawyer,"[53] was the brother-in-law of Thomas's half-brother Michael Jones. Thomas and Sprigg were two of the three territorial judges who in 1812 had fought Governor Edwards and the territorial legislature over an increase in their workload, in the process becoming Edwards's mortal political enemies.[54]

In Consequence of a Mistake

Like Cook, all of these candidates were denizens of Illinois who came recommended by avowedly partisan advocates. Joseph Philips stood in stark contrast to his rivals first by virtue of his status as a true outsider, hailing as he did from Tennessee rather than the territory or from Kentucky, the traditional incubator for so many aspiring Illinois politicians. Furthermore, Philips came armed with the recommendations of twenty-four prominent men in his home state, including Senator John Williams and future representative Thomas Claiborne.[55] Philips's supporters, in fact, far outnumbered those of all of his rivals for the position combined, and they acted on his behalf far earlier as well; at least ten of the letters were dated 30 August 1816, close to a week before Pope resigned as territorial secretary on 5 September. This backing was decisive, and it fit well into President Madison's past history of appointing outsiders to territorial offices. From 1809 through 1815, of the six men whom Madison selected to serve in the Illinois judiciary, one was from Georgia, one from Virginia, one from Connecticut, one from Missouri Territory, and one from Kentucky. Only one—Governor Edwards's bitter foe Jesse B. Thomas—was native to the territory (if hailing from the eastern portion of Indiana Territory could be considered native).[56] It seems unlikely that Madison's decision was a complete surprise to Cook.

Whether a surprise or not, Cook was sorely disappointed. He believed there was an additional dimension to the political context that had resulted in Philips's selection. He later told John Quincy Adams that Philips had been slated for retention as an army officer at the close of the War of 1812, "but in consequence of a mistake which happened in the War Department, he was left out, and as a reparation for the injury, Mr. Madison determined on conferring the appt. on him."[57] Governor Edwards sought to mollify his young protégé, writing on 19 January 1817 to Secretary of State (and soon-to-be president) James Monroe to recommend Cook for appointment as a territorial judge should a vacancy become available. Cook's frustration was heightened by the always fragile state of his health. In his letter to Monroe, Edwards implied that the strength of Cook's constitution was an impediment to his ability to engage in a more extensive law practice.[58] A long-term, successful career in public service seemed more elusive than ever. His apprenticeship in the territorial legislature, his time as auditor of public accounts, his temporary service as territorial secretary, and his careful cultivation of the likes of Edwards and Pope were all seemingly to no avail. What Daniel Pope Cook needed now was time to think.

4

A BEARER OF DESPATCHES

Consumed by weariness and plagued with doubt, Daniel Pope Cook sought to place some distance between himself and the scene of his personal and political stalemate. To that end, sometime in late December 1816 or early January 1817 Cook sojourned back to his birthplace in Scott County, Kentucky, where he spent time with his family, nursing his wounds and renewing old acquaintances. Chief among the latter was ex-senator John Pope. Here was a source of sage advice and counsel. In the privacy of Pope's Frankfort home Cook could tell the tale of his territorial successes and frustrations. Perhaps Pope could even provide insight into Governor Edwards's seeming nonchalance in the cause of Cook's advancement. If he could do little to allay his protégé's uncertainty, however, Pope could still act as his champion.

Accordingly, he wrote on 11 February 1817 to President-elect James Monroe:

> Dr SIR My young friend Mr. Daniel P. Cook of the Illinois Territory goes to Washington City & has probably in view some appointment in some of the Territories—I have to assure you that he is a gentleman of fine understanding correct habits & incorruptible integrity—I shall really be obliged by any services you can render him.[1]

It is significant that Senator Pope referred to Cook's interest in political appointment not in Illinois but in "some of the Territories." In other words, Cook felt that he had reached the limits of what he could accomplish in Illinois and was contemplating making a fresh start elsewhere. Any such territorial appointments would be made in Washington, and so Cook turned his sights eastward. On 6 February he wrote Ninian Edwards: "I am just starting to the City of Washington, partly on my own account and partly on account of my father, who has business in Virginia. I expect to return in April."[2] Presumably Cook had no specific plan in mind upon his arrival in Washington other than to avail himself of Senator Pope's contacts and hope for the best.

One of the Best Cathartics in the World

At long last in early March 1817 Daniel Pope Cook found himself face to face with the new president. Cook was not a prepossessing figure. "In his personal appearance, Mr. Cook was a small spare man, considerably under the ordinary hight [*sic*]," remembered William H. Brown, one of Cook's contemporaries as well as one of his successors as editor and publisher of the *Illinois Intelligencer.* "His usual weight did not, probably, exceed one hundred and twenty pounds." Nevertheless, Brown found something compelling in the man: "He was straight and erect in his person, and quick and active in his movements. His features were plain, but marked—and so indicative of intelligence and kind feeling as to render them agreeable and pleasing."[3]

At all events, the letter of introduction from Senator Pope—who was, after all, a loyal member of Monroe's political party—proved persuasive to the president, who assured the younger man—as Cook later reported—of "a perfect willingness to render me any service in his power."[4] As it happened, Monroe had just declared his intention on 6 March to appoint John Quincy Adams as his secretary of state. Adams was then serving as American minister to Great Britain, and so it would be necessary to send the appointment to London via diplomatic courier. Would Mr. Cook be willing to assume this responsibility? He thought for a moment. Monroe had been president for only three days, after all, and there would be ample opportunity to lobby for a territorial sinecure upon his return. Yes, Mr. Cook would be very interested in a trip to London.

The president wrote a letter to Adams, noting that the courier was "a respectable young man from Kentucky,"[5] and presumably directed Cook to see the interim secretary of state, John Graham, for the complete diplomatic portfolio. Cook now began a frenzy of preparations for his journey. He wrote to Governor Edwards on 7 March resigning his position as auditor of public accounts and "to return my grateful acknowledgements for the friendship rec[d.] at your hand."[6] Cook likewise penned a note to the *Western Intelligencer* announcing his appointment and promising that all business entrusted to him would be "punctually attended by J.D. Cook, Esq. residing at Shawneetown."[7] On 10 March he received his passport as "Dan[l] P. Cook, bearer of despatches to England."[8] He then proceeded via steamboat up the coast, and his arrival in New York City was announced in the *New-York Gazette & General Advertiser* of Thursday, 13 March, which added that Cook "will, we understand, sail from this port on board the United States' sloop of war Hornet, Captain Ballard, now fitting for the purpose of carrying out a Minister, and to bring home Mr. Adams."[9]

As it turned out, Cook was slated to sail to England not in a naval sloop but rather in a "packet boat." These vessels, largely devoted to carrying mail across the Atlantic at regular intervals, served simultaneously as passenger vessels—primarily used by diplomats and well-to-do passengers, as the cost of passage was typically beyond the reach of most average citizens. They ran regular routes between New York and Falmouth in Cornwall on the southwest coast of England.[10]

Once in New York, Daniel Pope Cook had three days to catch his breath and make final preparations for his upcoming thirty-five-hundred-mile sojourn to London. On the lookout for any opportunities that might arise, he placed a notice in the *New-York Gazette & General Advertiser* announcing his trip: "*Daniel Pope Cook*, on his way to England, with despatches from government, is at present at No. 321 Pearl-street. As he intends to remain in England some time, he will receive orders to transact any commercial business with which he may be entrusted."[11]

Some sense of his other arrangements may be gleaned from a letter of advice written around the same time by Evan Thomas Jr., a Baltimore Quaker and businessman, to his brother-in-law Elisha Tyson Jr. in preparation for the latter's upcoming journey to the British Isles.[12] Thomas counseled Tyson to obtain a Russia leather portfolio containing "paper, pens, ink, sand, wafers, pins, needles, silk, thread and in short every kind of useful instrument for a Traveller."[13] He suggested inspecting the captain's list of provisions to ensure a plentiful supply of water and cider, and he declared that ducks and pigs were to be preferred over chickens, turkeys, and sheep in the matter of shipboard livestock. He advised treating seasickness—a matter likely to be of no small interest to the delicate Mr. Cook—by drinking glasses of warm water or taking doses of "Henry's Calcined Magnesia." If all else failed, he wrote, "A glass of Sea Water occasionally is one of the best cathartics in the World." Most importantly, he counseled, "Leave every Local prejudice & opinion at home—and become a citizen of the world; let thy mind become like a Blank Sheet of paper—try all things, hold fast that which is good."[14]

Cook was sailing, as it happened, during a time of year in which the duration of the transatlantic voyage was a trifle shorter than at other seasons. Eastbound voyages during March averaged twenty-three days (as opposed to thirty-six days for a voyage in the opposite direction).[15] His chosen packet-boat, the *Marchioness of Queensbury*, was brig-rigged—that is to say, it possessed two masts with square sails—and "at 188 tons," remarked historian Tony Pawlyn, "she was about the standard size for a Falmouth packet." The captain, James Richardson Hannah (or Hennah), one of the owners of the *Queensbury*, had been commissioned as a Post Office packet commander in 1813.[16]

This was the vessel that departed New York City on Sunday, 16 March 1817 bearing one Daniel Pope Cook, diplomatic courier to John Quincy Adams.[17] The *Queensbury* first meandered down the East River to the open sea, and thence east-northeast toward Halifax, Nova Scotia, where she discharged and admitted passengers, took on additional mail, and then embarked on 27 March for the final leg of her voyage.[18]

Daniel Pope Cook's first ocean voyage—indeed, his first departure from the United States—provided him with an opportunity for reflection. Bouts of seasickness would have helped concentrate his mind wonderfully. Kaskaskia, the petty internecine squabbles over patronage, the nature of his relationship to Governor Edwards—all these receded into the horizon as the *Queensbury* sailed eastward and the Cornish port town of Falmouth came gradually into view. On Wednesday, 30 April 1817 Cook disembarked and departed for London.[19]

Future Allies

On Saturday, 3 May John Quincy Adams returned from attending the annual exhibition dinner of the Royal Academy/Somerset House—"Altogether the dinner was dull," he wrote—to discover that during his absence Mr. D. P. Cook had left his dispatches at the American minister's lodgings in Craven Street. Adams recorded in his diary that among these papers was his commission as secretary of state, a missive from John Graham, a letter of recredence (i.e., recalling Adams from his ministerial position) to the prince regent (the future King George IV), and letters of introduction on Cook's behalf from W. S. Smith (Adams's nephew) and Timothy Pitkin, a Federalist congressman from Connecticut.[20]

Adams and Cook met for the first time on the following day, when Adams recorded that the courier spent much of the morning at the minister's residence. It marked the beginning of a remarkable relationship with the future president who encouraged him, cultivated him, and introduced him to a wider world of politics and high culture. And it commenced that very same evening, when young Mr. Cook dined with the Adams family and afterward ventured forth to the theater—almost certainly for the first time in his life—with John Adams Smith, the minister's twenty-nine-year-old nephew and *chargé d'affaires*. It must have been a heady experience for Cook to survey the wide variety of entertainment venues suddenly available to him at the end of his first day in London: "King Richard the Third, Duke of Gloucester" starring Edmund Kean at the Theatre Royal in Drury Lane; "the new tragedy, called THE APOSTATE" featuring Charles Kemble at Covent Garden; "Every One Has His Fault" at the Theatre Royal in Haymarket; and "the Equestrian Melo-Drama of URANDA the ENCHANTER of the STEEL CASTLE."[21]

Adams and Cook already had at least one contact in common: the minister's wife, Louisa Catherine Johnson Adams, who was the sister of Senator John Pope's wife, Eliza Johnson.[22] But if John Quincy Adams was taking an interest in the young novice from Illinois Territory, it may also have had something to do with his recent contacts with two other men who were soon to become influential figures in early Illinois and political allies to Daniel Pope Cook. Edward Coles of Virginia had most recently been private secretary to President James Madison, and consequently Madison had entrusted him with a delicate diplomatic mission to Russia in late 1816. Coles was at that time already making arrangements to immigrate to Illinois, partly for the purpose of freeing his enslaved persons,[23] but at Madison's urging he agreed to undertake the journey to St. Petersburg. Coles ultimately brought the crisis to a successful resolution, and he thereupon embarked on a grand tour of European capitals that eventually led him to London and encounters with John Quincy Adams in March and April 1817.[24]

Minister Adams in turn introduced Edward Coles to Morris Birkbeck, another future Illinoisan who would one day become his political ally in the effort to prevent the legalization of slavery in the Prairie State. In 1858 Coles recalled that Adams made the introduction at Birkbeck's request after the latter learned of Coles's extensive travels, especially out West. Adams informed Coles that the Englishman was considering immigrating to the United States "and would be a great acquisition to it, as he was not only one of the best practical and scientific agriculturalists of Great Britain, but had much literary taste and knowledge."[25]

Birkbeck visited Adams to take his leave two days before the former's departure westward. "Birkbeck," wrote Adams, "is going with a view to settle in the United States, under the apprehension that troublous times are approaching in this Country."[26] It was his intention, the Englishman recorded in his journal, to settle in western Pennsylvania, Ohio, Indiana, or Illinois Territory, since slavery had not taken root in any of those places.[27] Ultimately he settled in Edwards County near the Wabash River—the "English Prairie," he called it—establishing the towns of Albion and Wanborough.

An Opportunity of Empowerment

Meanwhile, Daniel Pope Cook had not been idle during the nearly five weeks he patiently awaited the minister's departure. He seems to have explored London extensively. The scenes of desperation and deprivation that he witnessed reawakened his natural empathy. This product of the western frontier, accustomed to the rough equality of the backwoods and witnessing for the first time the spectacle of extreme poverty and unchecked wealth living cheek by jowl, wrote to his brother in a white heat of anger:

> Would you believe me, that the news papers [*sic*] gave an account of nineteen being hung in one week for larceny, and most of them no doubt urged by the gauling hand of necessity—to starve to death, or steal and run the risk of being hung, are often the alternatives of many of the poor wretches; and the latter as nature dictates, is often resorted to. . . . But while distress in every possible shape presents itself before you, at the same instant your feelings, if they are human, are insulted by the display of wealth and "pampered luxury." . . .
>
> Thus are the people divided into very rich and very poor. . . . To continue long in this situation is impossible. Hunger like fire enveloped in combustible matter, will ultimately seek satiety, it will explode.[28]

The day of departure finally arrived on 5 June 1817, when the ship *Washington*—Captain Jacob Forman commanding—left the London dock with the first members of the Adams household, and probably at this point Daniel Pope Cook, on board. John Quincy Adams himself traveled nearly ninety miles overland to embark at East Cowes on the Isle of Wight on 12 June. The *Washington* at long last turned its prow westward two days later.[29] Daniel Pope Cook was headed back home.

Such westbound voyages—in the days when ships relied upon wind power—were typically longer in duration than the eastward journey. The necessity of laying a course outside the Gulf Stream and "tacking against contrary winds," wrote historian Robert Greenhalgh Albion, meant adding upwards of 550 extra miles to the journey. The month of June—when the *Washington* began its journey—was in fact one of the worst months for the homeward passage due to ice fields, fogs, and calms.[30]

On board were thirty-four passengers encompassing nine members of the Adams household, ten cabin passengers—including Daniel Pope Cook, Henry Bradshaw Fearon (a London merchant), a Major Lamb, a Dr. Tillary, George A. Otis, a Mr. Shields, W. G. Cutting, and a Mr. Romanis—and fourteen travelers in steerage.[31] Fearon, who subsequently wrote an account of his travels in America, recorded that his passage cost forty guineas ("exclusive of wines, &c.") and that steerage passengers paid twelve pounds apiece.[32]

Aside from its longer duration, Cook's homeward journey differed from his first voyage in one particularly significant respect: this time, at least, he was not alone, and there were ample opportunities to divert his mind between spells of seasickness during the sixty-one days between London and New York. He was ill during much of the first three weeks of the trip, although that was also the case with most of the other passengers. Adams noted on 30 June, however, that "[t]he other passengers excepting M$^{r.}$ Cook have become enured to the motion and ceased to be sick." By the following day none of the passengers was ill, apparently even including Daniel Pope Cook.[33]

Having finally gotten his sea legs, Cook now had the chance in such close quarters to become better acquainted with John Quincy Adams. There were evening card parties in the cabin; there was a debating society started in steerage by a Mr. Davis that met twice weekly—on Monday and Thursday evenings—and solemnly discussed such lofty topics as "Which is the best form of government, a democracy or a monarchy?" "It was strongly contested on both sides," wrote Henry Fearon, "and at length determined in favour of the former by the casting vote of the chairman, who was seated in presidential state on a water-cask."[34] There were endless games of chess; on 21 July Adams recorded that "while my wife and the other cabin Passengers were at cards, Charles [his son] and I were playing over Philidor's first game to teach Mr. Cooke [*sic*] the elements of the game."[35] Cook also seems to have become close to sixteen-year-old George Washington Adams, the secretary's eldest son, advising him in matters of the heart. "I unbosom to you as to a friend," young Adams wrote to Cook upon his return home.[36]

There were likewise opportunities for extended, animated conversation with other cabin passengers. "We have frequent discussions at table after breakfast and dinner," Adams wrote, "upon various topics of Literature, Politics, Morals, Religion, and miscellaneous as they arise." The erudite but eternally self-critical Mr. Adams admitted: "In these Conversations I am sometimes led perhaps to take too great a share."[37] Young Mr. Cook drank it all in. It seemed a world away from Kaskaskia and opened his eyes to a multitude of possibilities.

Sensing that he had a narrow window of opportunity in which to act, on 4 August—two days before landfall at New York—Cook penned a heartfelt, almost desperate missive to John Quincy Adams, "beg[ging] leave to solicit your friendship and patronage in procuring some public situation, that will assist me in defraying those expenses which I am compelled to incur during my inability to prosecute my professional business." He touched on his experience as deputy territorial secretary and as clerk of the territorial legislature for three successive sessions. Cook worried aloud about whether his health would ever allow him to safely continue his law practice; "I should prefer some situation," he confided, "at the seat of the general Government, for a while at least, for the sake of the superior facilities which present themselves at that place of acquiring that knowledge of public business which will be necessary to enable me to fill a more responsible and lucrative situation than I am at present qualified to fill. . . . The situation therefore of *private Secretary* to yourself," he declared none too subtly, "if you should have one, or some other situation in your Department would be most desirable."[38]

Having thus appealed to Secretary Adams, Cook stepped ashore on the New York dock on 6 August 1817, his arrival duly noted in local newspapers as one of the passengers aboard the *Washington*.[39] On 8 August he wrote his brother of his safe arrival and reported that more than one hundred emigrants from Europe had arrived in the city in the two days since his own return.[40] He spent some time shopping in the city with Henry Fearon (who described Cook as a "very pleasant young man"), purchasing a fashionable narrow-brimmed hat for ten dollars.[41]

Cook continued to cultivate his acquaintance with John Quincy Adams, accompanying him on a visit to the studio of the artist John Trumbull on 10 August and dining together on the fifteenth.[42] Cook must have journeyed south to Washington, D.C., sometime shortly after this to wait patiently for Adams's arrival. Certainly he was back in the nation's capital by 10 September, when he was visited by his fellow Kentuckian Henry Clay. The following day Cook speculated in a letter to Edwards that Clay's visit was connected to the fact that he "has an eye on his popularity in the Territories, as they will become States before an opening presents itself for the gratification of his ulterior views in politics."[43] Clay's visit may also have been connected to two letters Cook wrote to the *National Register* on 10 and 14 September warning of the dangers of slavery and emphasizing the importance of national unity. "In a country so vast in extent," Cook argued, ". . . a great similarity in manners, habits, and mode of thinking, must be preserved, as the strongest cement of our union and safeguard of our tranquility. But slavery destroys this similarity in each of those particulars."[44]

Meanwhile Secretary Adams, after visiting friends and family in Cambridge and Quincy, Massachusetts, departed on 9 September, arriving in the nation's capital eleven days later. And one of his first visitors the next morning—Sunday, 21 September—was Daniel Pope Cook.[45] To the extent that Cook had discussed his professional ambitions with Adams, he had—up to this point—intimated a desire to stay permanently in Washington. Now, he confessed, he had changed his mind. Now it was his ambition to attain the position in the newly created Alabama Territory that had been denied to him in Illinois: he wanted to become territorial secretary. Cook wrote to Adams on 22 September that "the reason is that upon incidental inquiry I am induced to suppose there is no situation, vacant here, that I could think of getting into which would probably afford me an opportunity of improvement equal to the situation [of territorial secretary]." His background, experience, and ambition rendered him particularly suited for the position: "The duties of the office which I now solicit are familiar to me, having discharged them for three years as a deputy, and they are not laborious but afford all necessary time for study, which is a great object with me."

Warming to his subject, Cook foreshadowed the case he would soon be making for transforming Illinois Territory to statehood and, coincidentally, making an explicit connection between admission to the Union and his own ambition. He predicted that Alabama's population would presently entitle the territory to statehood, at which point "the advantages of a reputation established by correct deportment, (which I shall always aim to observe), will perhaps be greater than from any character which my talents would enable me to establish at this place [Washington, D.C.]" He nonetheless steeled himself against inevitable disappointment. "If however any other situation appears to you to be better fitted for me . . . which it will be practicable for me to obtain, and you are not unwilling to make a selection for me I beg of you to make such selection."

It Would Not Satisfy My Ambition

Clearly Daniel Pope Cook was searching for a compelling alternative to an uncertain future if he returned to Kaskaskia. He counseled haste to Secretary Adams, worrying that President Monroe was scheduled to leave town soon, and as it was Cook's understanding that an appointment to the position of secretary of Alabama Territory was to be made immediately, "delay might be injurious."[46]

Cook saw a great deal of John Quincy Adams over the next several days, soliciting the secretary personally in his office on 23 September and visiting him again at home on the evenings of the twenty-fourth and twenty-fifth.[47] His lobbying was beginning to make an impression. Adams assured Cook of his continuing willingness to act as his advocate as opportunities became available. Indeed, in later years they became close both personally and politically. In 1821 Adams deemed him "a man of fair mind and honourable principles, and makes a very handsome appearance in the House [of Representatives] as a speaker. He is yet under thirty and gives the promise of a useful and distinguished Statesman, but his health is very infirm and his Constitution so feeble that its duration is more than ordinarily doubtful."[48]

For now, however, Cook's ambitions remained unrealized and his fate uncertain. He expressed his ambivalence in a letter to Ninian Edwards on 25 September: "I can get a clerkship in the State department with a good salary, but I won't go into it; it is too confining. I shall know in a few days whether I go as Secretary of Alabama Territory or not. The President, it is feared, has made up his mind; if so, I shall fail; there is no situation vacant at present for me but that."[49]

Cook may have been putting on a brave face for Governor Edwards, however. On the very same day, a letter authored by Cook under the pseudonym "Americanus" appeared in the triweekly edition of Gales and Seaton's *National Intelligencer* decrying the presence in several federal departments of "a great number of foreigners, who have, as it were, but just landed on our shores, and who cannot, by any possibility, have become citizens of the United States." "[B]y showing a preference for foreigners," he wrote bitterly, "we at once sour the minds of our own citizens, and estrange them, in a certain degree, from the government, and thereby produce that dissatisfaction which may ultimately be of vital injury to our political institutions." He deemed government departments as a political training ground "in which the future pillars of the government should receive their strength and polish. But it is to be hoped that these pillars are not to be formed of exotic materials; for however fond we may be of the manufactures of foreign countries, for the use of our wardrobes . . . we would fain hope that a predilection will always exist for domestic manufactures to fill our *political cabinets*."[50]

Cook was seemingly at the end of his rope, stymied by political developments out west and now—as he perceived it—crowded out by foreigners given preference of place for federal sinecures. Already he was weighing his options against a worst-case scenario. "I am not yet well," he continued in his letter to Governor Edwards. "May it not be better for me to return to Kaskaskia and wait for prospects in that country if I don't go to Alabama?"[51]

Cook's fears proved well-founded. On 27 September, at the end of a lengthy note from President James Monroe to Secretary Adams dealing with a variety of foreign policy issues, Monroe—almost as an afterthought—referenced the petition of Adams's protégé: "The claim of Mr. Cook comes to late [*sic*] . . . to have the attention, bestowed it, it merits."[52] So much for Cook biding his time as a diplomatic courier. Presumably he received the bad news that very evening when he encountered Adams at the home of Nathaniel Frye, husband of Adams's wife's younger sister.[53] Adams seems to have shown Cook the president's letter, as Cook quoted parts of it almost verbatim in another letter to Ninian Edwards dated 2 October 1817. "I could get into the State Department as a clerk," he added, "but experience tells me it won't do to engage in close, laborious writing, and it would not satisfy my ambition to be buried in an office—merely as a servant as it were—where the world, perhaps, would never hear of such a being."[54]

But before he arrived at a final resolution, he turned once again to John Quincy Adams for advice "as the step which I may now take, may form an important epoch in my life." Cook had decided to head homeward the following Sunday (5 October), but he wondered, he told Adams, whether he should return "this fall with Mr. Pope . . . running the risque of getting some situation in the government that may better suit me than my professional business. . . . [I]t is necessary for me to decide now whether to relinquish my professional pursuit or to hasten in resuming it." He concluded: "May I request you to think on this subject and be kind enough when I have the honor of seeing you to give me your advice."[55]

That opportunity presumably came on the evening of 2 October, when Cook dined with Adams and his wife once again at the home of Nathaniel Frye. Whatever the course of that conversation had been, Cook had now come to a decision. He told Governor Edwards that as he had been unable to secure a position in the federal government, "I am advised by my own judgment, as well as by his [Adams's], to return to the West, and remain there until an opportunity presents itself for my advancement." He now planned to travel directly to Kaskaskia with no stopover in Kentucky, thus allowing him to return in time for the fall court sessions and for the meeting of the territorial legislature.[56]

Cook encountered John Quincy Adams once more before his departure, walking with the secretary and Mrs. Adams on 4 October to the home of W. S. Smith and then again to Nathaniel Frye's. "He goes tomorrow for Kentucky," Adams reported in his diary.[57]

As Cook had prophesied, however, he did not linger long in his home state en route to Kaskaskia during the forty-four-day journey. And by the time he arrived at the territorial capital, his resolution had become crystal clear. Cook had had ample opportunity to think about his ambitions by looking far afield from Illinois Territory. He had considered—and rejected—the dim prospects of a diplomatic career. Starting all over from scratch in a new territory was beyond his power and therefore out of the question. He had hobnobbed with men of influence and consequence and had developed a much clearer sense of himself, his station, his abilities, and his role among his political peers. The attempt to obtain a government appointment in Alabama had had one significant outcome. Cook realized now that the same arguments supporting the future admission of the Cotton State could be applied with equal justice to Illinois. His mind was made up. If he could not satisfy his ambitions in a territorial government, then only one last avenue remained open. Illinois must gain admission to the Union, and Daniel Pope Cook would be the agent of that transformation.

5
THE GRIEVANCES OF TERRITORIAL GOVERNMENT

Daniel Pope Cook had chosen a particularly propitious moment to inaugurate a movement for admission to the Union. Having observed the political machinations both within the territorial legislature and as the loyal protégé of Ninian Edwards and Nathaniel Pope, Cook was intimately aware not only of *what* was politically possible and desirable but also of *when* it was appropriate to take action. Returning to Kaskaskia in November 1817, Cook was preoccupied with finding some way of overcoming his own limited range of possibilities for personal advancement. As he saw it, accomplishing that purpose was a matter of convincing territorial leaders that Illinois faced similar obstacles for which statehood was the only solution.

Cook's territorial colleagues shared his frustrations. Benjamin Stephenson, Nathaniel Pope's predecessor as Illinois territorial delegate to Congress, had complained to his constituents about that body's unresponsiveness the previous year. Preoccupied with the War of 1812, Congress, he reported, had largely ignored territorial matters. Having presented the territorial legislature's petition asking Congress to curtail the powers of the territorial governor, Stephenson grumbled that "the most that I could obtain, was commendations on its decorous temperate and dignified style."[1] Even when Congress acted—such as passing a law to regulate the duties of territorial judges—they only reinforced the impression that Illinois Territory ultimately depended upon the whims of the federal government, who governed by a policy of what Michael Bakalis deemed "salutary neglect." Congress only reacted, he wrote, when "the numerous petitions of disgruntled settlers or the pleas of a bewildered territorial governor" became so numerous as to require attention.[2] Stephenson's fruitless term in Congress served to further underscore this flaw in the federal-territorial relationship.

In the midst of Nathaniel Pope's campaign for territorial delegate to Congress, "Aristides" had enlarged upon Stephenson's complaints in a letter to the

Western Intelligencer, referring to Illinois's "colonial and degrated [*sic*] state . . . under the government of the [Northwest] Ordinance, that accursed badge of despotism, which withholds from the people . . . a participation in those rights guaranteed by the constitution of every state in the union." In the face of this intolerable state of affairs, he prophesied: "The present rapid influx of population . . . justifies the belief that it will not be more than 3 or 4 years before we will burst the chains of despotism, by which we are now bound, and stand a sovereign and independent state."[3]

Cook had to be likewise aware that there was a strong possibility that the territory to the west might succeed in gaining admission to the Union in advance of Illinois. Petitions praying for statehood had already begun circulating in Missouri a mere month or two earlier. "There was every reason to believe," wrote Solon Buck, "that Missouri would come in as a slave state, and if that should happen before Illinois was admitted, the existence of slavery there would be the strongest argument for allowing it in Illinois also."[4] From a national perspective, those who—like Cook—opposed the extension of slavery viewed this prospect with genuine alarm. Since 1791 Congress had, after all, generally alternated between admitting free and slave states, and with the most recent addition of Mississippi earlier in 1817 the total stood at ten each. Time was of the essence. "If by some remote chance Missouri's entrance into the Union as a slave state would open the door to the admission of Illinois as a slave state there was but one thing to do—beat Missouri into the Union."[5]

Semi-monarchical Government

The time was thus ripe for Illinois's transformation. The slavery issue and the perception of the territory's "degraded" colonial status, taken together with the prospect of renewed opportunities for political power and patronage freed from the restrictions of the Northwest Ordinance, provided more than enough incentive for a nascent statehood movement. A single persuasive voice just might be enough to convince the territory's political leadership to act.

Cook's resolution became a matter of public discussion in the columns of the *Western Intelligencer* a mere two days after his return. Given the difficulties of publishing a newspaper in the early nineteenth century—the setting of type by hand, for example—it seems clear that Cook had been carefully composing his comments on the subject ever since his departure from Washington. The people of Illinois Territory, he argued, were saddled with what he termed "semi-monarchical government," and consequently, Cook asked, "[M]ight not our claims to a state government be justly urged? That part of our Territory which must ultimately form a state, will no doubt be willing to take the burthen of a state government upon themselves at this time, rather than submit any longer to those degredations [*sic*], which they have so long been compelled to put up with." He promised in the next number of the *Intelligencer* "to present to our readers, such a view of the subject as will induce our fellow citizens, as well as the legislature, to take such measures as will bring it before the national legislature, at their approaching season."[6]

A Sufficient Portion of Civilization

If the existence and administration of Illinois was governed by the Northwest Ordinance of 1787, so too were the processes for its admission to the Union. Cook studied Article V of the ordinance with particular care, as it specified that states could be formed from the Northwest Territory provided that they had a population of sixty thousand. However, "so far as it can be consistent with the general interest of the confederacy," the ordinance declared, "such admission shall be allowed at an earlier period, and when there may be a less number of free inhabitants in the State than sixty thousand."[7]

The issue of whether Illinois Territory met the necessary threshold for population cannot have been encouraging, given that the most recent federal census (1810) recorded a mere 12,282 inhabitants. Consequently, Cook—writing in the *Western Intelligencer* under the pseudonym "A Republican"—marshaled his arguments to deemphasize the population requirement and instead underscored the more nebulous (but, he thought, compelling) general interest of the nation. True, he estimated the territory's population as numbering between forty and forty-five thousand—certainly well below sixty thousand—but this, Cook argued, was comparable to the population of a number of other states at the time of their respective admissions.

Of greater importance, in his view, were the potential costs of state government. Based upon the salaries provided by the federal government for territorial officials—the governor, the secretary, and the judges—Cook estimated that analogous state officers would require no more than $6,200 annually. He confidently predicted that this amount could be provided out of revenues from salt production in the new state. Other officials—legislators, county officers, etc.—were already paid out of local monies, which would preclude the need for any additional revenues.

Cook admitted that in the early days of American governance, the French settlers of Illinois Territory were unaccustomed to a republican regime. "[T]he then inhabitants were familiarized to monarchy," he wrote, perhaps acknowledging that in those earlier days the presence of European interests in the region offered them alternative choices. It had been uncertain at that earlier date, he continued, as to whether the territory would ever attract enough settlers loyal to the United States to merit admission to the Union. Cook believed that Congress had settled upon sixty thousand as the population figure that "would unquestionably secure to the people, a majority in their conventions, in favor of the true principles of republicanism." Now Illinois had attained that majority, he declared, although he admitted that "all the original inhabitants are yet friendly to monarchy." And that majority had made a definitive choice: "[T]he late war, as well as the general deportment of these inhabitants prove that they are firmly attached to the principles of our government, and are justly entitled to the privileges and blessings of American citizens."[8]

The lack of a representative government was all the more offensive and objectionable. "[A]n executive officer," Cook complained, "owing no responsibility to the people, has the power of closing their deliberations at pleasure, by a dissolution of the assembly. . . . [T]he arm of an omnipotent executive may at one stroke, destroy and annihilate the effects of their labor by the exercise of his absolute veto." Congress had habitually admitted new states with fewer than sixty thousand inhabitants for this very reason, especially if "'the interests of the confederacy' would not be affected by such admission." Cook added—perhaps slightly tongue-in-cheek—that Congress itself stood to benefit by no longer being obliged to focus on territorial issues "and thus exempt congress from an irksome and uninteresting part of their deliberations."[9]

The Inconveniences of the Territorial Government

The great unknown was, of course, the future status of slavery in Illinois. "And many on both sides of the question," Cook wrote, "are remaining in the anxiety of suspense, to know how it will be settled." It was ultimately desirable, in his view, to resolve the issue as soon as possible in the interests of those wishing to immigrate to Illinois. "One of the richest and finest portions of the continent," he confidently asserted, "would soon be made to yield its proper tribute to the comfort and wealth of society—a new field for the enlargement of the human understanding would be opened, and the strength and respectability of the nation would be greatly augmented."[10]

On the following Monday—1 December 1817—Daniel Pope Cook strode into the two-story brick building that served as the home of the territorial legislature and again assumed his duties as legislative clerk. It was not long before it was clear that his efforts to awaken the sensibilities of Illinois's political leadership had borne fruit and that they recognized—on all sides and in every political faction—that statehood was not only desirable but achievable. On the second day of the session—2 December—William H. Bradsby of St.

Clair County came forth with a resolution to appoint a committee "to draft a memorial to congress praying for this territory to be admitted into the union, with all the rights and privileges of a state government."[11] The motion was approved, and Bradsby, Charles Reynolds Matheny of St. Clair County, Willis Hargrave of White County, and Samuel Omelveny of Pope County were selected to compose the petition.

The fact that members of all factions were eager to see Illinois enter the Union was reflected in the composition of this committee. A native Kentuckian, William Bradsby had trained as a physician "but disliked the profession and became rather a public character," according to John Reynolds, who had fought alongside Bradsby in the War of 1812. Bradsby and fellow committee member Charles R. Matheny were likewise antislavery as well as politically aligned with Ninian Edwards. Born in Virginia and largely raised in Kentucky, Matheny had been a Methodist "circuit rider" or itinerant preacher since 1805, when he was assigned to minister to scattered communities in the Illinois counties of Madison, St. Clair, and Monroe.[12] Over the years, Matheny served in a variety of public offices, including justice of the peace, county treasurer, and circuit attorney.[13]

The other two members of the memorial committee represented the opposing political faction led by Judge Jesse B. Thomas. Samuel Omelveny, a native of Ireland, was a prosperous jack-of-all-trades who engaged in farming, flatboating, ferrying, and general trade despite a lack of education. Immigrating to Illinois from Kentucky in 1804–5, he subsequently served in a variety of public offices such as justice of the peace.[14] Willis Hargrave, a native of South Carolina who immigrated to Logan County, Kentucky around 1790 and served as a captain in that state's "Cornstalk militia,"[15] had arrived in Illinois in 1808; he later served as captain of a company of mounted volunteers during the War of 1812. Hargrave served in public offices in White County as a judge, a county commissioner, and a justice of the peace. He was most prominent as a manufacturer of salt in the saline districts of Gallatin County, owning or renting numerous enslaved persons for that purpose, and simultaneously served as general inspector of the saltworks for the United States.[16]

The committee's work was buttressed by words of support from Ninian Edwards. Seemingly taking no offense at the characterization of his office as an omnipotent executive accountable to no one, and recognizing the political opportunities that statehood would afford, Edwards was effusive in his praise for the initiative. He was convinced, the governor declared, "that our present temporary government must soon give place to one more congenial to the principles of natural liberty, under which, being elevated to the rank of a member of the great American Union . . . our fellow citizens will have their just weight in the great councils of the nation, and may freely legislate for themselves as their interest and happiness may require." Recognizing the centrality of the population question to the admission process, Edwards recommended that a census be conducted to provide Congress with the most accurate information possible.[17]

Within a week the memorial committee had completed its work. Cook's influence upon the wording of the petition was unmistakable: "The inconveniences of the territorial government cannot be estimated except by those who live under it. . . . It is a species of despotism in direct hostility with the principles of a republican government; and in the opinion of your memorialists it ought to exist no longer than *absolute necessity* may require it." They underscored that with the nation at peace, it was an opportune time to extend statehood to Illinois, and then once again echoed Cook in estimating that the territory's population amounted to more than forty thousand, "among whom there is an unusual coincidence of sentiment as to the propriety of forming a state government." They argued that admission would be consistent with the general interest of the confederacy: "The citizens of the territory are mostly composed of those who have imigrated [*sic*] hither from the atlantic and western states: from principle and by education they are attached to the inestimable constitution of the United States, and to a republican form of government."[18]

Confident that they had set forth a compelling case for admission, the memorialists requested a grant of the lead mines and salt springs within the territory as well as a grant of section 16 reserved from sale in each township for the use of schools; part of the proceeds from the lands lying within the state to be appropriated in laying out and making public roads; and all grants previously given to Ohio, Indiana, and Mississippi "upon the like conditions." The memorial was approved by both houses of the legislature, which further ordered that fifty copies be printed and sent to Governor Edwards, who would forward them to Nathaniel Pope for distribution to members of Congress. The territorial delegate was further instructed "to use his best exertions to procure the object of said memorial."[19]

The man who had been more responsible than any other territorial leader for the success of the statehood initiative became increasingly confident as it moved toward passage. Writing to John Quincy Adams in the opening days of the legislature, Cook expressed a hope that his mentor would support the petition; "[W]e cannot conceive," he argued, "of the impropriety of granting our petition." Enclosing a copy of his original *Intelligencer* editorial advocating statehood, he added: "[S]ince my return I find myself more engrossed already in professional business than I am willing to attend to if I could without giving offence refuse to embark in it." Indeed, he "rejoice[d] that I did not go to Alabama—Never has there been such an opening for speculation & for a few good lawyers in the western country as now presents itself here."[20]

With the legislature's passage of the statehood petition, Cook was jubilant. "The vigilence [*sic*]," he told the subscribers of the *Intelligencer*, "with which the representatives of the people appear to act in striving to throw off the shackles of a colonial government affords a pleasing prospect. . . . When such unanimous promptitude is manifested in praying for a state government, I think our prayer will doubtless be granted."[21] This was the consummation of Daniel Pope Cook's year of uncertainty and contemplation. There was no need after all to look elsewhere to build a successful political career. There was every prospect that statehood would open up a floodgate of opportunities for patronage and public office.

An Act of Justice

There were still political realities to be confronted, however. On the day before the memorial's final adoption, committee member Charles Matheny introduced a bill to repeal the territory's indenture law under which Black enslaved persons were regularly brought to Illinois—mostly from Kentucky—under the pretense that they had voluntarily agreed to enter into contracts to work in the territory. Matheny's colleague William Bradsby was blunt in his support for repeal: "I hold it a clear proposition, that, any servitude which is required, that is not perfectly *voluntarily* [*sic*], is in violation of this [Northwest] ordinance, and therefore unconstitutional. . . . I am actuated by a love of the equal rights of man, those rights which it appears to have been the great object of this article in the ordinance to support."[22]

T. Walter Johnson speculated that Matheny's introduction of the repeal bill simultaneously with the memorial petition was no accident. In this fashion Matheny hoped "to prevent the constitutional convention from continuing indefinitely the system of indentured servitude."[23] George Fisher, Speaker of the House of Representatives, was having none of it, arguing that as the territory "has been much benefited by the introduction of negroes and as their situation has been much ameliorated thereby, I think it will not be good policy, now, to inflame their anxiety for freedom." Repeal would, he maintained, "render them restless" and would also "injure many, who have emigrated to the Territory, under the belief that the law was a good, or a constitutional one. . . . As it has stood so long I see no impropriety in leaving it to be settled by the convention who shall frame our constitution which will not be long hence."[24]

The bill was ultimately passed by both houses and sent to Governor Edwards, who vetoed it on 1 January 1818 and characterized the repeal as "a mere nullity and with every possible aid of legal construction and intendment would leave in full force the act of 1812." Perhaps thinking ahead to the struggle for admission, Edwards nevertheless hedged his bets: "I am no advocate for slavery, and if it depended upon my vote alone, it should never be admitted in any state or Territory, not already cursed with so great an evil."[25]

Taking up the governor's earlier suggestion, on 7 January the legislature approved a law to conduct a census from 1 April to 1 June that would enumerate the total number of white inhabitants as well as free people of color and servants or enslaved persons. It was further amended on 10 January to extend the census period to 1 December as "a great increase of population may be expected" during that time.[26]

The deed was done; the territorial legislature's petition was safely on its way. They had determined to seek admission to the Union in the face of a greater imbalance of power with the federal government than had been the case with their predecessors to the east. They had unburdened themselves of their ostensible resentment as a colony chafing under the tyranny of a "semi-monarchical government." In the absence of any prospect for transferring their loyalties to the newly departed European powers, they understood that their best hope lay in convincing the federal government that territorial issues were national in scope and that the time was ripe for Illinois's admission to the Union. They had begun—if only haltingly—to deliberate their ambivalence toward slavery as the implications of statehood for the institution became manifest. They had striven to facilitate access to natural resources and to land ownership. They had fulminated against the narrow distribution of power in the form of public contracts and patronage. They had attempted to reconcile the myriad conflicts between the Northwest Ordinance, the Constitution, territorial laws, and local conditions. They chose to advance the argument that admission "would be an act of justice, and not inconsistent with the general interest of the Republic"; indeed, "the union itself will assume additional importance."[27] Their long-term path toward statehood—like Cook's voyage of self-discovery—had been a frequently maddening effort to bring clarity to their ambiguous status. They sought—as he did—"to fill a more responsible and lucrative situation" and thereby to rise above that indeterminate condition. In the face of such mounting frustrations, once all other options had been exhausted, it was the decision of a moment to petition for elevation to the full rights and privileges of citizenship within the Union. Now it was up to Nathaniel Pope, their representative in the nation's capital, to argue that case convincingly—to run the congressional gauntlet and somehow cajole that body to produce legislation that would bring the dream of statehood that much closer to realization.

The man who had brought the statehood movement to fruition felt a new surge of self-confidence, bolstered by a pending appointment from Governor Edwards on 13 January as a judge for the territory's Western Circuit.[28] And so on 6 January 1818 Daniel Pope Cook announced that in fifteen or twenty days he intended to start another journey, this time for Richmond, Virginia, whence he planned to visit Washington, Philadelphia, and maybe even New York. "I will undertake the transaction of any business which may be confided to me," he told his fellow citizens, "which may come in my route."[29]

PART II

Nathaniel Pope and the Roads Not Taken

6

TRULY AN AMIABLE CHARACTER

The gentleman from Illinois was perturbed. On a cold day in Washington, D.C., in January 1818, Nathaniel Pope—former secretary of the territory and now its delegate to Congress—composed an uncharacteristically chiding letter to Governor Ninian Edwards, his close friend, first cousin, and political ally (the roles were hardly mutually exclusive):

> You are but a poor correspondent owing I suppose to being exclusively absorbed in mercantile speculations—It is however not a little surprising that upon the subject of . . . state government you should have withheld from me your own views especially as when I left home it was not contemplated to take that step this winter—I looked over and opened all the letters . . . with an expectation of something from yourself but I looked in vain.[1]

The statehood campaign had begun on a hopeful note, spurred on by the enthusiastic and determined advocacy of Daniel Pope Cook, energized by local indignation over the territory's second-class status within the Union, and solemnly endorsed by the territorial legislature and the governor. But that political fervor had its limits. During December and January the petition for admission traversed more than eight hundred miles stretching between Kaskaskia and the nation's capital to reach the delegate's desk. To bridge the remaining distance between territory and statehood—to negotiate the most favorable terms governing control of public lands and resources, to integrate Illinois into the larger national infrastructure, to calm the fears of the East over the rise of the western frontier, to devise an enabling act that would codify the changes in governance—these challenges required flexibility, focus, determination, and clear-headedness. It was Illinois's good fortune that their congressional champion in the winter of 1818 was their erstwhile territorial secretary, Nathaniel Pope.

It is no exaggeration to say that the territorial legislature's statehood petition—the brainchild of Pope's protégé Daniel Pope Cook—was a complete surprise to the congressional delegate. Not in the long haul, perhaps; anyone with political skills and extensive experience wheeling and dealing in Kaskaskia—which Pope possessed in abundance—would have understood the advantages and attractions of admission to the Union. Nearly five years earlier Pope had presided at a Fourth of July banquet on the banks of the Kaskaskia River where, after a stirring address by William C. Greenup, a toast was offered to "The Illinois Territory—May she soon rise and join the Federal Confederation."[2]

But the motivations for admission went well beyond patriotic platitudes at a backwoods picnic. Nathaniel Pope and his Kaskaskia cohorts—on both sides of the partisan divide—knew quite well that statehood represented yet another opportunity for political gain. And at first glance, admission may have appeared to be a relatively simple matter. In reality, however, the prospects for that accomplishment were—as Pope understood—ensnared within a bewildering array of issues encompassing internal improvements, sectional tensions, and suspicions of the burgeoning West. No one was better fitted for negotiating these obstacles than Nathaniel Pope, born and bred in Louisville, Kentucky, and apprenticed to political maturity in Ste. Genevieve and Kaskaskia.

An Agreeable Society

The Falls of the Ohio River represent the most troublesome stretch of this unpredictable waterway. These shallow rapids descend a slope of almost twenty-four feet over only three miles, rendering them tentatively navigable—if fearfully so—to the pirogues, bateaux, flatboats, and other shallow-water craft employed by early explorers and settlers. Later steam-powered vessels that required a deeper draft called for a keen eye and an especially steady hand for those who dared venture into these waters.[3] Here the banks of the Ohio abound in native bear grass, a yucca-like perennial rising upward of five feet, ornamented with rough-edged leaves and crowned with clusters of "small, creamy white flowers."[4] They lend their name to nearby Beargrass Creek, which flows into the Ohio. The intersection of these two waterways forms the foundation of what is now Louisville, Kentucky.

It was here that Nathaniel Pope was born on 5 January 1784. Perhaps no other region of Kentucky held the same degree of importance for Illinois's early development. Indeed, it played a pivotal role in the Illinois Country's original incorporation into the United States. When George Rogers Clark marshaled his ragtag troops to take Kaskaskia and Vincennes—and thus all of the Old Northwest—from the British in 1778, he settled on this site as his base of operations. It was ideally situated, he later explained, to serve as "a post of communication on the river between the Illinois country and Kentucky"; indeed, the Falls of the Ohio "would also protect in great measure the navigation of the river, since as every vessel would be obliged to stop some time at this place they would always be exposed to the Indians." Clark drilled his green troops on nearby Corn Island under the pretense that they were cultivating gardens and creating settlements for their accompanying families. Once established, word of these communities reached other pioneers along the Ohio and Monongahela Rivers; "This," wrote Clark, "was one of the chief causes of the rapid settlement of Kentucky."[5]

One of these settlers was a Virginian by the name of William Pope. His precise reasons for emigrating and bringing his family to Louisville are unclear. What is known is that Nathaniel Pope's father was present as early as 24 April 1779—less than a year after Clark's expedition—during a lottery for town lots. William Pope was among those appointed as trustees to lay out the town, and he apparently had sufficient skills in cartography to create an early map of the area.[6]

In all likelihood the elder Pope recognized the location's economic potential along the lines suggested in a 1783 letter from John May—founder of Maysville, Kentucky—to Barthélemi Tardiveau, a French trader: "As the Falls of Ohio is the place where all vessels both coming up, and going down the river, must call to unload, when it is not very high; and as this place has a large extent of fertile country to support it; larger and richer than any other place in the united states, I am of opinion it will be one of the greatest trading towns in america."[7] Louisville was fated to become a crucial linchpin in east-west commercial transportation and trade, surrounded and supported by the immensely fertile and productive soil of Jefferson County.[8] Born, raised, and educated upon this landscape, Nathaniel Pope understood the importance of such topography in the winter and spring of 1818 as he contemplated the proper placement of Illinois's prospective state boundaries.

Historian Paul Angle observed that evidence suggests "that even at an early date, life in the Pope family was above the general level." William Pope was lieutenant colonel of the county militia, he represented Jefferson County in the Virginia legislature in 1785, and he served as justice of the peace as well.[9] He was sufficiently well-to-do that in the federal census for 1810 he was recorded as the owner of nine enslaved persons.[10]

Nathaniel Pope was the fourth child of William Pope and Penelope Edwards and the first of their children to be born in Louisville.[11] Angle deemed the pioneer village "a rough, precarious environment":

> Everyone in the settlement lived in small log cabins with puncheon floors and unglazed windows. Furniture was of the simplest kind. Clothing was for protection only—buckskin breeches and coon-skin caps for men; linsey-woolsey for women. Settlers cultivated their crops in the small clearings adjacent to the stockade with rifles always close at hand, for the threat of Indian attack and massacre was ever-present.[12]

To some extent it was very similar to the community in which Pope's future protégé Daniel Pope Cook grew to maturity in Scott County, just seventy miles to the northeast.

William Pope's relative prosperity made it possible for Nathaniel to attend private schools under the tutelage of local teachers such as the Reverend George Leach, "who taught the classics as well as English studies."[13] This training provided an adequate foundation for young Pope to enroll at Transylvania University in Lexington, Kentucky, which had been founded in 1780 and where the curriculum encompassed classical and modern languages, "mathematics, geography, belles-lettres 'and every other branch of learning. . . .'" Although it is not known for certain that he graduated, Pope nevertheless emerged from Transylvania with a facility for French and a fondness for the classics.[14]

If Nathaniel Pope did not in fact graduate from this institution, it may have been because a more concrete opportunity presented itself: the chance to study law in the offices of his older brother John, the future U.S. senator from Kentucky, who had come to Lexington to practice law in November 1803.[15] Much like Daniel Pope Cook a dozen years later, Nathaniel Pope understood that the legal profession stood to provide a lucrative income as well as the prospect of useful political contacts. If there were any doubts, he needed only to look to the example of his cousin Ninian Edwards, or, for that matter, his brother.

At this point Pope might well have been expected to embark upon a practice within the Kentucky courts. He chose instead to travel westward in 1804 to the newly acquired Louisiana Territory. In this place, Paul Angle wrote, "A lawyer who could speak French should have no difficulty in securing enough clients to yield him a comfortable living, while the new states which would undoubtedly be formed from the province should afford more than sufficient opportunity for political position."[16]

The site Pope chose was Ste. Genevieve across the Mississippi River from Kaskaskia. At the time of his settlement the village encompassed about two hundred families, including about thirty Americans. The latter were apt to find the French inhabitants somewhat distant and aloof. Christian Schultz, a New Yorker who visited the region in 1808 in the course of a journey down the Ohio and up the Mississippi, reported that although the French settlers disdained Americans for their inferior religious devotion, they nevertheless "entertain a very high opinion of our knowledge, spirit, and enterprise. . . . There is a small circle of Frenchmen, who, from a familiar intercourse with the Americans, have conquered both their local and religious prejudices, and may be considered as agreeable society, when absent from the *card-table*."[17]

Nathaniel Pope's willingness to immerse himself successfully in this new culture helps to illustrate why American settlers might have been willing to transfer their loyalties away from their native country. He quickly developed a congenial relationship with the French settlers. Not only was he chosen to serve as a trustee of the newly established Ste. Genevieve academy, but he was also selected in August 1808 as the town's secretary.[18] Pope also received his first federal government appointment as treasurer of the Ste. Genevieve district some time before 30 September 1807.[19] He developed a steady law practice at first on his own largely in Ste. Genevieve and in Cape Girardeau some sixty miles to the south. In 1806 he joined forces with John Scott, a native of Virginia who had moved to Indiana Territory in 1802. Scott was later to serve as Missouri's territorial delegate to Congress from 1816 to 1821 and then as the new state's representative in the House until 1827.[20] They expanded their practice in 1807 to Kaskaskia, where the citizens were inordinately fond of going to court; "[T]hey adjudicated neighborhood quarrels upon the slightest provocation," Paul Angle remarked, "and apparently preferred to pay their debts by court order rather than voluntarily."[21]

In Kaskaskia Pope began to cultivate the social and political contacts that were to serve as the basis for his subsequent lengthy career of public service in Illinois. He became aligned with supporters of Indiana Territory governor William Henry Harrison in opposition to partition of the territory and to land speculators such as John Edgar, Robert and William Morrison, and John Rice Jones and his doomed son Rice. Pope's allies included Shadrach Bond, James Gilbreath, Robert Robinson, and Elijah Backus. Indeed, his alignment illustrates the extent to which the political became personal in territorial Illinois, for on 13 December 1808 he married Backus's daughter Lucretia. That same month Pope took up residency in Kaskaskia, although he continued as Ste. Genevieve's town secretary until resigning on 11 February 1809.[22]

Universally Esteemed by His Acquaintances

Events soon justified Pope's judgment in removing to the eastern shore of the Mississippi. He relocated permanently to Kaskaskia at the very moment that Jesse B. Thomas was maneuvering to separate Illinois from Indiana Territory.

There was some irony in the fact that the latter was soon to become an advocate for Pope's elevation to yet another public office, for Thomas was destined to become a bitter political opponent of Pope's cousin and ally, Ninian Edwards. But for now, Indiana's delegate to Congress was willing to endorse the twenty-five-year-old Nathaniel Pope for the office of secretary of the new Illinois Territory, reporting that in the course of his law practice Pope had cultivated a wide-ranging circle of acquaintances: "[H]e is universally esteemed by his Acquaintances He is truly an amiable Character has been Liberally educated and possesses very respectable talents."[23]

The extent to which Pope and Thomas were previously acquainted is unclear, given that the latter's sphere of political activity was primarily in Vincennes to the east. Certainly they would have been aware of each other's reputation. But it is also true that Senator John Pope—Nathaniel's older brother—wrote a recommendation two weeks later endorsing Thomas—successfully—for a territorial judgeship.[24] Nathaniel Pope was likewise endorsed for territorial secretary by Richard M. Johnson, representative from Kentucky, who would later play an important role in the congressional admission process for Illinois. Buckner Thruston, John Pope's fellow senator from Kentucky, and Representative Benjamin Howard of Virginia wrote a joint recommendation for Nathaniel Pope's appointment as well.[25]

The other major territorial office awaiting an appointee was the position of governor. John Boyle, who had lived in Kentucky since 1779, had served in that state's legislature, and had represented the Bluegrass State in Congress from 1803 to 1809, seemed to be a fitting choice.[26] Recommendations on his behalf were forthcoming from Johnson, Thruston, and Howard as well as from Thomas and Senator Pope.[27] The nature of his support for the position, taken in context with the recommendations for Thomas and Pope, adds detail to the larger pattern of influence surrounding the distribution of territorial positions and therefore of territorial political power. The same names appear repeatedly as advocates. Benjamin Howard recommended Boyle and Pope as well as Walter Reid, an unsuccessful candidate for territorial judge. Richard M. Johnson supported Boyle, Pope, and Thomas. Buckner Thruston supported Boyle and Pope as well, and he also recommended David Holmes, an outgoing Virginia congressman, for governor of Mississippi Territory. Holmes for his part supported Thomas's elevation to territorial judge in concert with Thomas Kenan, a North Carolina congressman. The next day Kenan obligingly joined Thruston's endorsement of Holmes for the Mississippi vacancy. Senator John Pope was responsible for endorsing no less than six candidates for office—one for governor (Boyle) and five for judge, albeit of these only Jesse B. Thomas was selected.[28]

The offices thus filled wielded substantial power. The governor, as chief executive, was able to appoint local county and township officials, and he likewise possessed the authority to name officers below the rank of general in the territorial militia. The secretary of Illinois Territory was charged with keeping, maintaining, and preserving all laws and public documents, and he assumed the governor's duties in his absence.[29] All in all, it was a sobering challenge for Nathaniel Pope.

The situation was rendered all the more daunting by a practical reality: John Boyle never actually assumed the duties of territorial governor (although he drew a paycheck). On 3 April Boyle informed the secretary of state that he had decided to step down, and three days later he wrote an apologetic letter to President James Madison, explaining that upon returning to Kentucky he had learned that a position on the state's court of appeals had become vacant and needed to be filled immediately lest an entire term be lost. At the urging of "the gentlemen of the bar & by the wishes of my family & friends" and out of concern for his family's delicate health, Boyle decided to forego the governorship and remain in his native state. He recommended his fellow Kentuckian Ninian Edwards as "a man of great talents & of unquestionable integrity" who would be "willing to accept the appointment & will be ready to proceed immediately to the territory should he be honoured with the appointment." The case for Edwards's appointment was bolstered by an additional note written in pencil on Boyle's letter: "M^{r} [John] Pope has strongly recommended Mr Edwards." Edwards also apparently expressed his interest in the post to Henry Clay, who advocated for his appointment in letters to the president, the secretary of state, and the attorney general.[30]

Nathaniel Pope had come a long way in the five years since he had departed his birthplace near the Falls of the Ohio. He had shown a remarkable knack for seizing opportunities as they arose—relocating in the newly acquired Louisiana Territory, ingratiating himself with the local French inhabitants, and building a successful regional legal practice. And although he aligned himself (both personally and politically) with the faction that had opposed partition of Indiana Territory, he nevertheless found himself elevated to high office in the new territorial government at the tender age of twenty-five. Now—with John Boyle nowhere to be found and Ninian Edwards not due to arrive until summer was well underway—the exercise of executive authority lay entirely within his hands. And so young Nathaniel Pope found himself—in effect if not in name—the first territorial governor of Illinois.

7
THE SNARL OF SUSPICION

As a young student steeped in belles-lettres at Transylvania University, Nathaniel Pope must have been familiar with the works of William Shakespeare. "Uneasy lies the head that wears a crown," the Bard of Avon declared in *Henry IV, Part II*, and so it was with acting governor Pope. The trials he faced went well beyond his youth and relative inexperience as a public official. Pope's appointment had come, Paul Angle reported, "in spite of local opposition";[1] the young Kentuckian had, after all, aligned himself with the coalition supporting Governor William Henry Harrison during the Indiana period. The situation was worsened by the uncertainty surrounding the selection of a permanent governor. Pope had been appointed secretary on 7 March 1809, but the inevitable delay in communicating that selection held up his taking the oath of office until 25 April, when he likely learned of the governor's resignation for the first time.

In the wake of John Boyle's decision, Pope assumed the duties of governor as well as that of secretary for six weeks until 11 June, when Ninian Edwards was sworn in.[2] In the meantime Pope was not idle. In one of his first official acts he decreed that the two existing counties—St. Clair (established 1790) and Randolph (established 1795)—would continue largely unchanged save for the fact that their boundaries now ended to the east at the border with Indiana Territory.[3] He appointed nearly one hundred men to militia leadership posts and to local civil offices such as sheriff, justice of the peace, and coroner. Recognizing the ambiguity of the situation, Pope was careful to underscore that all those appointed were to serve "during the pleasure of the Governor for the time being." Nevertheless, Pope restricted his selections to his political allies.[4] Thus it was not surprising that members of the opposing faction began a whispering campaign to the effect that the secretary had not been properly sworn into office and therefore lacked the official authority to act. Pope was rattled. Anxious about the potential for eroding public trust in territorial government, he wrote Secretary of State Robert Smith requesting his opinion as to the validity of his oath of office.[5] There is no record of any response from Smith. But the damage was done; there was to be no letup in the factionalism that had originated during the Indiana territorial period. All that had changed, Angle observed, was that "the old Harrison faction had transferred its allegiance to Pope, while the Edgar-Morrison group made him the object of attack."[6]

Their hostility was founded upon a healthy respect for Nathaniel Pope's talents; some members of the opposing faction, especially William Morrison, had engaged his legal services.[7] Once Boyle's resignation was made public, they feared that the secretary was in a position to assume the governor's office permanently. To ward off that possibility, Edgar and the Morrisons penned an acid-tinged missive to Congressman Matthew Lyon of Kentucky. Lyon was the father-in-law of John Messinger, who had been one of the members of the Indiana territorial legislature advocating for division of the territory the previous year, and Lyon himself had played an important role in securing the passage of that measure in Congress. Edgar and the Morrisons disparaged Pope as "a Boy without the talents to assume the reins of Government, as the violent partizan [*sic*] of a sinking faction, engagd [*sic*] by the ties of consanguinity to its leader [i.e., as the son-in-law of Elijah Backus] and desirous of propping its declin'g power—is altogether an unfit Character to become our Governor." Should such an appointment come to pass, they warned, "the evident dislike of the people to anyone tinctured with the politics of the murdering faction . . . will drive them instantly to arms."[8]

Edwards did his best to calm the waters upon taking his oath of office. The Edgar-Morrison partisans formally protested the appointment of men such as Michael Jones—who had been named adjutant of the Randolph County militia—as one of the "'murdering faction' whom they charged with the death of Rice Jones."[9] They likewise regarded James Gilbreath, a member of the pro-Harrison coalition whom Pope had appointed sheriff of Randolph County, as a "'highly improper character,'" and they asked that Edwards vacate all of the secretary's appointments to be filled only by their membership.[10]

The governor's response was deft. He rescinded Gilbreath's appointment to ensure that the man who occupied the office of sheriff would be above suspicion. By choosing Benjamin Stephenson—Edwards's old colleague from Kentucky—as his replacement, the governor shored up his own political power while seemingly making a concession to Pope's enemies. He further mollified them by ordering the mustering of all militia companies and calling for the election of officers, at the same time affirming the secretary's selections as necessary and appropriate under the circumstances. "I am free to declare that the Course he adopted was precisely such as I myself should have pursued under Similar Circumstances. . . . I therefore take up the business as if it had not been acted on at all."[11]

This was not the end of the factionalism, of course, but it enabled Edwards to assert his own authority, create at least a veneer of bipartisanship, and allow Pope to retain a modicum of dignity, thereby gaining his loyalty. The secretary could now begin focusing upon his own official duties. In compensation for his work Pope received 500 acres of land during his four-year appointment. The total budget for his office amounted to $350 per year, out of which the secretary paid for rent, stationery, office furniture, fuel, and the printing of laws.[12]

Pope professed to have had some initial difficulty in understanding and navigating the rules established by the federal government overseeing these expenditures. The challenge was compounded by the territory's remoteness; a letter typically required three to four weeks to travel from Kaskaskia to Washington, D.C. Pope wrote Secretary of the Treasury Albert Gallatin that he lived and worked rent free in a house owned by his father-in-law Elijah Backus; "[I]t being a personal favour it is no argument," he contended, "against his charging the Government a reasonable price for the occupation of it." Consequently, he submitted a receipt—payable to Nathaniel Pope himself—for office rent dating back to 7 March 1809.[13] Gallatin responded that any such receipts needed to be signed by Backus, and in any case office rent should not exceed forty dollars per year.[14] Incredulous, Pope maintained that he could not find office space for less than sixty dollars per year, and he noted that in any case he—Pope—was Backus's business agent and should therefore be eligible to sign receipts. "It is impossible that I can make a Bargain with Mr. Backus on this point," he concluded, "I consider it the same as making a Bargain with myself."[15] Gallatin ultimately approved the higher figure, but he balked at paying for rent retroactive to 7 March: "As you could not have occupied an office before you received your commission, and as this was not probably received before the first of April, I do not perceive how you can charge office-rent before that day."[16] Pope pleaded ignorance: "Being unacquainted with the regulations concerning the [territorial] Secretaries, I supposed that I was as much entitled to Office rent as to my Salary previous to the receipt of my Commission."[17]

A Strong Original Character

With that issue resolved, Nathaniel Pope directed his energies to familiarizing himself with the duties of his office and continuing to adjust to an unruly political environment. As had been the case in Ste. Genevieve, he came to be highly regarded and well-respected by his peers. One described him as "a strong, original character" who "had a head like a half-bushel, with brain enough for six men," possessing "a wonderful knowledge of human nature, and [he] was utterly without fear. . . . He was what Dr. [Samuel] Johnson calls a good hater. In fact, he was strong in everything—his likes and dislikes."[18] Another remembered him as "rather above than below the medium height and rather corpulent."[19] All were consistent in remarking upon his intellect and his legal abilities, which he kept sharp by maintaining his law practice simultaneously with his duties as secretary. Even political adversaries such as John Edgar continued to seek out his services.[20] "[I]n legal Science in firmness of Mind, respectability of Character and Solidity of Understanding he is second to no Lawyer in this or any of the adjacent Territories." Such was the joint judgment of Jesse B. Thomas, Ninian Edwards, and Alexander Stuart, Thomas's fellow territorial judge, in February 1810, recommending Pope to the secretary of state to fill a vacant territorial judicial position.[21] Ultimately, however, the president chose another candidate.

Pope's performance as secretary was sufficiently capable that in early 1813 he was reappointed for a second four-year term, partly upon the recommendation of Shadrach Bond (by now Illinois's territorial delegate to Congress), territorial judge Alexander Stuart, and Edward Hempstead (the congressional delegate from Missouri). They deemed Pope "a Gentleman of the first intelligence, talents, worth, and integrity," whose abilities uniquely suited him above all other candidates to hold the office.[22] His retention in this capacity was just as well, for with the recent onset of war with Great Britain, the territory was sorely in need of capable leadership. Ninian Edwards, always something of an imperious character, absented himself from the territory for the last six months of 1813 in a state of high dudgeon after his authority over territorial defenses was superseded by a military district commanded by William Henry Harrison and encompassing Illinois, Indiana, Missouri, and Michigan. During that period Pope stepped into the role of acting governor with characteristic moderation, making relatively few appointments. When the territorial legislature met in November 1813, he made his executive recommendations to modify the territorial code and abolish two offices, but for the most part he limited himself to exhorting legislators to act harmoniously in the interests of their constituents.[23]

Pope's legal talents and attention to detail proved valuable when he was tasked with the responsibility of revising and publishing the territorial code in 1815. What came to be known as *Pope's Digest* went beyond merely presenting the body of contemporary law. He organized the code in the topical/alphabetical arrangement that is still implicit in the Illinois state code. For this he was paid three hundred dollars.[24]

The secretary's ambitions, however, extended beyond the narrow confines of his office. On 22 May 1816 the readers of the *Western Intelligencer* were greeted with the news of Pope's intention to be a candidate for territorial delegate to Congress. Now under the editorial guidance of Daniel Pope Cook, the *Intelligencer* praised the secretary as a public servant of whom "no man has ever been heard to say that he has not faithfully and satisfactorily discharged his duty," and went on to deny that Pope was in any sense aligned with any clique or party.[25] Writing in the following issue, one prospective opponent, Russell Heacock, was careful not to attack the secretary directly, but he nonetheless fumed that service in public office should not immediately entitle the office-holder to other sinecures. Heacock outlined five issues of central importance in the campaign. First, he alluded to the need for reducing the price of public lands. Second, he emphasized the importance of excluding British traders from the frontier. "[T]he Indian trade is valuable," he wrote, "and belongs exclusively to us, as a matter of right." Third, Heacock advocated renewed attention to land claims—i.e., claims held by speculators such as John Edgar and William and Robert Morrison—rejected by a board of commissioners several years earlier. Some of these, he argued, "must have been good; they therefore, require the particular attention of the delegate." This marked Heacock as an ally of the land speculators who had been aligned in opposition to Pope. Fourth, he advocated federal land grants to frontier rangers to compensate them for their service in the War of 1812. Finally, Heacock argued for setting aside lands dedicated for school funding for the immediate benefit of the poor.[26]

Pope responded publicly in a handbill dated 29 August 1816. Portraying himself as above partisanship, he wrote: "It is asked with the snarl of suspicion, 'What induces Mr. Pope to offer for congress? He has a good office, &c.'" He had no intention, he declared, of promoting private interests, and his only inducement was "the honor of representing the free people of Illinois territory in congress."

Pope's campaign platform focused upon attracting new settlers by promoting prosperity, extinguishing Indian land titles, building new roads and bridges, and raising funds for public education in a more expeditious manner. Noticeably absent in all this rhetoric was anything substantive relating to the territory's admission to the Union, other than Pope's single reference in his handbill to "this (will be) state."[27] Heacock was completely silent on the issue. Only the pseudonymous "Aristides" touched on the question in the *Intelligencer* on 21 August 1816, and then only in a general way as a prospect within the next three to four years, at which point the people of Illinois would "burst the chains of despotism, by which we are now bound."[28]

If there were no particularly substantive areas of disagreement between Pope and Heacock—who subsequently withdrew from the contest—the campaign was nonetheless not without controversy. On 2 September 1816, William Russell, a St. Louis "surveyor and land speculator," published a handbill charging Pope with having falsely accused Russell of conspiring to purchase land claims—at a discount—from victims of the New Madrid Earthquake of 1811. Russell and his fellow conspirator Rufus Easton would then submit the claims to the federal government for compensation and in the process pocket a healthy profit. Russell also accused Pope and his old law partner, John Scott, of having stolen $4,000 from an orphan's estate.[29]

In the end Russell's charges went nowhere. This was partly because there was no opponent in the race capable of sustaining the case, but it was also because Pope had already refuted the charges in his handbill of 29 August with the testimony of five arbitrators who had examined the evidence and had cleared both Pope and Scott of any wrongdoing.[30] At all events, when the election was held on Thursday, 5 September, Nathaniel Pope emerged victorious over his single challenger, John Caldwell, "by a majority of 928 votes."[31]

Pope resigned as secretary of Illinois Territory on the same day. It is unlikely the vote totals were compiled with enough speed that the results would have been known so soon. More probably, Pope was supremely confident he would prevail; his letter to President James Madison characterized his resignation as attributable to "[h]aving offered to serve the people of Illinois in Congress"[32]—not that he had been chosen or elected, but that he had *offered* to serve. Once that outcome was certain, he commenced preparations for his journey eastward. On 30 October 1816, the *Western Intelligencer* notified the citizens of the territory that as the upcoming session of Congress was likely "to be a short one from necessity, and if they have petitions of any description to forward to that body to which they wish the attention of our Delegate, it would be well for them to forward such petitions to him at as early a period as possible."[33] Pope was still in Kaskaskia as of 2 November 1816, when Ninian Edwards gave him a letter of introduction to President James Madison lauding his cousin as "a lawyer . . . certainly second to no gentleman of the bar of this, or his own Territory": "As a politician," he continued, "I think he is sincerely a republican, though he may not in all cases have been an unqualified admirer of all the measures of the administration . . . and it is within my own personal knowledge that he has been uniformly a zealous advocate for your election to the Presidency—which," Edwards added slyly, "I mention merely for the purpose of characterizing his politics."[34]

A Pestilential Quagmire

Pope was present at the opening of the second session of the 14th Congress on 2 December 1816, standing side by side with his friend and law partner John Scott, who was now Missouri's territorial delegate. Together they produced their credentials and took their seats. They lodged together at Davis's Hotel, located at what is now 601 Pennsylvania Avenue.[35] Nathaniel Pope soon found that the glory of serving as territorial delegate was substantially mitigated by the reality that was contemporary Washington, D.C. Pennsylvania Avenue, wrote historian David L. Lewis, was regularly transformed into a "malodorous, pestilential quagmire," swamped and overwhelmed by the surging swells of Tiber Creek, the *de facto* "municipal sewer." The Capitol building where Pope spent most of his time was "jerrybuilt and poorly engineered": "Columns split under the weight of spectators' balconies in the House and Senate. The forced-air heating system, conceived as the last word in modern domestic engineering, was so thermal that the legislators had to turn it off. The glass-domed ceiling in the House chamber leaked water on the tobacco-chewing solons below."[36]

The *Western Intelligencer*'s exhortations to its readers to quickly send Pope their petitions underscored his central function in Congress as the territory's lobbyist, "charged," wrote Paul Angle, "with the duty of securing favorable legislation, warding off inimical acts, transacting business at the departments and performing personal favors and errands."[37] This was illustrated in a letter written by Pope on 6 January 1817 to Elias Kent Kane concerning a claim of Kane's father-in-law. "[T]he time is unpropitious. The demands upon the Gov[t] usually from the late war are so numerous as to be alarming and besides occupy so much of the attention of Congress (the session being short) that I cannot hope to get this claim through."[38]

Pope attempted to make good on promises implicit in his campaign for delegate. On 19 December 1816 he moved the adoption of a resolution to instruct the House Committee on Foreign Relations "to inquire into the expediency of excluding foreigners from trading with the Indians residing within the limits of the United States." "Such a course," he asserted, "would relieve the Indians from their present dependence upon the British traders, the ill effects of which were at present very evident."[39] He likewise forwarded a petition on 24 January 1817 from the Illinois territorial legislature asking that frontier inhabitants who had engaged the enemy during the War of 1812 "be allowed the pay and emoluments of soldiers of the army of the United States."[40] Earlier the previous month Pope had visited the War Department to ensure that payments to the

Illinois militia had been properly processed and sent westward.[41] On several occasions he forwarded requests from his constituents asking for confirmation of land titles or for relief from paying the full amount for such lots.[42] And after his friend John Scott was unseated on 13 January 1817 when the House ruled that his election as Missouri's delegate had been illegal, Pope frequently represented the interests of Scott's constituents.[43]

A Useful Template

Of particular relevance during the second session of the 14th Congress was the admission (or preparation for admission) of two new states—Indiana and Mississippi. Congress had passed an enabling act for Indiana by a vote of 108–3 during the spring of 1816,[44] and now that that territory had drafted a constitution, elected a general assembly, and sent representatives to Congress, the only remaining hurdle was the final admission of the new state into the Union. The Senate accordingly passed a resolution to that effect on 6 December 1816, the House concurring three days later and President Madison signing the measure into law on 11 December.[45] And although Nathaniel Pope only witnessed the closing stages of the statehood process for Illinois's neighbor to the east, Indiana's underlying enabling legislation nevertheless served as a useful model for Pope a year later.

Mississippi's admission proved to be more challenging, and in some ways it may have been more instructive for the delegate from Illinois. Mississippi's territorial legislature had repeatedly petitioned Congress for statehood since 1810, meeting with mixed results. The House's select committees charged with evaluating the petitions consistently emphasized the expediency of admitting Mississippi to the Union, and they drafted admission enabling bills in each of the 11th through 14th Congresses. Opponents focused on issues that would have been familiar to Pope. Easterners feared that the admission of yet another western state would mean "the diminution of their [states'] relative weight in the scale of the Union."[46] They criticized the lack of accurate population figures; the census of 1810 counted 40,352 inhabitants, including 17,088 enslaved persons[47]—well below the threshold of 60,000 inhabitants deemed necessary for admission. This was particularly troubling in light of the size of the prospective state, which encompassed not only Mississippi but Alabama as well. During a debate in the 14th Congress in 1816, Richard Stanford of North Carolina deemed it "entirely too large, considered in relation to the other States, and in time would be too powerful if it continued an undivided State."[48] There were similar concerns in the Senate, where each of the four bills proposed during the 11th through 14th Congresses were postponed for later consideration. In 1816 the upper chamber's select committee on statehood for Mississippi warned that the new state "with its present very extensive limits, and dispersed population would subject many of its citizens to serious inconveniences." Consequently they recommended that the territory be divided in half, with a line running north and south, and that a census be conducted.[49]

Congress followed this advice and—despite some opposition among territorial leaders out west—provided for the more heavily populated western half of the territory to begin the process of admission. In a separate bill they established the eastern half as Alabama Territory. The bills were passed by both houses and signed by the president on 1 and 3 March 1817.[50]

Nathaniel Pope was thus able to observe the challenges inherent in the pathway to statehood. He witnessed the practical limits of a territory's ability to obtain the best possible terms for admission. He saw how the final bill set geographic boundaries, authorized a constitutional convention, defined voting standards for selecting representatives in that body, and provided funding for roads and canals both within Mississippi and leading to the new state.[51] And he recognized that geography, population, and political expediency would be determinative in governing a territory's incorporation into the Union.

It was a useful template for Pope to follow for Illinois statehood should the opportunity arise. To the extent that he gave the matter any consideration, there was no reason to believe that the process was likely to play out in any different way. For now, Nathaniel Pope's focus was on heading homeward where he could once again devote his energies to his law practice and confer with his political cohorts.

Missing from that circle, of course, was Daniel Pope Cook, who had left the territory earlier in the year and was by now somewhere at large in London. There is no evidence relating to whether Cook and Pope crossed paths in the nation's capital in early March, but any encounter would have been necessarily brief.[52] It is quite certain that they did not see each other before Pope departed Kaskaskia once more for Washington around 10 October 1817,[53] or more than a month before Cook's return home, consequently leaving no opportunity to confer on the issue of statehood or anything else. The delegate and the protégé literally passed each other on the road.[54]

It was a long, weary journey for Pope, longer than Cook's westward trajectory home. (Cook had left the capital on 5 October and arrived in Kaskaskia on 18 November—a sojourn of forty-four days.)[55] Delayed by "bad roads and weather," it was not until 6 December—fifty-seven days after leaving Kaskaskia[56]—that the delegate from Illinois Territory strode into Davis's Hotel and took up residence once more alongside his friend and colleague John Scott, who by now had been restored to his position as Missouri's territorial delegate. Pope resumed his seat again when Congress was called to order on the eighth,[57] presumably steeling himself for another few months of the legislative routines and banalities that fell to the lot of a nonvoting delegate. Where Illinois Territory was concerned, however, Nathaniel Pope was about to find out that the 15th Congress would ultimately prove to be anything but typical.

8

CANDOUR AND GOOD FAITH

Like his predecessor Benjamin Stephenson, Nathaniel Pope was coming to fully understand the intrinsic limitations of the position of territorial delegate in his second year of service. Section 12 of the Northwest Ordinance declared that the delegate would "have a seat in Congress, with a right of debating, but not of voting."[1] He would be the territory's eyes, ears, and voice in the nation's capital. He could plead, argue, advocate, cajole, persuade on behalf of his fellow Illinoisans both individually and as an undifferentiated constituency, but that was the extent of the powers of a territorial delegate. Building influence was ultimately a matter of time and patience. Stephenson observed that he had worked to become "more familiarized with the proceedings of congress, having enlarged my acquaintance and acquired the confidence of friends who are both able & willing to afford their useful co-operation; without which, it is a melancholy truth, that a delegate of a territory, whatever may be his talents, cannot be very successful in advancing its interests."[2] It was good advice, and Nathaniel Pope was determined to make the most of it.

In his first days back in Washington, D.C., Pope devoted substantial time and effort to forwarding petitions from his constituents to Congress. Petitions dealing with land issues were common; on 10 December, for example, he forwarded a "petition of sundry inhabitants of the territory of Illinois, concerning land titles, confirmed by former governors of the north western territories."[3] Another petition originated with Morris Birkbeck, the English agricultural entrepreneur who had finally arrived in America to pursue his dream of creating a settlement of like-minded "farmers, labourers, and mechanics" on the western frontier. Birkbeck sought to purchase public lands for that purpose, and so in late December Pope dutifully presented his petition.[4] Pope had already responded to Birkbeck in support of the proposal: "I can not fail to indulge an ardent wish that you may succeed in your plan."

Pope's enthusiasm for Birkbeck's scheme stemmed in part from conversations he had had with Secretary of State John Quincy Adams, who, Pope wrote, "speaks of you [Birkbeck] in the most flattering terms." Pope's only concern, he confided to the Englishman, was that the fear of speculation might defeat his application, and he expressed regret at the lack of more explanatory details in the petition. Nevertheless, Illinois's congressional delegate pledged to do everything possible to bring the matter to a successful resolution.[5]

The opportunity of making Secretary Adams's acquaintance was an important byproduct of Birkbeck's petition. They were already related by marriage; former senator John Pope's wife Eliza was the sister of Adams's wife Louisa, and by now, of course, they shared a mutual connection to Daniel Pope Cook. The delegate from Illinois spent a great deal of time over the next several months socializing with Adams, frequently in the company of fellow legislators such as David Trimble and George Robertson of Kentucky and John Scott of Missouri. The secretary of state's diary provides a valuable record of their association, chronicling conversations on a variety of topics—Adams was particularly struck by Pope's mastery of western politics—and it affords some evidence as to Pope's state of mind at the time.[6] He was not preoccupied in late December and early January with initiating a successful statehood admission process. Nathaniel Pope was instead planning a trip to the northeast—to New York City and Boston. On 21 December John Quincy Adams confided to his diary that he had written a number of letters of introduction on Pope's behalf.[7] They included missives to William Gray, president of the Boston branch of the Bank of the United States; Adams's cousin and Boston bibliophile William S. Shaw; John T. Kirkland, president of Harvard University; Dr. Thomas Welsh of Boston, who was married to a cousin of Adams's mother; Daniel McCormick, a Wall Street businessman and a director of the Bank of New York; the painter John Trumbull; and the secretary's father, former president John Adams.[8] The secretary's letter to Dr. Kirkland remarked that Pope "is making a short visit to Boston, and has I believe a particular motive for obtaining information respecting the University over which you preside—I avail myself with pleasure of the opportunity of introducing him to your acquaintance, and of recommending him to your kind attention."[9] He added in a separate letter to his father that Pope would be joined in his travels by Senator John Crittenden of Kentucky, who had been a political ally of Ninian Edwards in that state and was appointed by the governor as Illinois Territory's attorney general in 1810.[10]

Pope's own rhetoric at this time implicitly emphasizing statehood as a long-term goal strongly supports the notion that he was not aware of the admission campaign. In a letter to the *Western Intelligencer* dated 10 December 1817—at almost exactly the same time as the territorial legislature was in the act of approving the statehood petition—Pope alluded to speculation that President

James Monroe supported increasing public land prices, "but it is hoped no such measure will be adopted—indeed I will oppose it with all my strength. It would check emigration and might have the effect of postponing our admission into the union."[11] And if there were any remaining doubts regarding Pope's foreknowledge of the initiative, they were dispelled by a letter he later wrote to Senator Rufus King in April: "I had no agency in the petition to Congress but I have supported the application with that candour and good faith becoming my station. I cannot however suppress my regret that the application was made at this time, least it may fail [*sic*]."[12]

My Hopes Are Sanguine

Nathaniel Pope's visit to the Northeast was more limited in scope than he had originally envisioned. He left the nation's capital on or shortly after 22 December, carrying in his luggage skates, books, and brushes for delivery to ten-year-old Charles Francis Adams in Boston, courtesy of the secretary of state and his wife.[13] Pope reappeared in Washington on the evening of 16 January at Adams's home; the secretary confided to his diary that Pope had "just returned from New York, having been no farther."[14] And one of the first items of business greeting the delegate from Illinois upon his return was the territorial legislature's petition, which had probably arrived in Washington around 8 January. Pope lost no time in acting upon the summons, presenting it to the House of Representatives on 16 January. The House thereupon appointed a select committee to consider the issue and develop appropriate legislation, choosing Pope, Richard M. Johnson of Kentucky, New Yorker John C. Spencer, Ezekiel Whitman from the District of Maine in Massachusetts, and Thomas Claiborne of Tennessee.[15]

Richard M. Johnson was a particularly important influence on the statehood process, given his connections to numerous Illinois political leaders, including Pope himself. Like Pope a native of Louisville, Kentucky, Johnson was a hero of the War of 1812—he had killed Tecumseh at the Battle of the Thames, so it was claimed[16]—was a strong supporter of protective tariffs and internal improvements, and later was elected vice president under Martin Van Buren.[17] He was regarded by his contemporaries as a pleasant, congenial fellow; Margaret Bayard Smith, an early Washington socialite, described him in 1816 as "[t]he most tender hearted, mild, affectionate and benevolent of men. . . . His eloquence is not that of imagination, but of the heart. His mind is not highly cultivated, or rather I should say his taste."[18] Nearly twenty years later the British writer Harriet Martineau encountered him at a dinner party in Andrew Jackson's White House and recounted bemusedly: "His countenance is wild, though with much cleverness in it; his hair wanders all abroad, and he wears no cravat. But there is no telling how he might look if dressed like other people."[19] Johnson had ties to both Pope and Governor Edwards, having previously recommended the former for his original appointment as territorial secretary: "[N]o man of his age in the Western Country has a higher reputation as to moral character, his abilities or his information."[20] Johnson had helped Illinois advance to the second stage of territorial government in 1812, after Edwards had written Johnson requesting his assistance in Congress to obtain the popular election of territorial delegates as well as an expansion of voting rights beyond the provisions of the Northwest Ordinance.[21] Johnson's connection to Edwards and his own western background support the notion that—except for Pope—he had perhaps a clearer understanding of the situation in Illinois Territory than any of the other committee members.[22]

John Canfield Spencer, from Canandaigua, New York, was in the middle of his only term as Congressman. Described as "a man of great abilities, industry, and endurance, curt manners and irascible temper," he had been active in New York legal circles since 1809. While in Congress he was a member of the Committee on the U.S. Bank, which wrote a report highly critical of that agency. After he left Congress, Spencer served several terms in the New York legislature; he later became an Antimason and subsequently a Whig. Spencer also served as both Secretary of War and Secretary of the Treasury under President John Tyler, who nominated him (unsuccessfully) to the U.S. Supreme Court.[23]

Ezekiel Whitman, from Portland in the District of Maine, Massachusetts, was the only Federalist on the committee. He was in his second term in the House, having previously served from 1809 to 1811. In the interim he had been a member of the executive council of Massachusetts. He ran for election to Congress again in 1816 on a ticket of Federalists touting themselves as "disciples of your revered WASHINGTON" and blaming their opponents for plunging the country "into an impolitic and ruinous war" that had saddled the United States with debt; as a result, "the people now are and will be for years to come loaded with numerous vexatious and oppressive TAXES."[24] He was subsequently the only member of the committee to vote against Illinois's admission to the Union, probably because he felt Illinois's new constitution failed to adequately prohibit slavery.[25] Although an erstwhile supporter of Maine's separation from Massachusetts and admission to the Union, Whitman actively opposed the Missouri Compromise in 1819–20 that admitted these two regions to statehood. The compromise, he argued, meant that "the South was engaging in political blackmail by linking the admission of the two states" and would thus "establish a dangerous precedent in national politics."[26]

The fifth member of the committee was Thomas Claiborne, a Democrat from Nashville, Tennessee. A lawyer by training, he had served on Andrew Jackson's staff in the Creek War and had been a member of the Tennessee General Assembly. He was described at the time of his death as "rigid, uncompromising, and out-spoken" and that he held "what have been usually considered extreme positions on political subjects." Like Spencer, he served only one term in Congress.[27]

Illinois's prospects for statehood, then, lay in the hands of men representing all the major regions of the nation. It was ostensibly their responsibility as national legislators to accomplish that end in a manner beneficial to the country as a whole; but at this early point in America's history the reality was than any given representative was far more likely to think of the admission of a new state in terms of the effect upon his own state, his own region. Nathaniel Pope was not focused upon such rivalries, however. Noting in his letter to Edwards that the committee would begin meeting the following day (22 January 1818), he predicted: "I think a bill will be reported and my hopes are sanguine that it will pass. . . . If I fail it will be on the ground that the Legislature has not acted upon such Testimony as enables it to decide with certainty the amount of population in the territory."[28]

Pope, Johnson, Claiborne, Spencer, and Whitman quickly drafted an admission enabling bill that Pope presented to the House of Representatives on 23 January. The shortness of their labors and a careful reading of that first draft support the conclusion that the committee relied heavily upon the recent statehood bills for Mississippi and—especially—Indiana, with substantial reference to the Northwest Ordinance and the territorial legislature's original petition. The bill's second section set the boundaries of the new state mostly as they exist today, with the Mississippi River to the west, the Ohio River to the south, and a line originating from the Wabash River pointing northward on the east. The northern boundary, however, was designated as an east-west line drawn through a point ten miles north of the southern tip of Lake Michigan, or about fifty miles south of the modern border with Wisconsin.[29]

Upon first glance this would seem to be in violation of the Northwest Ordinance of 1787, which empowered Congress to establish a northern and a southern tier of states divided by "an east and west line drawn through the southerly bend or extreme of Lake Michigan."[30] The ordinance does not say, however, that the line *must* be located at this point. In a letter to the *Western Intelligencer* a few days later, Pope observed that the boundary extended no further north than that of Indiana. "When the bill is taken up," he continued,

"I will endeavour to procure twenty or thirty miles farther north, and make Lake Michigan a part of our eastern boundary. I shall not attempt to explain the importance of such an accession of territory as it is too obvious to every man who looks to the prospective weight and influence of the state of Illinois."[31] At all events, as if to allay any lingering doubts as to its legality, Pope and his colleagues took pains to include a provision underscoring that the new state's constitution must not be repugnant to the ordinance "excepting so much of said articles as relate to the boundaries of the States therein to be formed." They also required the state's constitutional convention to ratify these boundaries, "otherwise they shall be and remain as now prescribed by the Ordinance."[32]

Section 3 dealt with qualifications for voting and the election of a state constitutional convention. It was in some ways the most liberal suffrage provision of its day anywhere in the United States, but it was in keeping with a long-term loosening of such qualifications as newer states to the west were admitted to the Union; "The general sentiment in the west," wrote Solon J. Buck, ". . . was in favor of allowing immigrants to vote as soon as possible."[33] Whereas Indiana had given the ballot to all male citizens aged twenty-one and older who had been residents for one year and paid a county or territorial tax,[34] the first draft of the Illinois enabling bill shortened the residency period to six months and eliminated the tax requirement. It differed further from the Indiana bill in one subtle but important respect. In the first draft the word "white" is marked for insertion in the phrase "all male citizens."[35] It is likely that the committee based this change on Mississippi's enabling act that enfranchised "all free white male citizens."[36]

In providing for the election of a constitutional convention, the draft bill decreed that delegates would be selected by county. The precise number of representatives for each of the twelve counties was left blank for the moment. Three days—a Monday, Tuesday, and Wednesday—of a month still to be determined were set aside for the election of the convention.[37]

Section 4 authorized the formation of a constitution and state government that would be "republican and not repugnant" to the Northwest Ordinance of 1787. The bill also departed from the Indiana model by including a requirement that "it shall appear from the enumeration hereinafter directed to be made that there are within the limits of the proposed State not less than _____ thousand inhabitants."[38] This was a matter of particular concern for Nathaniel Pope. He wrote to the *Western Intelligencer* on 24 January that his only concern was "whether we have the population supposed by the Legislature. . . . In order to evade that objection the bill contains a *proviso*, that the census shall be taken previously to the meeting of the Convention—I hope however to have that feature of the bill struck out before its final passage, if it passes at all, of which I have strong hopes."[39]

The source of Pope's unease about the population provision was twofold. First, Article V of the Northwest Ordinance decreed that admission to the Union for any state created from portions of the Northwest Territory was conditioned upon that prospective state having "sixty thousand free inhabitants therein." His hopes for abandoning this requirement rested upon the provision in Article V that a state could gain admission with fewer than 60,000 "so far as it can be consistent with the general interest of the confederacy."[40] Second, Pope was aware that no similar requirement had been present in either the Indiana or the Mississippi bills. The Indiana territorial legislature had conducted its own census documenting that its population exceeded 60,000 and incorporated the results into their petition to Congress.[41] Mississippi's 1814 legislative petition cited the previous 1810 general census figure of 40,352 and maintained that substantial in-migration in the meantime would have brought the total population to upward of 60,000. In any case, the reports from the select committees on Mississippi statehood over the years consistently emphasized that this provision was not written in stone, focusing especially upon the provision in the original cession agreement between the United States and Georgia that admission could take place even if the territory's population fell short of 60,000, "if Congress shall think it expedient."[42] By contrast, the Illinois territorial legislature had limited itself to merely expressing its opinion that the territory's population amounted to at least 40,000.[43] The 1810 census had calculated this figure at 12,282, which would help to explain why the legislature felt its best hope lay in obfuscation.

Section 5 specified that the new state would have one representative in the U.S. House until the next general census in 1820. Section 6 was among the most consequential portions of the bill, setting forth four propositions offering specific grants and gifts to Illinois. First, monies realized from the sale of section 16 in each township would be granted to Illinois for local residents for funding schools. Second, "All salt Springs & Lead mines within the said Territory and the land reserved for the use of the same" would provide a source of revenue. Leases of such resources were not to extend beyond ten years at a time. Third, "five per cent of the net proceeds of the lands lying within the said Territory and which shall be sold by Congress . . . shall be reserved for making public roads and canals." Three-fifths of these funds would be devoted to internal improvements that were entirely within the boundaries of Illinois, and the remaining two-fifths would be reserved for interstate roads and canals. Finally, land sales from one entire township (thirty-six sections) would be "reserved for the use of a seminary of learning and vested in the Legislature of the said state to be appropriated solely to the use of such seminary." These propositions were largely identical to passages from the Indiana bill, differing only in that the latter made no reference to lead mines.[44] The Mississippi bill only contained the passage regarding the use of land sales revenues for funding roads and canals.

The first and last of these propositions—providing funding for local schools and for the support of a "seminary of learning" through land sales—were rooted in a late eighteenth-century consensus among the Founders that there was a profound connection between an educated populace and a vital republic. "They felt that providing a public education," wrote historian Alexandra Usher, "was the only means by which to ensure that citizens were prepared to exercise the freedoms and responsibilities granted to them in the Constitution and thereby preserve the ideals of liberty and freedom."[45] In 1779 Thomas Jefferson, then governor of Virginia, authored "A Bill for the More General Diffusion of Knowledge" in an effort to encourage the development of a publicly funded education system within the state. Such a system, he declared, would help prevent tyranny by illuminating "as far as practicable, the minds of the people at large, and more especially to give them knowledge . . . [so that] they may be enabled to know ambition under all its shapes, and prompt to exert their natural powers to defeat its purposes." It was therefore "expedient for promoting the publick [*sic*] happiness that those persons, whom nature hath endowed with genius and virtue, should be rendered by liberal education worthy to receive, and able to guard the sacred deposit of the rights and liberties of their fellow citizens."[46]

The federal government began providing for funding of public education in the Land Ordinance of 1785, which sought to systematically apportion public lands in the Northwest Territory and make them available for sale. It specifically reserved lot 16 in every township "for the maintenance of public schools."[47] Two years later, Article III of the Northwest Ordinance decreed: "Religion, morality, and knowledge being necessary to good government and the happiness of mankind, schools and the means of education shall forever be encouraged."[48] As a result, beginning with Ohio in 1803, the federal government granted lands for the use of schools to thirty states, going well beyond the five carved out of the original Northwest Territory. Not every new state was granted thirty-six sections, or one entire township, to fund a seminary of learning; Indiana had been the first state admitted with that proviso, and every subsequent state except for Texas and Hawaii was a beneficiary of such land sales. Without such funding and the "federal government's endorsement of free public schooling for all citizens and legislation specifically setting aside land and money for the establishment of schools," Usher wrote, "the expansive territories and nascent states may have struggled to sustain education as a monetary and political priority."[49]

This was certainly the reality in Illinois Territory. In 1816 the *Western Intelligencer* decried the lack of any public school in the territorial capital in spite of a clear and pressing need: "Such carelessness bespeaks an unpardonable indifference in parents about the welfare of their posterity, or an egregious ignorance of the necessity and utility of education." The good citizens of Kaskaskia, the *Intelligencer* implied, were too stingy to support a school providing even the most rudimentary education for the community.[50]

The draft enabling act offered the ideal solution: perhaps frontier citizens might be persuaded to change their minds if someone else—those purchasing land, for example—were to provide the money. It was an early example of a cooperative venture between the state and federal governments foreshadowing later initiatives such as the Morrill Land Grant College Act and the National Defense Education Act. Federal, state, and local governments alike had roles to play. The federal government, Alexandra Usher wrote, offered "a national vision, motivation and a sense of purpose, as well as some funding"; states stood ready to shape policies within their local environments and provide additional funding; and local governments would implement and influence these policies.[51]

Nathaniel Pope was already familiar with the potential value of federal subsidies for promoting education on the western frontier. Ten years earlier, as one of the trustees of the Ste. Genevieve academy, Pope had signed a petition to Congress asking for a donation of vacant lands that would serve as an additional source of funds for the school. The trustees were, they said, "induced to look up to the Government of the United States for such aid & support in accomplishing so desirable an object, as to Your wisdom may seem just & proper."[52]

Finding the wherewithal to fund governmental functions likewise inspired the provision to grant salt springs and lead mines to the new state. Historian Frederick Jackson Turner wrote: "The early settlers were tied to the [East] coast by the need of salt, without which they could not preserve their meats or live in comfort." Turner argued that the discovery of salt springs in the interior was one of the factors that enabled further westward migration.[53] Salt that had been produced overseas was still imported to the interior via Philadelphia and Baltimore. However, over time the advantages of naturally occurring salines—pools of seawater left behind from a much earlier period when, as

John Jakle observed, Illinois was "covered by an inland sea"—in modern-day Gallatin and Saline Counties provided an incentive to develop a robust and lucrative salt manufacturing industry.[54] The federal government encouraged and facilitated its development; in 1809 U.S. secretary of the treasury Albert Gallatin told Ninian Edwards that the government placed a high priority on reducing the price of salt by renting the salines at a low cost and by requiring that a minimum amount of salt be produced annually.[55]

Manufacturing the salt was complicated by a difficulty in securing an adequate labor supply for this purpose. In 1812 the territorial legislature passed a resolution calling upon Illinois's congressional delegate to work for the passage of a federal law authorizing the introduction of enslaved persons into the saline districts, given that "Labor in this territory is abundant and Laborors [*sic*] at this time [are] extremely scarce so much so that the Lessees [of the salines] and others engaged in making Salt at the Saline near Shawney Town cannot progress only on a small scale."[56] In 1813 Senator George Mortimer Bibb of Kentucky introduced a bill to enable this purpose, "any ordinance or act of Congress for the government of said territory to the contrary notwithstanding."[57] No further action was taken by Congress on this bill, however. Consequently, in December 1814 the territorial legislature approved "An Act Concerning Negroes and Mulattoes" declaring that "experience has proved that the manufacture of salt in particular, at the United States Saline cannot be successfully carried on by white laborers, and it being the interest of every description of inhabitants to afford every facility to the most extensive manufacture of that article." Under its provisions, any enslaved person from elsewhere could "voluntarily hire himself or herself, within the Territory, by the consent of his or her master, for any term not exceeding twelve months."[58]

Salt, then, was a crucial commodity, but it was also a lucrative source of revenue for the government. Over the course of the period 1811–15 the lessees of the Wabash saline near Shawneetown paid rent in the amount of $28,160.25. From 1807 to 1818, the federal government also received more than 158,000 bushels of salt for rent as well, which it could then sell at a profit.[59]

Nathaniel Pope was familiar with the parameters of the salt industry, the factors influencing its price, and the ways in which the government might maximize its own profits from the "rent salt" it collected. In an 1816 letter to Josiah Meigs, commissioner of the U.S. General Land Office, the territorial delegate advocated that "the clear profits of the saline ought to be expended in improvements in the Territory to which it belongs, say in roads." He emphasized that this would ultimately have a beneficial influence upon settlement:

"The General Government will be well remunerated in the appreciation of its public lands through which the roads shall pass. Every road would throw into demand all the lands on or near its borders."[60]

Potential revenues emanating from lead mines in Illinois were similarly promising. The mineral was extraordinarily abundant in what are now the counties of Jo Daviess and Carroll in the northwestern corner of the state, especially along the banks of the Mississippi and the Fever (or Galena) River. European explorers and settlers had sought to exploit these lead deposits from their earliest incursions into the Illinois Country.

By the time that Nathaniel Pope and his fellow representatives on the committee were drafting the statehood enabling bill, a variety of factors rendered granting of the lead regions to the new state an attractive and valuable prospect. Historian Reuben Gold Thwaites reported that in 1816 Colonel George Davenport had shipped "the first flat-boat cargo of lead ever avowedly emanating from the Fever River mines." By that time, Thwaites observed, lead had become "quite as useful as currency in the financial operations of the country."[61] Steamboats began to traverse the Mississippi the following year, and by 1818 there were twenty-three such crafts navigating that river and its tributaries, underscoring the potential for easily transporting lead ore over long distances.[62] In the same year that Davenport shipped his first cargo, the United States signed a treaty with the Ottawa, the Chippewa, and the Potawatomi granting those tribes all territory between the Illinois and Wisconsin Rivers with the exception of an as-yet-unidentified tract "five leagues square" on the Mississippi River that was specifically intended to encompass the lead region, which the federal government's negotiators described as "immensely valuable."[63] Sometime between 1819 and 1821 Colonel James Johnson—incidentally, a brother of Pope's fellow committee member Richard M. Johnson—began mining operations in the Fever River region that relied in part upon enslaved labor and paying rent to the federal government in the amount of nearly sixteen tons of lead in the year ending 30 September 1823 (the first year such records were kept).[64] In the end, however, the lead mines provision was struck from the bill in its second draft.[65] It is possible that there was a sentiment that reserving these resources for the new state would amount to asking for too much, but it is equally conceivable that (unlike the salines) in 1818 the committee felt there was not enough information available on prospective revenues.

The next provision reserving 5 percent of land sales revenues for roads and canals—three-fifths to those completely within the state and two-fifths to those connecting to other states—was perhaps the most momentous section of the bill, although there was no reason for the drafting committee to think so at the time. After all, the enabling acts for Indiana and Mississippi had contained—and those for Alabama and Missouri (the next two states admitted after Illinois) would later contain—almost precisely the same language.[66] And Nathaniel Pope already had some familiarity with the issue, having directly observed the extent of Illinois's reliance upon its existing waterways—the Illinois, the Mississippi, and the Ohio Rivers in particular—to develop a communication and transportation network. Thus it would hardly have occurred to him or anyone else on the committee that providing for internal improvements—which was standard operating procedure in the statehood process—would be controversial. Subsequent events would prove that judgment to be premature.

Acceptance of these four provisions by Illinois Territory was conditioned upon the new state agreeing to exempt all federal land sales from any taxation for five years.[67] Section 7 declared that federal laws would have "the same force and effect" in Illinois as in the other states. And the final sections 8–12 prescribed the appointment of U.S. District Court judges, the U.S. attorney, and U.S. marshals. This had not been present in the Indiana or the Mississippi bills, and these provisions were later stricken from the Illinois bill as redundant.[68]

With the Zeal Becoming His Station

Nathaniel Pope presented the draft bill to the House of Representatives on Friday, 23 January 1818, where it was read twice and committed to the Committee of the Whole for the following Monday (26 January). Whatever sense of elation he may have felt in clearing this first major hurdle was only heightened by that body's rejection—by the narrowest of margins—on the same day of a bill that would have exempted military bounty lands from taxation and thus shut off another funding source. This plan, he wrote, "I hope is abandoned by its friends; but at any rate I have no fears that it will succeed. So that we may calculate upon a handsome revenue from that quarter."[69]

At this point there was every reason for confidence about the prospects for statehood, concerns about population notwithstanding.[70] Nathaniel Pope could call upon fellow members of the House such as Richard Johnson, William Henry Harrison of Indiana, and George Poindexter of Mississippi (the latter two both former territorial delegates) for assistance in the lobbying that was soon to follow.[71] The *Intelligencer* observed the following summer that Pope "had no agency in putting on foot the application to congress for a state government. But when he received the memorial for that purpose, he supported it with the zeal becoming his station. No blame can attach to him if we fail; the fault consists in our want of numbers, over which he had no control."[72] Illinois's congressional delegate had successfully parlayed his talents as an advocate to create a rudimentary legislative vehicle for admission to the Union, much as previous territorial delegates had shepherded enabling acts for Indiana and Mississippi through Congress. The past was prologue as far as he was concerned. Nevertheless, circumstances had changed, and Nathaniel Pope would know soon enough how treacherous the road—or roads—ahead would prove to be.

Garrison Hill Cemetery looking east, Fort Kaskaskia State Park, Ellis Grove, Illinois. Those who lie here were moved from their original last resting place in old Kaskaskia in 1891 when their graves were endangered by erosion and flooding. *Photograph by James A. Edstrom, 28 October 2002.*

Daniel Pope Cook (1793–1827), architect of the statehood campaign, first state attorney general, and member of the U.S. House of Representatives. *Image courtesy of the Abraham Lincoln Presidential Library and Museum, Springfield, Illinois.*

Nathaniel Pope (1784–1850), mentor to Daniel Pope Cook, first cousin to Ninian Edwards, secretary of Illinois Territory, territorial delegate to Congress, and U.S. federal judge.
Image courtesy of the Abraham Lincoln Presidential Library and Museum, Springfield, Illinois.

Elias Kent Kane (1794–1835), the "principal member" of the first Illinois constitutional convention, the first Illinois secretary of state, and U.S. senator from Illinois.
Image courtesy of the Abraham Lincoln Presidential Library and Museum, Springfield, Illinois.

Ninian Edwards (1775–1833), mentor and father-in-law to Daniel Pope Cook and first cousin to Nathaniel Pope, governor of Illinois Territory, U.S. senator, and governor of the State of Illinois. *Image courtesy of the Abraham Lincoln Presidential Library and Museum, Springfield, Illinois.*

Jesse Burgess Thomas (1777–1853), rival to Ninian Edwards, mentor to Elias Kent Kane, Illinois territorial judge, and U.S. senator from Illinois. *Image courtesy of the Abraham Lincoln Presidential Library and Museum, Springfield, Illinois.*

John Quincy Adams (1767–1848), sixth president of the United States, U.S. secretary of state under James Monroe, and mentor to Daniel Pope Cook. Portrait by Gilbert Stuart in 1818, around the time of Adams's first acquaintance with Daniel Pope Cook and Nathaniel Pope. *Original portrait in the White House Collection, Washington, D.C. Gilbert Stuart / Wikimedia Commons / Public Domain.*

The packet ship *Swiftsure* by Nicola Camilleri, 1817. It was very similar in construction and appearance to Daniel Pope Cook's ship the *Marchioness of Queensbury*; like the *Queensbury*, the *Swiftsure* ran a regular route between New York, Halifax, and Falmouth. *Image courtesy of the National Maritime Museum Cornwall, Falmouth, United Kingdom, FAMMC OC936.*

Map of Daniel Pope Cook's voyage home from London aboard the *Washington* in the summer of 1817, reconstructed from John Quincy Adams's daily record of the ship's latitude and longitude in his diary. *Map by James A. Edstrom.*

Edward Coles (1786–1868), diplomat who advised Morris Birkbeck on immigrating to America at the behest of John Quincy Adams in 1818. Coles himself settled in Illinois later that same year and freed all of his enslaved persons upon his arrival. Daniel Pope Cook served as his legal advisor in the matter. During his one term as the second governor of Illinois, Coles attempted to fully prohibit slavery in the state. *Image courtesy of the Abraham Lincoln Presidential Library and Museum, Springfield, Illinois.*

Morris Birkbeck (1764–1825), English agriculturalist who established the "English Settlement" in Albion, Illinois, partly on the advice of John Quincy Adams and Edward Coles. Birkbeck was a leading voice opposing an 1824 campaign to revise the state constitution to legalize slavery. *Image courtesy of the Abraham Lincoln Presidential Library and Museum, Springfield, Illinois.*

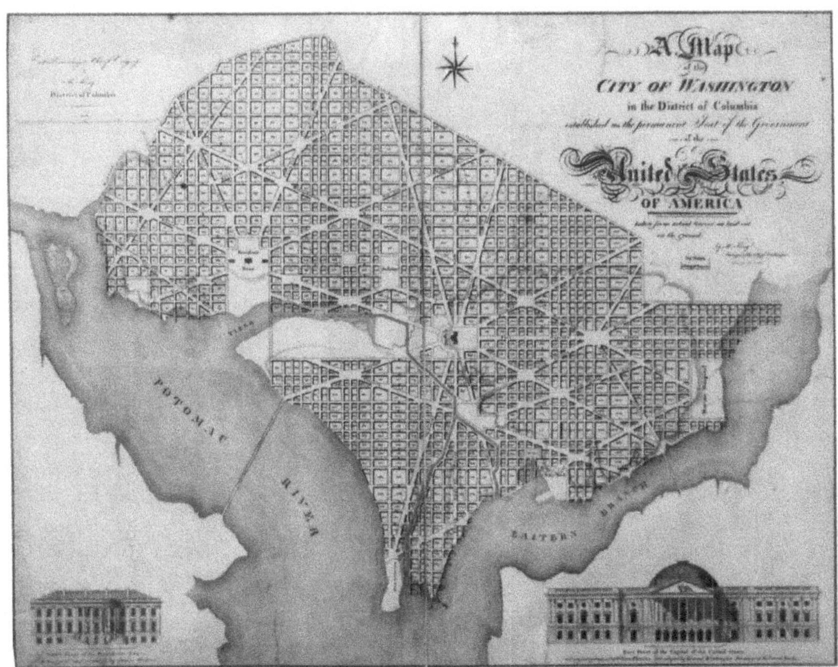

Map of Washington, D.C., at the time of the Nathaniel Pope's tenure as territorial delegate in Congress. Davis's Hotel, where Pope lived at the time, was located roughly halfway between the White House and the Capitol. *Image courtesy of Library of Congress, Geography and Map Division, G3850 1818. K5.*

Rufus King (1755–1827), Federalist senator from New York, was a target of Nathaniel Pope's lobbying effort for statehood. King opposed the initiative and spoke out against it during the debate over the enabling bill. Portrait by Gilbert Stuart, circa 1819–20. *Original portrait in the National Portrait Gallery, Washington, D.C. Gilbert Stuart / Wikimedia Commons / Public Domain.*

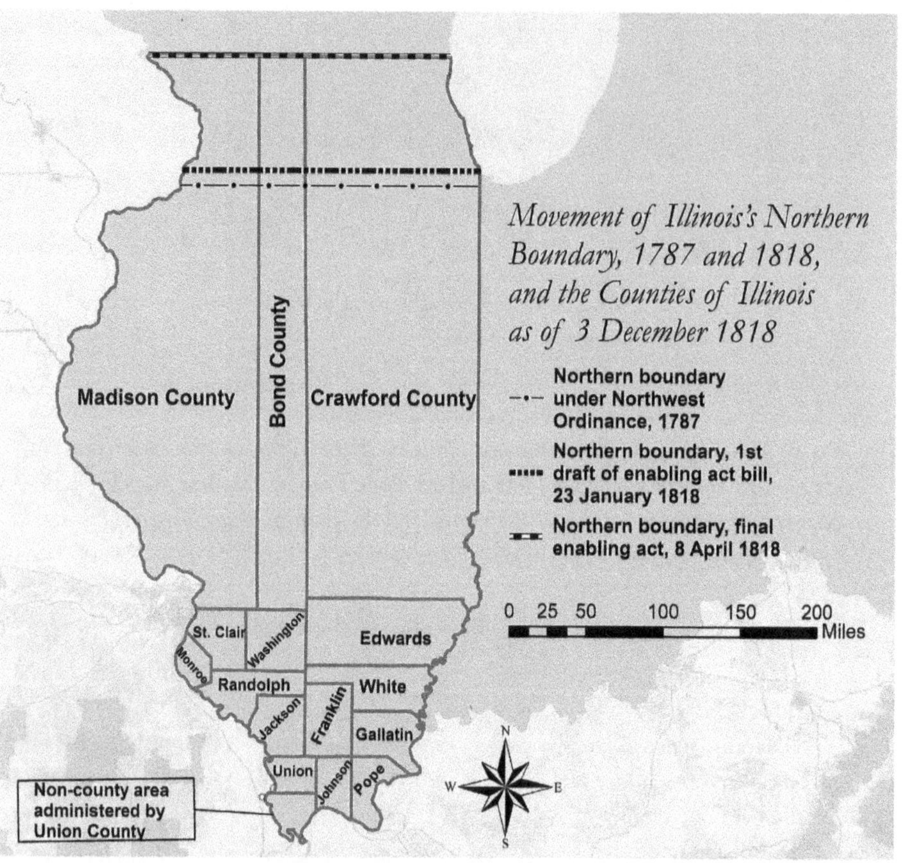

Nathaniel Pope revised Illinois's northern boundary twice in different drafts of the enabling bill, moving it further northward from the original location at the tip of Lake Michigan. Illinois's counties are depicted as they existed at the time of statehood in December 1818. *Map by James A. Edstrom.*

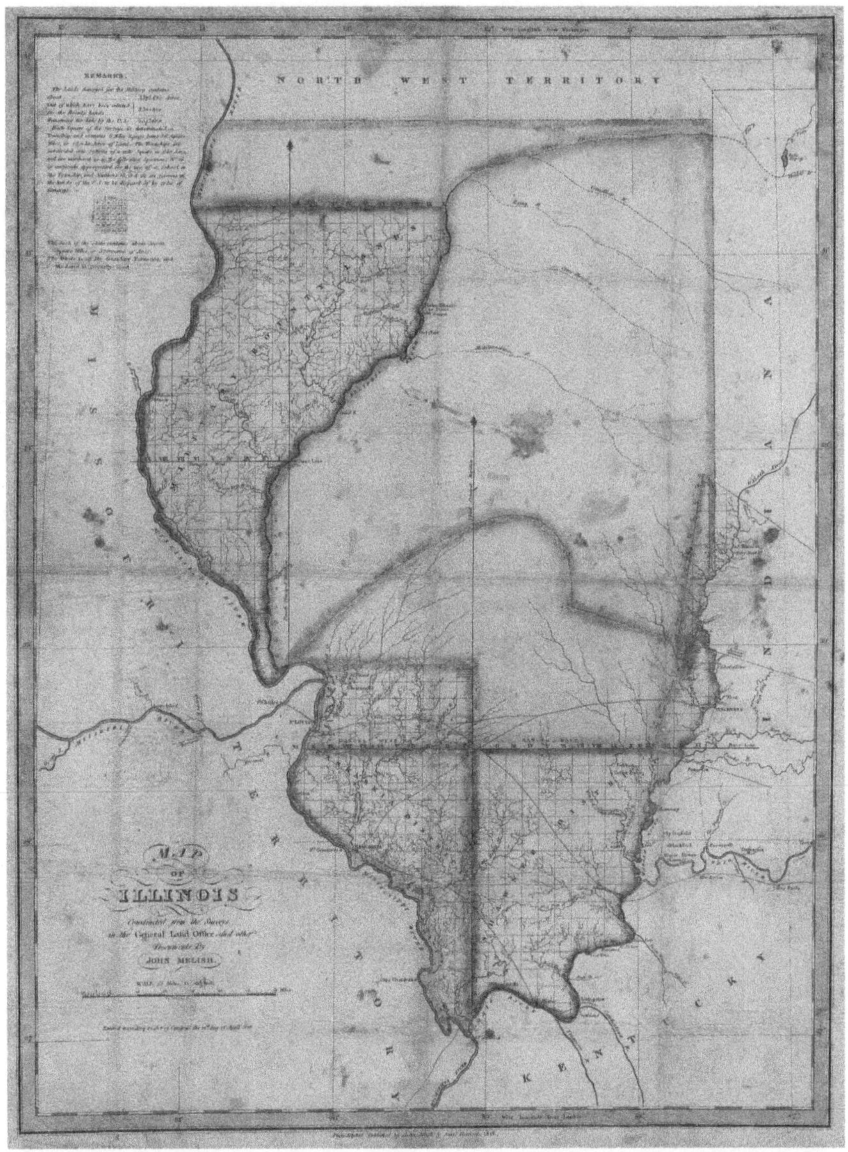

First map of the state of Illinois, published by John Melish on 16 April 1818, two days after congressional approval of the statehood enabling bill and two days before it was signed by President Monroe. Melish may well have created the map before the final passage of the bill, given that he located the northern boundary at approximately 41°42′ N, or slightly south of the boundary originally proposed by Pope (i.e., ten miles north of the southern tip of Lake Michigan). *Image courtesy of the Map and Geography Library, University of Illinois at Urbana-Champaign, G4100 1818 .M4.*

Site of Illinois's first constitutional convention, Kaskaskia (photo circa 1890). The building had previously housed the territorial legislature and served as the first state capitol building until the seat of government was moved to Vandalia in 1819. The structure was completely gone by 1901, a casualty of flooding and erosion from the Mississippi River. *Image courtesy of the Abraham Lincoln Presidential Library and Museum, Springfield, Illinois.*

Kaskaskia about 1857. *This image was published in* Meyer's Universum, oder Abbildung und Beschreibung des Natur und Kunst auf der ganzen Erde, *Achzehnter Band (Hildburghausen: Bruck und Verlag vom Bibliographischen Institut, 1857), plate 330 following page 156. David MacDonald and Raine Waters believed that this was a copy of a lithograph by J. C. Wild originally published in* The Valley of the Mississippi Illustrated in a Series of Views *(St. Louis: Chambers and Knapp, 1841), plate 13 opposite page 61. David MacDonald and Raine Waters,* Kaskaskia: The Lost Capital of Illinois *(Carbondale: Southern Illinois University Press, 2019), 86.*

9

NOTHING CERTAIN CAN BE CALCULATED ON

In the winter of 1818 Nathaniel Pope was flourishing in his role as Illinois Territory's territorial delegate to Congress despite the fundamental limitations of the position. He had somehow mitigated the shock of the territorial legislature's statehood petition and engineered a draft admission enabling bill in a remarkably short time. On 21 February he wrote to the *Intelligencer* with cautious optimism that he expected Congress to begin consideration of the statehood bill in early March: "Its success will have a great influence on the emigration to that [Illinois] country. I cannot describe the interest Illinois awakens in the minds of the Atlantic people. I have no hesitation in hazarding the opinion that next season will add greatly to our population."[1]

In reality Nathaniel Pope was feeling plagued with doubt. He confided to Elias Kent Kane on 8 March 1818: "I have delayed for several days to write you in the hope that my bill would be taken up and acted upon, but the question of Roads and Canals continues to engage the attention of Congress. My prospects of success in making Illinois a State are not diminished—Nothing certain however can be calculated on—."[2]

A Wilderness of Impassable Roads

The entire question of roads and canals was in some ways a stand-in for a variety of subjects lacking a clear national consensus. On its face, it was tied in with constitutional issues—i.e., whether or not the federal government had the power to subsidize, construct, and maintain a national infrastructure. It was, however, just as closely connected to questions of individual state sovereignty, political power, and sectionalism, especially with regard to the growing population and influence of new states to the west in relation to the original members of the Union. Pope had good reason to fear that Illinois statehood was potentially in jeopardy. For now he was powerless to influence the course of events. All he could do was to watch and wait—and hope.

Pope was well aware that developing an accessible transportation network was of paramount importance in Illinois at this early period, when, as Theodore Calvin Pease observed, "the means available for it necessarily influenced the state's contact commercially and intellectually with the outside world. . . . Not till 1819 was a stage line from Kaskaskia to St. Louis in operation [a distance of some 80 miles]. In the summer of that year a second line from Shawneetown to St. Louis was projected."[3] A "postal-route advertisement" in May 1814 specified that the distance between Shawneetown and Ste. Genevieve amounted to 120 miles, with mail leaving the former every Sunday at 2:00 PM and arriving in the latter the next Wednesday by 6:00 PM.[4] The members of the territorial legislature, however, had their own opinions on how frontier conditions might affect the postal service and the swift completion of its appointed rounds. In December of that same year they considered a bill to construct a road that would run from the territory's eastern salines to Kaskaskia. The proposal described a wilderness of impassable roads, the difficulty of navigating "turbulent streams which often extend some miles beyond their Beds," and the reality of travelers who were frequently "obliged to encamp often for Weeks in woods, wanting often the necessary sustenance for Man & Horse." New roads, they maintained, would attract settlers, facilitate the creation of ferries, toll bridges and amenities, and expedite the movement of the mails.[5] The proposal ultimately went nowhere, but it nevertheless painted a vivid portrait of the territorial conditions that led Westerners in general and Illinoisans in particular to favor vigorous, proactive governmental intervention in the development of infrastructure. Nathaniel Pope shared that sentiment; he had directly witnessed the extent of Illinois's reliance upon its own resources to develop a communication and transportation network that was based upon navigable streams and easy access to the rest of the nation via the Illinois, Mississippi, and Ohio Rivers. The bulk of early settlement occurred along such waterways.[6]

This natural infrastructure had disadvantages that went well beyond muddy roads and a lack of amenities. The citizens of Illinois Territory could send their produce to markets in the East primarily over two routes—either down the Mississippi River to New Orleans or up the Ohio River and from there by land, "from Wheeling to Baltimore or from Pittsburgh to Philadelphia." The distance and expense meant that neither route was practical except for commodities having a high value proportional to their weight and bulk, few of which originated in Illinois.[7] The *Eastern Argus* in Ezekiel Whitman's hometown of Portland, Massachusetts, was merely expressing the contemporary consensus in doubting the West's ability to compete with the East "when the mere expense of transporting many of the principal productions of the country from the banks of the Ohio or Illinois [Rivers] to New-York or Boston, will very nearly equal the usual market price of those articles in all the principal ports of the Atlantic."[8]

Illinoisans also favored building a canal between the Great Lakes and the Illinois and Mississippi Rivers to encourage development. Accomplishing this goal was a central purpose of the 1816 treaty with the Ottawa, the Chippewa, and the Potawatomi that had resulted in the acquisition of the lead region of northwestern Illinois.[9] That judgment was supported by Major Stephen Long's 1817 report to the secretary of state arguing that the construction of a canal "would be attended with very little expense compared with the magnitude of the object."[10] Daniel Pope Cook echoed these sentiments in April 1818, underscoring the connection between canals and Illinois's future prosperity; without federal assistance, however, the project "must remain long unopened." Thus, the provision of the statehood bill allocating money from public land sales to roads and canals was of special importance.[11] Cook must have been gratified when the House of Representatives approved a resolution in December 1817 instructing the House committee on internal improvements to examine the possibility of constructing what later was to become the Illinois and Michigan Canal.[12]

Support for government-subsidized internal improvements was thus a function of local conditions and needs. Western settlers heartily approved of Henry Clay's "American system" that sought to tie the nation more closely together economically—and therefore politically—through infrastructure subsidies. Clay and his ilk advocated that the federal government should actively encourage such development in the interest of promoting the general welfare. Those who opposed such innovations, wrote historian John Lauritz Larson, were "localists and ideologues" who were "[f]rightened by rapid change, high mobility, the proliferation of new western states, and the emergence of a less local, more national identity among young Americans." They worried about strengthening the federal government at the expense of state sovereignty. Internal improvements provided them with a convenient target.[13] Consequently, it was Illinois's misfortune—insofar as admission to the Union was concerned—that these partisans chose this moment to vigorously oppose an effort to approve and subsidize a national infrastructure.

As a result, when the House delayed consideration of statehood, the ensuing debate over internal improvements reinforced Nathaniel Pope's conviction that developing and subsidizing infrastructure was intrinsic to the prosperity of the future state of Illinois. When Congress was once again ready to consider statehood in April, the nature of Pope's efforts on behalf of Illinois statehood suggests that the House's deliberations over internal improvements had made a strong impression.[14]

The Apple of Discord

Pope had been present during Congress's debate in December 1816 over John C. Calhoun's proposal "to set apart and pledge, as a permanent fund for internal improvements, the bonus of the National Bank, and the United States share of its dividends."[15] The bill passed both the House and the Senate. However, President James Madison doubted the bill's constitutionality, and on the day before leaving office—3 March 1817—he vetoed it, observing that "it does not appear that the power proposed to be exercised by the bill is among the enumerated powers [of Congress], or that it falls by any just interpretation within the power to make laws necessary and proper for carrying into execution those or other powers vested by the Constitution in the Government of the United States."[16] Privately, Madison made a clear distinction between the constitutionality and the desirability of federally funded roads and canals. In late 1817, when James Monroe informed his predecessor that he planned to suggest amending the Constitution to grant Congress the power to subsidize and construct internal improvements, Madison approved: "The *expediency of vesting in Congs* a power as to roads & Canals I have never doubted, and there has never been a moment when such a proposition to the States was so likely to be approved."[17]

Monroe raised the issue directly in his annual message to Congress on 1 December 1817. "When we consider the vast extent of territory within the United States," he wrote, "the great amount and value of its productions; the connexion of its parts, and other circumstances . . . we cannot fail to entertain a high sense of the advantage to be derived from the facility which may be afforded in the intercourse between them, by means of good roads and canals." He added that there had never been a clear consensus of opinion on whether Congress had the power to fund and construct roads and canals; consequently, he concluded that Congress did not possess the right.[18]

Monroe's message elicited reactions in both chambers of Congress. On 3 December 1817, the House referred "so much [of the President's message] as relates to roads, canals, and seminaries of learning" to a select committee.[19] In the Senate, James Barbour of Virginia proposed a constitutional amendment on 9 December that would have been more restrictive than Monroe suggested, enacting improvements only with the consent of states and distributing funding according to states' representation in the House.[20]

On 15 December the House committee reported its conclusion that, contrary to the president's belief, Congress (provided it gained the assent of the states) already possessed the capacity to "lay out, improve, and construct, post roads," "open, construct, and improve, military roads," and most importantly, "to cut canals through the several States . . . for promoting and giving security to internal commerce, and for the more safe and economical transportation of military stores &c., in time of war. . . ." The committee consequently recommended that Congress appropriate money to internal improvements to "promote and give security to the internal commerce among the several States; to facilitate the safe and expeditious transportation of the mails . . . to render more easy and less expensive the means and provisions necessary for the common defence, by the construction of military roads" and for any other internal improvements "within the Constitutional powers of the General Government."[21] The *Eastern Argus* editorialized against the proposal, arguing that Congress did not possess the power to fund internal improvements "for the mere local benefit of a particular section of the country. . . . [W]e should say that before Congress can constitutionally appropriate money for roads or canals, it must be shewn *generally* that they will contribute to render the country more secure or more formidable in war."[22]

This was the conflict troubling the collective mind of the House of Representatives as they began deliberating the committee's report on 6 March 1818, first as Committee of the Whole and then as the full House. While they considered internal improvements both constitutional and desirable, they were exceedingly reluctant actually to appropriate money. And it is clear that Nathaniel Pope followed the course of the congressional discussion closely, ultimately adopting components of the arguments both for and against internal improvements into his strategy for gaining statehood.[23]

The question of internal improvements was centrally concerned with the exploitation of the country's natural resources and how (and by whom) it was to be controlled. Proponents understood it to be a national problem. Internal improvements, together with "protection of American interests, labor, industry, and arts," were one of the primary means for bringing Henry Clay's "American system" to life.[24] In such a scenario, the federal government was the appropriate—indeed, the only—agent capable of accomplishing this purpose.

Those who supported subsidized roads and canals dwelled in the course of the debate upon their value as a protection against the perils of disunion. Congressman Henry St. George Tucker of Virginia, who had chaired the improvements committee, declared: "It is to the preservation of this Union, that national improvements will chiefly tend." Once internal improvements were accomplished, "we may look to a degree of permanence in our institutions."[25]

Tucker's fellow Virginian Ballard Smith spoke to the possibilities of greater national unity: "No longer will that supposed dissimilarity of interests . . . between the various sections of this Union, be a pretext of jealousy and complaint on the one part, or a source of fear and alarm on the other." Unity was of paramount importance in the context of the nation's experiences in the War of 1812. During that time, Smith argued, "its interior was but the weeping image of its own decayed and withered state, for the want of those vehicles of safe, easy, internal intercourse, which it is now the object of this resolution to afford." Smith and John Cushman of New York addressed objections that the bill overstepped constitutional bonds. The former pointed to Article I, section 8 of the Constitution giving Congress the authority to "establish post offices and post roads," while the latter emphasized that the appropriation of federal funds for roads and canals had been an integral part of the admission process in Ohio, Louisiana, Indiana, and Mississippi.[26]

To those who supported the principle of internal improvements, the most important issue was facilitating the transportation of goods from producers to the marketplace. Francis Jones of Tennessee asserted: "[O]pen roads, cut canals, clear the channels of rivers, and you afford facilities to commerce, give stimulus to industry, the effect of which will be individual and national wealth."[27] At the same time, the pro-improvements faction acknowledged the potential misuses of the funding they proposed. Charles F. Mercer of Virginia admitted that there were those who felt "that, if a fund be provided for internal improvement, it will be misapplied, to gratify local and sectional interests." Nonetheless, he felt that this danger could be lessened with strict accounting measures.[28]

Herein, however, lay the most serious reservations of those who were opposed to internal improvements. Where Mercer's allies saw infrastructure development as an important foundation of national unity, those who opposed it, such as Archibald Austin of Virginia, feared its potential for sowing dissension and sectionalism; where there was now peace and harmony between the states, "the moment Congress assumes this power of internal improvement, you throw out the apple of discord among the States; they will then begin to scramble, and quarrel who shall get the most, and where shall be the places of this internal improvement; and . . . it would turn out to be an internal division and commotion, instead of internal improvement."[29]

Alexander Smyth, also of Virginia, saw internal improvements as a states' rights issue. "The power which it is now proposed to exercise is, the power to legislate respecting internal police and local interests, with the assent of the States, and to appropriate the money of the whole nation to the disposal of particular States, for the advancement of local interests." He feared that the proportional allocation of funding for improvements tied to representation in the House would set a bad precedent for any future appropriations. Were Congress to assume the power of constructing roads and canals, "it seems obvious that there will be such a conflicting of jurisdiction and of interests, such an interference with the internal and local concerns of the States, as the people, in adopting the Constitution, never intended to produce." Internal improvements were not measures for the general welfare but rather were strictly of local concern, and thus appropriations for them, he asserted, "ought to be made by local impositions."[30]

Historian John Lauritz Larson maintained that such sentiments were rooted in Americans' pervasive suspicion "that some other class, party, or region was gaining advantage behind the smiling mask of public amity." Americans constantly searched "for the agents of corruption that their ideology led them [to] expect. Often they found what they were seeking. . . . As a result, public works seldom were seen as simply roads or river improvements, and policy initiatives easily stood condemned as stalking horses for interested factions and their sinister designs."[31]

In the course of the debate four resolutions concerning internal improvements were approved by the Committee of the Whole on 10 March for consideration by the full House of Representatives. These propositions deemed Congress as having power under the Constitution to:

1. appropriate money for constructing postal, military and other roads, and for building canals and improving water courses;
2. build such roads and canals;
3. build roads and canals necessary for commerce between the states; and
4. construct canals for military purposes.

Resolutions 3–4 provided furthermore that no private property could be taken for such public use without just compensation.[32]

The full House's final decision four days later reflected the divisive nature of the debate. After rejecting a motion to postpone a vote, the House approved only the first resolution by a vote of 90–75. The second and fourth resolutions were each turned down by only two votes, while the third was roundly rejected by a vote of 95–71.[33] This demonstrated that the House was more comfortable with internal improvements that facilitated the movement of the mails and the military. They were less confident of their power to facilitate interstate commerce, as shown by their rejection of the third resolution.

A close examination of the internal improvements votes reveals intriguing regional patterns. Representatives from New England (Vermont, New Hampshire, Massachusetts, Connecticut, and Rhode Island), and the South Atlantic states (Virginia, North Carolina, South Carolina, and Georgia) rejected all four of the propositions by an overwhelming margin. Those from the Middle Atlantic states (New York, Pennsylvania, New Jersey, Delaware, and Maryland)—all with close economic ties to the West—favored them in similarly significant percentages, while the free western states of Ohio and Indiana supported them to a greater degree than anyone else. Representatives from the western slaveholding states (Kentucky, Tennessee, Mississippi, and Louisiana) were the most closely divided, supporting resolutions 1, 2, and 4 by narrower proportions and rejecting resolution 3.[34]

The members of Pope's Illinois statehood committee mirrored these regional alignments. John C. Spencer of New York voted in favor of all of the resolutions. New England's Ezekiel Whitman voted to postpone consideration of the question and for the first resolution (appropriating money for constructing postal, military, and other roads, and for building canals and improving water courses) but rejected resolutions 2–4. Thomas Claiborne of Tennessee and Richard M. Johnson of Kentucky reflected the divisions in the slaveholding West. The former, like Whitman, supported postponing consideration of the resolutions. He was, however, absent for the vote on the first resolution, and he opposed resolutions 2–4.[35] Richard M. Johnson was consistently in favor of internal improvements, in part as a result of his experiences in the War of 1812[36] and perhaps—like Pope—owing something to his having been raised in Louisville near the Falls of the Ohio. He had in fact spoken at length in support of the proposals on the very day of the vote. "Bring your mind to reflect on the immense advantages to be derived from a connexion between the waters of the Atlantic with the upper Lakes," he declared. "What is there alarming in the General Government having it in its power to accomplish these and similar objects?"[37] Unsurprisingly, Johnson voted against the motion to postpone and for each of the four resolutions.

As a nonvoting delegate, Nathaniel Pope had been forced to the sidelines during the course of the debate. Now he faced a dilemma. The original bill for Illinois statehood made possible the appropriation of funds from public land sales to construct roads and canals both within the state and leading to Illinois. This was based upon the precedents established in the cases of Indiana, Ohio, and Mississippi, but those states' admission to the Union had occurred in a far different context. The House of Representatives had made its position quite clear: for now, such extensive funding of internal improvements was out of the question. And two of his colleagues on the statehood committee—Whitman and Claiborne—were unalterably opposed. The passage of the enabling act—and, indeed, the entire prospect of Illinois's admission to the Union—was anything but a foregone conclusion.

10

TO ACCOMPLISH THIS OBJECT EFFECTUALLY

In the waning winter of 1818 Nathaniel Pope had amply demonstrated his intuitive grasp of Benjamin Stephenson's insight that a successful territorial delegate to Congress should develop a familiarity with congressional protocols and practices as well as a facility for networking. Pope had shown a remarkable degree of patience throughout the internal improvements debate. Now he recognized that although the debate had complicated the prospects for the enabling bill, it nevertheless offered opportunities as well. And so on Saturday, 4 April 1818—a day when John Quincy Adams, an inveterate weather watcher, recorded spring rainstorms and the appearance of the first apricot blossoms[1]—Nathaniel Pope stood at long last before Congress's Committee of the Whole to speak on behalf of Illinois statehood.

The day had not begun auspiciously. There was a nervous moment when Arthur Livermore, a Democratic-Republican from New Hampshire, proposed a constitutional amendment declaring that "[n]o person shall be held to service or labor as a slave, nor shall slavery be tolerated in any State hereafter admitted into the Union, or made one of the United States of America." It was a political warning shot and a potentially perilous moment for Illinois statehood. Happily for Pope, Livermore's proposal was rejected, and the delegate from Illinois was free to proceed.[2]

Pope first moved to amend the bill by changing the boundaries outlined in section 2. The initial draft had set the northern boundary as an east-west line ten miles north of the southern tip of Lake Michigan—that is to say, from 41°30′ to approximately 41°45′. He proposed to set that boundary instead at 42°30′—one whole degree of latitude that would place it a trifle over 61 miles north of the original border established in the Northwest Ordinance. Pope drew an explicit connection between the contours of the new state and the continued cohesion of the Union. This amendment, he remarked, would "gain, for the proposed State, a coast on Lake Michigan. This would afford additional security to the perpetuity of the Union, inasmuch as the State would thereby be connected with the States of Indiana, Ohio, Pennsylvania, and New York, through the Lakes."[3]

Pope could have added that Illinois's extant economic connections to the South via the Mississippi River bound it just as securely to that region as well. Governor Thomas Ford, who knew Pope, declared that if Illinois had been solely confined to watercourses via the Mississippi, Ohio, and Wabash Rivers, her economic interests would have inclined the state to join a southern and western confederacy if the nation were to be torn asunder. It was Pope's aim, therefore, to create a rival interest binding Illinois to the North. "To accomplish this object effectually," Ford wrote, "it was not only necessary to give to Illinois the port of Chicago and a route for the canal, but a considerable coast on Lake Michigan, with a country back of it sufficiently extensive to contain a population capable of exercising a decided influence upon the councils of the State."[4] Pope acknowledged that he was thinking of economic connections as much as sociopolitical ones. "The facility of opening a canal between Lake Michigan and the Illinois river," he told Congress, "is acknowledged by every one who has visited the place. Giving to the proposed State the port of Chicago . . . will draw its attention to the opening of the communication between the Illinois river and that place, and the improvement of that harbor."[5] Having been born and raised—like Richard M. Johnson—in Louisville, Nathaniel Pope understood the advantages of a geographic location that straddled a link between two natural highways. Chicago, he foresaw, had the potential to perform the same function for the waterways encompassing the Great Lakes and the Mississippi River basin as his birthplace had for the Ohio River.

Pope's appeals to nationalism and economic objectives remained subsidiary to his central aim of accomplishing statehood under the most advantageous terms possible. This became especially apparent when Pope moved to amend the portion of the bill that dealt with funding internal improvements. The statehood committee's first draft back in January had provided that 5 percent of the net proceeds of public land sales would be devoted to building internal improvements, of which three-fifths would be devoted to the construction of roads and canals *within* the state and the remaining two-fifths would be applied to such projects connecting Illinois with other states. With congressional debates over government subsidies for such infrastructure still fresh in his mind, Pope proposed that the three-fifths be diverted instead to the encouragement of learning, of which one-sixth would "be exclusively bestowed on a college or university." The remaining two-fifths would remain as originally intended. The past application of such monies had not, he remarked, accomplished the desired outcome, having "been exhausted on local and neighborhood objects. . . . The importance of education in a Republic . . . was universally acknowledged; and that no immediate aid could be derived in new counties from waste lands was not less obvious; and that no active fund would be provided in a new State, the history of the Western States too clearly proved."

Here Pope was echoing the concerns of those who had stood in opposition to government-funded internal improvements. He seems to have concluded that if the statehood bill was endangered by the inclusion of funding for local internal improvements, the only logical response was to remove that provision. Committing those monies to the funding of education was a shrewd tactic—who could argue against it? Furthermore, Pope casually assured his colleagues, there was no pressing need to subsidize local infrastructure. Nature, he said, "had left little to be done in the proposed State of Illinois, in order to have the finest roads in the world. Besides, roads would be made by the inhabitants as they became useful, because the benefits are immediate; but not so with endowments to schools." "The effects of these institutions," he added, echoing the *Western Intelligencer*'s editorial of the previous year, "were too remote"—essentially saying that the citizens of Illinois could not be trusted to devote resources to education.

The removal of funding for internal improvements thus heightened the importance of extending the northern boundary. Incorporating Chicago and the land between Lake Michigan and the Illinois River into the new state would, in Pope's calculation, provide Illinois with a water transportation network that might in some measure make up for the loss of this funding. It was no accident that he introduced the provision to alter funding for internal improvements immediately after obtaining the Committee of the Whole's consent to extend the boundary. Both motions were agreed to "without a division."[6]

A Great Desideratum

A few more relatively minor changes were made to the bill. The number of delegates to the new state's constitutional convention was specified, and dates for their election and for the beginning of the convention were set for the first Mondays in July and August respectively. The minimum population qualifying the territory for admission was set at forty thousand—less than required under the Northwest Ordinance but more than Pope would have liked, given that he had hoped to remove the requirement entirely. The proposition turning over control of any lead mines to the new state was stricken, and the saline districts were left under Illinois's jurisdiction.

To Pope's chagrin, John W. Taylor of New York revived the proposal to exempt military bounty lands from taxation for three years from their date of issue as long as they were held by the patentees or their heirs, thus removing the prospect of what Pope had previously deemed "a handsome revenue from that quarter." The provision also decreed that lands held by owners not living in Illinois would never be taxed at a higher rate than that applied to owners living in Illinois.[7] All remaining territory beyond Illinois's and Indiana's northern boundaries was made part of Michigan Territory, and the final five sections of the bill dealing with courts, judges, U.S. attorneys, and U.S. marshals were removed as redundant. The amendments were accepted, and the Committee of the Whole reported the bill to the House, where it was ordered engrossed and read a third time on 6 April.[8] Pope dutifully wrote a letter to the *Western Intelligencer* afterward, repeating the same arguments he had made before the House urging the bill's passage and predicting its eventual passage in the Senate.[9]

Pope was simultaneously keeping an eye on developments in the upper chamber. On 26 March Senator James Barbour's proposal for a constitutional amendment addressing the issue of internal improvements came up for discussion in that body's Committee of the Whole. On motion of Senator David Daggett from Connecticut, the committee voted 22–9 to postpone consideration of the proposal until July.[10] Whether or not the Senate was taking its cues from the House's overall rejection of funding internal improvements, Nathaniel Pope could see that its inclusion in the statehood bill was at best problematic.

Upon its transmission to the Senate on 7 April, the bill was referred to the Committee on Public Lands, chaired by Jeremiah Morrow of Ohio. It was reported out on 9 April with three amendments and read a second time. The changes were minor. The word "territory" was replaced in two places with the word "state," and the superfluous section 7, which declared all federal laws "which are not locally inapplicable" to have the same force in Illinois as elsewhere in the United States, was removed.[11]

Nathaniel Pope had written a note to the Committee on Public Lands that focused particularly on the question of population. That note has not survived, but the nature of his lobbying efforts can be gleaned from a letter he wrote on 10 April to the venerable Senator Rufus King of New York. His argument was fourfold. Recognizing that the territory's precise population could potentially stand in the way of its admission, Pope confronted the issue directly by arguing that law and precedent favored statehood. Pointing out that the Northwest Ordinance allowed admission with a population under 60,000 "if it be *consistent* with the General interest of the confederacy," he reminded King that Ohio had entered the Union with fewer than 40,000 inhabitants and Mississippi had a population of 45,000, of whom 25,000 were free whites.[12] Pope later claimed that Congress's intention in enacting the population provision was that "if we have 40,000 at any period, during the time which the commissioners are authorised to take the census, that we shall then be able to form a state government."[13] At this point, of course, Pope had enough common sense not to make that argument to his colleagues in Congress.

He recapitulated Daniel Pope Cook's arguments concerning the deficiencies of "colonial government" as being "liable to infinite reproachs [*sic*]." Pope assured Senator King that the people of Illinois were well equipped to undertake the burdens of state government, and he implied that they were in fact better prepared than in places such as Missouri, which was also on the cusp of applying for statehood. He emphasized again that the extension of the northern boundary was rooted in his belief that Illinois could serve to draw the entire nation more closely together; "[T]he boundaries are designated," he wrote, "not less upon National principles than state advantages. . . . The state however will not be so large as has been supposed—But even if it were there is a propriety in it because but one state can be carved out of the extensive territory north of it."

Pope placed particular importance on the application of the three-fifths fund to education rather than internal improvements within Illinois. He argued that the mere presence of schools would enhance the value of public lands and would in fact "bring land into market that would not otherwise sell. I do not believe that its application [i.e., the three-fifths fund] to *local* roads . . . has ever enhanced the price of the public lands." This effort to fund public education, he contended, was the most valuable feature of the bill; "The diffusion of knowledge among the poor classes of society," he wrote, "is a great desideratum with me. . . . [T]he apprehension that postponement might effect a different application of that fund has infused into me a zeal bordering on importunity for the passage of the Bill at the present session."[14]

It is unclear why Pope specifically chose to lobby Rufus King. To the extent that he had any familiarity with the public record of the senator from New York, Pope would have had cause for concern about the statehood bill's prospects, and not just because King had at one point the previous year opposed Mississippi's admission to the Union.[15] King had had a long and distinguished career as a soldier, state legislator, representative to the 1787 federal constitutional convention from Massachusetts (serving on the convention's Committee of Style that created the final draft of the Constitution), vice presidential candidate (on the Federalist ticket) in 1804 and 1808, U.S. senator from New York, and the last Federalist candidate for president in the 1816 election against James Monroe. He had helped to draft the Northwest Ordinance; in fact, Rufus King had originated the idea that there should be neither slavery nor indentured servitude in the territory.[16] He was profoundly skeptical of the West's long-term potential for easy political integration into the Union. Thirty-two years earlier he had written to Elbridge Gerry expressing serious doubts as to whether there could ever be a unifying connection between the Eastern Seaboard and any new western states. "The pursuits and interests of the people on the two sides will be so different, and probably so opposite, that an entire separation must eventually ensue. . . . I know not what advantages the inhabitants of the Western territory would acquire by becoming members of our confederacy."[17]

He made his position public a year later at the federal constitutional convention when he seconded a motion put forward by Gerry "that in order to secure the liberties of the states already confederated, the number of representatives in the first branch, of the states which shall hereafter be established, shall never exceed in number the representatives from such of the states as shall accede to this Confederation." Gerry warned that future western states possessed the potential to seize control of the federal government from the thirteen original states and abuse that power by "oppress[ing] commerce and drain[ing] our wealth into the western country." The measure was defeated, but it underscored Rufus King's eastern sympathies at an early date.[18] "[H]is viewpoint," observed King's biographer Robert Ernst, "was that of an easterner concerned about the welfare and influence of the Atlantic seaboard, oceanic commerce, and the revival of the ailing merchant marine."[19]

Consequently, Nathaniel Pope's entreaties were to no purpose as far as the senator from New York was concerned. Nevertheless, Pope was present and watching with keen interest when the Senate resumed consideration of the question on 13 April. At his side was John Quincy Adams, who reported that he listened to the debates for two hours and remarked in his diary with some nostalgia: "It is within a few days of ten years since I left this body of which I had been five years a member. Mr. [John] Gaillard, of South Carolina, is the only member now who was a member then."[20]

Pope must have been alarmed when Charles Tait of Georgia commenced the debate with a motion to postpone further consideration of the bill until the next Fourth of July. Tait contended that he was not intrinsically opposed to the admission of Illinois; however, he supported postponement "on the ground that there was not sufficiently authentic information that its population was forty thousand." He was joined in opposition by David Daggett of Connecticut as well as by both of the senators from New York—Nathan Sanford and Rufus King.[21] Nathaniel Pope later characterized their disapproval of devoting the three-fifths fund to schools "as being altogether for the benefit of the state, and not for that of the United States. That it gave to Illinois greater advantages than was ever allowed to any other state admitted into the union. It was urged that we had no claims to such preference, that that fund was granted to the other states with a view of raising the price of the public lands."[22]

Pope's recapitulation of these arguments closely followed the train of thought in Rufus King's contemporary notes on the subject. King devoted particular attention to the proposed transfer of money from internal improvements within Illinois to education. In his letter to the senator, Pope contended that there was no relationship between local improvements and the price of public lands. In King's view such improvements would in fact increase the value of unsold lands belonging to the United States. He estimated the total current value of public lands in Illinois at $4.2 million, three-fifths of which was $2.52 million. All acknowledged the importance of public education, he wrote, and Congress was inclined to make provision for it in the new states, "but something sh[oul]d. be done by the state money chest and not all by the US because the new and old states are unassisted by Congress in providing for the public Education, and as the Fund belongs to all the states, it may not be easy to give a satisfactory explanation why these grants sh[oul]d be so liberally made to some and so wholly witheld from others." "There is no good reason," he added, "why the Road fund should be diverted—and the US as well [as] the Inhab[itant]s of Illinois, have a great Interest in the making of good Roads throughout the territory."[23]

Their Future Authority in the Union

Of even greater importance to King—who had been, after all, a member of the convention of 1787—were the constitutional difficulties in the way of admission. The admission of new states, he argued, was a generous action on the part of the original states, and as such it ought not to be abused, especially with regard to how it might affect apportionment. "In a matter of so much importance, and concerning which the States respectively are so attentive in apportioning their Representatives by equal & fixed Rules—it cannot be that the Constitution has left the same to the arbitrary Decision of Congress." Acknowledging that the Constitution placed no precise limitations on admitting new states, he nevertheless argued that such restrictions were implicit in Article I, Section 2 dealing with the apportionment of Representatives and direct taxes among the states. "[I]f a Territory sh[oul]^{d} have the number of Inhab[itant]s wh[ich] w[oul]^{d} enable a state to choose a Rep, Congress may admit such Territory into the Union—but not otherwise—because Reps are to be apportioned by an equal ratio." Illinois's population as enumerated at the time of the previous census in 1810, King wrote, was "a number quite too small to give a Right to the admission of the District into the Union at that time." He particularly objected to the provision in the statehood bill allowing the territory to conduct a special census. That responsibility, he argued, was reserved for the federal government. "Its numbers may now be 40 000, & perhaps more—but on the construction that has been given to the Cons$^{tn.}$ this gives no Right to admission before another Census." However, even he recognized that ultimately nothing could hinder the ascent of the western states. "Their Future authority in the Union cannot be questioned, & he is neither a wise man nor good Patriot who desires to retard the same—but let all be done in order and according to the Principles of the Constitution—in a few years, the thirteen old states will be a minority, & all this will be according to the true theory of our Cons^{t}."[24]

Pope faithfully recorded the responses of Senators John Crittenden and Isham Talbot of Kentucky, Jeremiah Morrow of Ohio, and James Burrill Jr. of Rhode Island to these arguments. They particularly emphasized the importance of public education in perpetuating republican government. Morrow contended that road funds "had been laid out most unprofitably, and that in education it would have been productive of the most important benefits. . . . [O]ne great objection to emigrating to new countries was the want of the means of education. Apply this money to schools . . . and then thousands will go who would otherwise stay."[25]

The most striking aspect of the exchange between Nathaniel Pope and Rufus King is that they based their arguments for and against statehood on two fundamentally different legal authorities. For Pope—as with his constituents who regarded it as "more significant to their individual destinies than the Federal Constitution of 1787"[26]—that authority was the Northwest Ordinance of 1787. For Rufus King, on the other hand—despite his role in the creation of the ordinance—the federal Constitution was unquestionably the supreme authority. As one of the statesmen responsible for its construction, King was suspicious of any actions that might undermine his work and thus jeopardize the bond of union.

As matters stood, the motion to postpone admission was defeated 29–4, the amendments were agreed to, and the bill was reported to the House.[27]

On the following day (14 April), the amended bill was read and referred to a select committee consisting of Nathaniel Pope, William Hendricks of Indiana, George Robertson of Kentucky, Francis Jones of Tennessee, and Wilson Nesbitt of South Carolina.[28] This time, however, there was no question of divisiveness on statehood with respect to the issue of internal improvements. All but Nesbitt (who was apparently absent that day) had voted to oppose postponing further consideration of the subject. Robertson and Jones had voted in favor of all four; the latter had spoken forcefully in favor of internal improvements. Hendricks had voted "nay" only on question three—i.e., whether or not Congress had the power to build roads and canals necessary for commerce between the states.[29] Furthermore, it may not be entirely coincidental that Pope, Nesbitt, and Robertson all lived at the same boarding house—Davis's Hotel on Pennsylvania Avenue; for that matter, Senator Jeremiah Morrow of Ohio, chair of the Senate Committee on Public Lands, lived there as well.[30] Robertson had even accompanied Pope on a visit to John Quincy Adams on 11 December 1817.[31] Thus, Nathaniel Pope had close personal associations with three Representatives on the select committee (as well as the chair of the relevant Senate committee), and could count on the support of the remaining representative.

And the select committee acted accordingly, reporting their agreement to the three Senate amendments on 15 April, which the full House approved. The bill was reported as enrolled on the following day and sent to the president, who signed it into law on 18 April.[32] There was some irony in the fact that thirty-two years earlier Monroe had been instrumental in establishing the principle that the Northwest Territory would be divided into no fewer than three or more than five states. He had spent some time visiting the region in the fall of 1785 and concluded: "A great part of the territory is miserably poor, especially that near lakes Michigan & Erie & that upon the Mississippi & the Illinois consists of extensive plains w$^{h.}$[ich] have not had from appearances & will not have a single bush on them, for ages." He doubted the likelihood that the territory would ever attract enough settlers to justify their full membership in the American nation; "[I]n the mean time, the people who may settle within them will be gov[erne]$^{d.}$ by the resolutions of Congress in w^{h}[ich] they will not be represented. In many instances I observ'd their interests will be oppos'd to ours."[33] In effect James Monroe had provided the basis for creating a colonial relationship between the federal government and the people of Illinois Territory. Now with a few strokes of the pen the president signaled the beginning of a new affiliation that would elevate the western pioneers to full citizenship within the Union.

Better Prospects than Any State

The effort to pass the statehood enabling act had been the agent of this transformation, and in the process it illuminated growing tensions between North and South, East and West. Disagreements as to the respective roles, rights, and responsibilities of the state and federal governments were manifest in the debate over internal improvements. Nathaniel Pope's deft legislative maneuvering had ensured that Illinois statehood avoided the taint of association with such federal largesse. Then, too, the ambiguous nature of slavery in Illinois Territory underscored the troubling reality that its fate was far from being settled as a national issue. The enabling act mandated that Illinois's constitution and state government be "republican and not repugnant" to the Northwest Ordinance. This, however, could only be effective to the extent that Congress and the people of the territory were in agreement as to the true meaning of Article VI. The very existence of an indenture system spoke to a concerted effort to circumvent the slavery prohibition.

Illinois's prospective statehood had withstood its first test in the national legislature. Under Nathaniel Pope's steady guidance, it had survived congressional egos, attempts to tie admission to the territory's inadequate population, the pitched battle over internal improvements, and eastern fears of the rising West. The enabling act's journey to President Monroe's desk underscored that admitting a new state into the Union had national implications going well beyond merely granting western settlers the full rights of citizenship. It was a sometimes heated dialogue encompassing social, political, and economic relationships between states, between regions, and between the federal and state governments. Against great odds Nathaniel Pope had skillfully leveraged Illinois's disadvantages in the admission process, most notably its insufficient population and the reduction in funding for internal improvements. He had made the case that the territory's loyalty now lay firmly with the United States, and that the admission of new states could help resolve internal conflicts by tightening the bond between their citizens and the older states of the Union.

Securing the successful passage of the enabling act was a major accomplishment, and it was with genuine pride and a palpable sense of relief that Pope wrote to the *Western Intelligencer* on 15 April:

> We may say with truth, that we will enter upon a state government with better prospects than any state ever did.—The best soil in the world, a mild climate, a large state, with the most ample funds to educate every

> child in the state; however poor, a man may well hope to see his child rise to the head of this mighty nation, if he have talents and virtue. Our avenues for navigation are towards the east and the west, the north and the south.[34]

He did not linger long in the nation's capital, although he made time to stop by the home of John Quincy Adams once more to bid the secretary of state a fond farewell.[35] By the time he returned to Kaskaskia on 15 June,[36] all eyes were once again upon the frontier settlements between the Wabash and Mississippi Rivers, where census agents were already diligently enumerating households in a patient effort to document that the population amounted to at least forty thousand people. Over the course of the next month and a half those same households would elect representatives to the prospective state's first constitutional convention, and in Kaskaskia's sweltering August heat that convention would commence the process of painstakingly devising a blueprint for Illinois's future governance as a full member of the Union.

PART III

The Enigmatic Mr. Kane and the Convention of 1818

11

A SPIRIT OF ADVENTURE AND ENTERPRISE

Three weeks had passed since Congress had given its final approval to the Illinois admission enabling act. On 6 May 1818 the *Western Intelligencer* broke the news by publishing a jubilant letter from Nathaniel Pope, who reported that the bill "is now beyond the control of both bodies [the House and the Senate], and will be signed by the President."[1] In an accompanying editorial, a writer styling himself "One of the People" praised "those who have heretofore holden [*sic*] high and important places under the territorial government . . . giving way, and soliciting those who are better qualified to render important services to the people, to come forward as candidates for the [upcoming state constitutional] convention." He cautioned, however, that a number of candidates "do not possess a single qualification to render any service to the public in that important capacity. . . . Each of these candidates has a *hobby horse* or two which he rides, as though he expected that it would carry him to the goal of his ambition, the convention."[2]

Somehow the dream of admission to the Union had emerged more or less intact from the congressional crucible. If the enabling act did not quite encompass everything the territorial legislature had requested, it nonetheless provided a greater measure of clarity on issues such as the boundaries of the new state, its sources of revenue and objects of public expenditure, its infrastructure, its access to natural resources, and the future status of slavery. But the central goal—gaining statehood—was a step closer to realization. Now the people of Illinois Territory were faced with the task of crafting a governmental structure to address these questions. How rigorous that structure would or should be was a matter for debate, owing to the reality that the enabling act had declared that the constitution—that state government—be "not repugnant" to the Northwest Ordinance. How was that phrase to be defined? How long would it apply? Was Illinois to be permanently constrained by the ordinance? To resolve these issues they turned their attention to electing delegates to Illinois's first constitutional convention and commencing the process of redefining their relationship not only with the federal government but with the other states of the Union as well.

A Brilliant Enigma

Old settlers and newly arrived immigrants alike sensed opportunity in the air. All understood that Illinois's metamorphosis from territory to state would bring with it a torrent of public contracts and patronage positions, from the low-hanging fruit of local sheriffs, justices of the peace, and county coroners to plum sinecures in the form of state legislators, congressmen, senators, and governors. And they were not slow in announcing their intentions. In that very same issue of the *Western Intelligencer* two of the most prominent local young men of ambition proclaimed their willingness to serve. One was the ubiquitous Daniel Pope Cook, then serving as judge of the Western Circuit (having been appointed to that position back in January).[3] Having surveyed the available political opportunities, he concluded that the proper arena for his talents lay to the east in the nation's capital, and consequently Cook professed himself a candidate for the U.S. House of Representatives.[4] And immediately below the notice of Cook's candidacy was this declaration: "We are authorized to announce ELIAS K. KANE, esq. a candidate for the Convention from the county of Randolph."[5]

It was fitting that the state political careers of two men who were destined to become political opponents should be launched simultaneously. Both were born around the same time—the mid-1790s—and both fit to a greater or lesser degree into what Theodore Calvin Pease termed "the young men who came to the frontier to seek a fortune."[6] Both impressed contemporaries with their powerful intellects. Governor Thomas Ford said of Cook: "His mind was uncommonly supple, wiry, and active and he could, as he pleased, shoot his thoughts readily over the great field of knowledge." More vaguely, he remarked of Kane: "His talents were both solid and brilliant."[7] John Reynolds was somewhat more forthcoming; Kane, he wrote, "possessed a strong mind and a benevolence and kindness of heart that are rarely surpassed."[8]

Such personal testimonies notwithstanding, Pease deemed Elias Kent Kane "the enigma of early Illinois politics"; among the few documents that exist "can be found not one human touch, not one phrase that can endow the man with a living personality. No anecdotes that would characterize him have survived. Catalogs of his political abilities, virtues, and vices can be found . . . but from all these can be drawn no picture of Kane himself."[9] The fact that this cipher was, in Ford's view, "the principal member" of the first state constitutional convention in the summer of 1818 renders what little is known of Kane all the more tantalizing.[10] If we cannot necessarily see the man himself with perfect clarity, we can certainly view his trajectory and impact upon his contemporaries. Kane's leadership proved crucial for his fellow delegates as they navigated the murky waters of the admission enabling act to create a workable governmental structure for the new state.

Elias Kent Kane stands out in one particularly distinctive way from the other principal movers of the statehood process. Daniel Pope Cook and Nathaniel Pope were both westerners by birth and upbringing, and like many other early Illinois leaders, spent their formative years in Kentucky. By contrast, Kane was a native New Yorker born on 7 June 1794, probably in Whitesboro in what was then Montgomery County.[11]

Kane has been portrayed as the genteel product of the more refined East Coast and thus distinctive from his political peers on the Illinois frontier. Pease described him as belonging to "a decayed aristocratic New York family."[12] The nature of the Kaskaskia settlement, however, was not necessarily so different from what he had known back home in Whitesboro. The latter village had, after all, been settled only a decade before, long after Kaskaskia was founded in 1700; it was, in fact, at that time (according to historian D. E. Wager) "the only white settlement in the State [of New York] west of what is now the village of Herkimer."[13] Kane's father, also named Elias, was the son of John Kane, an Irish immigrant who became a prosperous storekeeper in Dutchess County. John Kane's property had been confiscated by rebel authorities during the American Revolution, and he had moved his family to Nova Scotia with other Loyalists at the end of the war. His sons—including the elder Elias Kane—returned to New York a decade later and established their own chain of trading posts running from Albany westward to Canajoharie and Whitesboro, where (according to their descendant Elizabeth Dennistoun Kane) they bought wheat, furs, and potash and "sold the crockery and the broadcloths and the groceries and ironmongery and everything else" that John Kane's sons Oliver and John bought in Europe and New York.[14] They developed congenial relationships with the Oneidas of western New York, who nicknamed the elder Elias Kane "Tanatolas" ("Pine Knot"). The brothers were "enterprising business men" with "family connections as influential and as highly respected as any in the State." The father described himself in 1814 as having held a "proud standing" in society, and George W. Smith, who compiled the most authoritative biographical narrative of Elias Kent Kane, described the Kane brothers as "extensive merchants at New York, with branches at Albany, Utica and Whitesboro."[15]

James E. Davis has suggested that in later coming to the West Elias Kent Kane transformed himself from a northerner to a southerner, internalizing southern culture in Tennessee on his way to Illinois and learning to defend "slavery and other southern interests."[16] This assumes that the particular northern culture in which Kane was raised was thoroughly, distinctly, and intrinsically different from its southern counterpart in Kaskaskia. But in fact the Illinois frontier and rural New York shared at least one reality in common: the presence of slavery. It may be surprising to think of the Empire State as a bastion of the institution, but in fact it was quite widespread. In 1790 there were 21,324 enslaved persons throughout the state, with 588 in Kane's Montgomery County alone. (For that matter, the only state with no enslaved persons in 1790 was Massachusetts.) New York's total population of enslaved persons was not far short of Georgia's (29,264).[17] "In 1790," reported historian Shane White, "there were proportionately more households containing slaves in New York City's hinterland than in the whole of any southern state." In the Hudson Valley area encompassing Kane's birthplace, "Slavery had long been an established part of everyday life," playing an important role in agricultural production.[18]

And Elias Kent Kane had more than a passing acquaintance with the institution. His Kane grandparents owned at least two bondspersons. Other members of his extended family were recorded as slaveholders as early as 1800, when the federal census numbered two enslaved persons in the household of his uncle, Charles Kane, who resided at that time in Westfield (now Fort Ann) in Washington County, New York.[19] By 1810, when Elias Kent Kane's family resided in New York City, his father was listed as the owner of one enslaved person at a time when 1,686 were held in that city and its environs.[20] Ten years later, when the elder Kane resided in Albany, that number increased to three.[21]

In the end, Elias Kent Kane's passage through Tennessee seems to have been largely incidental to his defense of slavery. New York had only recently passed its Gradual Manumission Act in 1799, and that law only freed enslaved persons who were not yet born. An act to free all of them was not signed into law until 1817, and it did not go into effect until 1827.[22] On the issue of slavery, at least, given his experience of the institution and its legal status in the state of his birth, it seems likely that Kane needed little persuasion—and thus required no substantial transformation—to defend and perpetuate it in Illinois.

A Perfect Youth

Little is known of Elias Kent Kane's early life. Sometime between 1794 and 1802 his father moved from upstate New York to the state's largest city, where the elder Kane set up shop as "Elias Kane & Co.," an importer of tea, sugar, fine wines, and other liquors as well as "a constant supply of Anchors, of various sizes" at 182 Water-street.[23] Information on his early education is scanty as well. Certainly his family valued learning; his uncle James Kane wrote in 1849 that Elias's grandfather John Kane was a very capable Latin scholar.[24] We can glean some idea of the depth and range of his education based upon Elias Kent Kane's acceptance to Yale College in 1811 when he was seventeen years old (incoming freshmen were allowed to enroll as early as the age of fifteen). Yale's standards for admission at the time required that prospective students demonstrate the ability to "read, translate and parse Cicero's Select Orations, Virgil, and the Greek Testament, and to write true Latin in prose, and [students] shall also have learned the rules of Vulgar Arithmetic." The prospective student was likewise required to "produce satisfactory evidence of a blameless life and conversation" and to "exhibit proof that he is not guilty of using profane language." Once admitted, Kane navigated a rigorous curriculum, studying "Learned Languages, Arithmetic, Algebra, Geography, and Roman Antiquities" in the first year alone, and in his subsequent years he would have absorbed "Elements of Chronology and History, English Grammar, Logarithms, Geometry, Plane Trigonometry, Mensuration; Surveying, Navigation, Conic Sections, Dialing, and Spherical Geometry and Trigonometry."[25]

But Elias Kent Kane was not destined to take the full range of coursework, nor was he fated to complete a degree, at least at that point in time. (Later, in 1825, after he had become U.S. senator from Illinois, Yale finally bestowed a degree upon its alumnus, perhaps more in recognition of his political office than of academic accomplishment.)[26] He left Yale in 1812 without graduating, briefly studied law in New York, and then headed westward—probably in 1813—to Tennessee. George W. Smith speculated that Kane was "prompted by a spirit of adventure and enterprise, mingled with political ambition, but not induced by necessity."[27] It seems likely, however, that his family's economic circumstances played an important role. John Kintzing Kane later explained: "His father as well as mine had failed in business, or they were already involved in the vortex which carried them down soon after."[28] Indeed, John wrote to his cousin on 28 April 1814 that both of the elder Kanes had gone into bankruptcy; "I do not yet know for what sums," he related, "but evil report, ever magnifying, says your father was indebted more than he could pay five hundred thousand dollars. This of course, is false, although the amount was undoubtedly large."[29] Elias Kane later wrote his son that he had "been brought to this dire situation from being a man of very large fortune, by this untimely war [of 1812]," and the father's sister Sarah Kane Morris attributed their business failure to "commercial disasters brought on by the Embargo, Orders in Council, Berlin and Milan decrees."[30]

There are also hints that Kane may have become estranged from his family. John Kintzing Kane upbraided his cousin: "I have endeavored by every possible means to keep up the friendship which formerly prevailed between us, but in vain. You seem to have forgotten that you ever had a friend or connection, that you ever resided among civilized people, or were ever bound by the laws of civility. . . . We fear some devilish Indian has tomahawked you. . . . Do not suffer our fears to prevail."[31]

The possibility of a family rift is further suggested by the fact that his relatives believed Kane had decided to settle in Carthage, Tennessee, where they were directing their correspondence.[32] In truth, by July 1813 Kane had traveled instead to Nashville, where he established himself as "Elias K. Kane (attorney at law) . . . in an office adjoining the one now occupied by [Tennessee] Governor [Willie] Blount."[33] It is not readily apparent why he chose the state capital for commencing his legal career. One possibility is connected to a legal notice from the state's Supreme Court of Errors and Appeals that appeared in the Nashville *Democratic Clarion & Tennessee Gazette* for the first time on 11 August 1812. That court commanded Kane's uncle Oliver Kane, his wife Ann Eliza, and Ann's sister Harriett Clark to appear before it as defendants in a suit brought by "William L. Bledsoe & others."[34] It may be that Elias Kent Kane came west to represent his uncle's interests in the case. If so, his efforts seemingly came to naught; variations on the original notice continued to appear with some frequency over the years in the Nashville press, some as late as 1820.

In any case Kane's residence in Tennessee was short-lived, because by 4 August 1814 he was writing from his new home in Kaskaskia. That date marked Kane's first effort to contact his family in some time, writing of his "anxiety and concern" over the elder Kane's financial reversals. Judging by a letter from his father, it is apparent that Elias Kent Kane spoke with enthusiasm in his missives of his bright prospects and—as he announced to his father—of his impending marriage, neglecting, oddly, to share the name of his fiancée. Elias Kane responded approvingly, but he warned his son: "I hope you have maturely considered the boldness of the undertaking. You are very young, not more than twenty years old, without anything to rest on for your support but your own industry and talents in your profession, and although I think favorably of your capacity and talents, still I fear you have not had experience and practice enough."[35]

Kane's future spouse was Felicité Peltier, a Kaskaskia denizen of French ancestry and—according to some accounts—the owner of enslaved persons, although none were listed as belonging to her family in the federal census of 1810.[36] George W. Smith believed that such a personal interest helped to account for Kane's favorable disposition toward slavery, "although it is said of him that he afterwards was the means of giving them their freedom."[37] Kane was himself documented as indenturing an enslaved sixteen-year-old African American female from Kentucky named Rebecca on 6 December 1816 for a term of forty years.[38] The indenture system provided an effective means for evading the Northwest Ordinance's prohibition on slavery by establishing the fiction that enslaved persons were voluntarily entering into contracts for their labor. By the time of the 1820 federal census his household was listed as encompassing five enslaved persons, increasing to six in 1830. His widow was still listed as the owner of seven bondspersons as late as 1840.[39]

The speed with which he found himself betrothed and cultivating political alliances suggests an amiable, agreeable personality. His one extant portrait strengthens this impression, representing a young man of pleasant countenance framed by slightly wavy hair and a delicate chin. John F. Snyder—son of Adam W. Snyder, another of Jesse B. Thomas's protégés—described Kane as "tall, light complected and of prepossessing appearance, but not strong, physically."[40] Another more contemporary observer characterized Kane at the time of his arrival in Illinois Territory as "a perfect youth, poor and destitute both of money and patronage, and acquaintances, struggling against an opposition produced by his inflexible resistence [*sic*] of all attempts to buy him off to their corrupt *uses*."[41] Here he encountered a political terrain dominated by two factions "founded," wrote John Reynolds, "on the qualifications of men for office, and on the 'ins and outs' of power and place." These factions clustered around Ninian Edwards and Jesse B. Thomas. Governor Edwards, Reynolds recalled, "had the aged and sedate leaders of the people friendly to him, but Judge Thomas had the young, ardent, and energetic men, supporting him, who were mixing every day with the people."[42]

An Adroit and Winning Manager

It was Thomas with whom Elias Kent Kane chose to ally himself at an early date. The young New Yorker presumably made his acquaintance with the judge in the course of conducting his law practice. Virginia-born and Kentucky-bred, Thomas had a territorial political career reaching back to the days when Illinois was part of Indiana, playing a crucial role in their division into separate territories. Samuel Morrison described Thomas as "full six feet, with florid-brown complexion, dark-hazel eyes, dark-brown (nearly black) hair, with a well-developed muscular system, and weighed over two hundred pounds."[43] Thomas's contemporary Governor Thomas Ford deemed the judge "a large, affable, good-looking man, with no talents as a public speaker; but he was a man of tact, an adroit and winning manager. It was a maxim with him that no man could be talked down with loud and bold words, 'but any one might be whispered to death.'"[44] Born in Virginia in 1777, Thomas and his parents emigrated westward in 1779 to Bracken County, Kentucky. As a young man he worked in the Mason County clerk's office and—much as Nathaniel Pope did a few years later—studied law in the office of his elder brother, Richard Symmes Thomas. He was subsequently admitted to the bar and commenced his own practice in Brookville, Kentucky. His residence was short-lived, however. Thomas departed for Lawrenceburg, just across the Ohio River in Indiana Territory, after the death of his first wife, to whom he had been married for less than a year.[45] He became active in local politics and was elected in 1805 to represent Dearborn County in Indiana's first territorial legislature, where he was chosen as Speaker. He served in that body alongside future Illinois political leaders Shadrach Bond and George Fisher.[46]

Thomas proved to be a skillful political operator. He was initially close to territorial governor William Henry Harrison, although the two later became estranged. Thomas wrote Harrison in 1810 that "experience has already taught me that I have neither profited by our former correspondence nor by my acquaintance with you," and he accused the governor of having schemed to "crush" him politically in 1808.[47] This referred to Harrison's effort in that year to select a candidate to represent Indiana in Congress as its territorial delegate—in preference to Thomas—without consulting him or the Illinois faction in the legislature. Thomas's biographer Matthew Hall wrote that the region that Thomas represented in the territorial legislature—Dearborn County—was largely antislavery, but his constituents were uncertain as to the best means for ensuring that Indiana as a whole remained permanently slave free. In one scenario, Hall observed, "if the more virulently proslavery Illinois Country could be carved off [i.e., separated from the territory], then Indiana, at least, could be safely preserved free of slavery." Here Thomas saw an opportunity. Already miffed by Harrison's support for another candidate, Thomas perceived that he could best respond to his constituents by allying himself with local leaders in Illinois who desired separation as a means for improving the prospect of retaining slavery in that region.[48] To that end Thomas made a deal in writing with Illinois representatives in the Indiana legislature and with powerful Illinois leaders such as John Rice Jones and his son Rice to support separation in return for Thomas's election as congressional delegate. It was a successful maneuver, Thomas ultimately emerging victorious over Michael Jones of Kaskaskia, Harrison's candidate.[49]

There were immediate outcries against this result. Writing in the Vincennes *Western Sun* a week later, "Veritas" addressed Thomas directly, accusing him of taking different positions in different areas of his home county of Dearborn and of colluding with John Rice Jones, Rice Jones, William Biggs, and John Messinger to support division of the territory (despite publicly opposing it) in return for their votes to elect him as territorial delegate to Congress.[50] In a letter to Thomas dated 17 November 1808, Rice Jones reported speculation that "Veritas" was Thomas Randolph, Indiana Territory's attorney general. Jones told the territorial delegate that in a visit to Kaskaskia, Randolph had announced that Jesse B. Thomas had been burned in effigy in Vincennes "& said it had been determined on that you should not be delegate longer than this winter." He comforted Thomas with the observation that "*Veritas* & the burning in Effigy has had the effect of increasing your popularity in these counties [in Illinois]."[51]

Thomas's diligent efforts to accomplish the separation of Indiana and Illinois were ultimately successful. Recognizing that he had ended any prospect of a future political career in Indiana, Thomas obtained for himself an appointment as one of Illinois Territory's three judges on the strength of recommendations from Richard M. Johnson, Congressman David Holmes of Virginia, and—significantly—John Pope, brother of Nathaniel Pope and first cousin of Ninian Edwards, who was destined to become Thomas's political nemesis.[52]

That Thomas and Edwards should have come to a bitter parting of the ways was by no means inevitable. Joseph E. Suppiger wrote that both arrived in Illinois at approximately the same time "and were, for a brief period, close neighbors and friends." That relationship began to sour in 1812, when Illinois was reclassified to the second grade of government, qualifying its citizens to vote for a territorial legislature and to that extent reducing the powers of the governor. Suppiger observed that with that development "there came a greater public abhorrence of arbitrary authority"—to the detriment of Governor Edwards—and a great deal of criticism of Thomas and his fellow territorial judges for receiving princely compensation in return for light work. Thomas objected to efforts by the territorial legislature to regulate and modify his duties as a territorial judge. He regarded such actions as unconstitutional given that he had been appointed by the federal government, and he spoke out in support of candidates for the territorial legislature who agreed with that opinion.[53] Two years later Edwards wrote bitterly to his now former friend that "while I was engaged on the frontier in defending my fellow citizens [in the War of 1812], you disregarding the dignity and delicacy of your office was in the honorable employment of riding about from place to place electioneering, and using the most unjustifiable means to injure me." He added that he intended "*freely* and *publicly* to investigate your conduct towards me in 1812, and to exhibit to the world the motives by which you were governed."[54] The territorial legislature finally passed a law in December 1814 to form a supreme court composed of Thomas and his fellow judges, increasing their workload. When the governor defended the law, the breach between Thomas and Edwards became permanent.[55] Indeed, the two men had barely avoided fighting a duel with each other the previous summer.

Integrity and Firmness

This was the man who took Elias Kent Kane under his wing and provided him with a political apprenticeship in much the same way that Ninian Edwards and Nathaniel Pope were mentoring Daniel Pope Cook at about the same time. Kane became close to Thomas at an early date—so close, in fact, that in the summer of 1814, not long after arriving in Kaskaskia, he acted as the judge's second in his near-duel with Edwards. In a notice dated 3 August 1814 and written for publication in the *Kaskaskia Illinois Herald*, Kane defended his mentor's conduct during the conflict as bearing "an honourable testimony of integrity and firmness."[56] And when Thomas visited Albany, New York, the following year, he went out of his way to visit Elias Kane, who reported to his son in a letter dated 25 April 1815: "The manner in which he speaks of you is very gratifying to me indeed. I find him to be a very warm friend of yours, and I think it not altogether improbable that from that cause his account of you is rather a partial one, but be this as it may, coming from so reputable a source, it is highly flattering to me."[57]

Such had been the remarkable path traversed by Elias Kent Kane in an extraordinarily brief period. He had emerged as a mysteriously contradictory figure who was at once a product of the frontier backwoods of upstate New York, the state's largest city, and the rarefied environs of Yale College. Somehow his apparently aimless wanderings westward had enabled him to navigate with notable swiftness into Kaskaskia's most consequential political circles. Somehow he had managed to worm his way into the confidence of the leader of the territory's loyal opposition. The true dimensions of that journey from the old established Northeast to the Far West only became fully apparent with the willingness of Jesse B. Thomas to travel that same distance and bring an anxious father glad tidings of his son's good fortune.

12

THE RIGHT TO FRAME A CONSTITUTION

In 1820 John Kintzing Kane wrote to his cousin Elias of his gratitude at receiving a letter from him after a long and silent interval. "It was like one of the interviews," he observed, "which I have sometimes had with an old classmate in renewal of an old and warm friendship, at a time when our circumstances have changed and our situations in life become fixed. . . . Let us be correspondents. We were running *haud passibus equis* [with unequal steps], but our object was the same." He added wistfully, "We were intimates at college. Perhaps we may one day renew our personal acquaintance on a more distinguished theater."[1] Elias Kent Kane's father seems to have been similarly troubled by his son's detachment, writing to him in 1825: "I hardly know how to commence a letter to you. It appears to me you have taken offense at my neglect to write to you. . . . I acknowledge, my dear son, that you have cause to feel hurt at my neglect, but whether this ought to be a sufficient excuse for your not writing to me, I shall leave to your own feelings to decide."[2]

Perhaps this was the source of Kane's enigma—a seeming aloofness that was both personal and political. "We have heard something of your success in life," his cousin John wrote in his 1820 letter, "but it was only a traveler's report—always vague and often contradictory."[3] Such reserve may well have been a calculated strategy on his kinsman's part, for in spite of his association with Jesse B. Thomas—or perhaps because of it—Elias Kent Kane had little prospect of gaining appointment to any territorial offices. Thomas was, after all, a leader of the political cabal that opposed Governor Edwards, who controlled local patronage. Kane instead cultivated a law practice; John Reynolds deemed him "a profound lawyer and an agreeable and eloquent speaker"; legal historian Frederic B. Crossley described him as "one of the foremost lawyers in the state at the time of the adoption of the Constitution of 1818."[4] Kane's association with Thomas was not, however, a completely insurmountable barrier to political advancement or, for that matter, to collaboration with those on the opposite side of the aisle. George W. Smith wrote that he was "deservedly popular even to the degree of commanding the support of political opponents."[5] Indeed, in late 1816 he asked Ninian Edwards's ally Nathaniel Pope for assistance in bringing forward a claim from his father-in-law for action by Congress, an action that was unsuccessful despite all of Pope's best efforts.[6] In January 1817 he was designated to oversee "the printing of the laws of this session of the Legislature and to furnish a copy thereof for the printer" as well as to devise an index for those laws. He was ultimately paid sixty-five dollars for these services. And in January 1818 the territorial legislature passed a measure appointing Kane and four other men—including Shadrach Bond, a fellow member of the Thomas faction—as Kaskaskia town trustees. Kane also benefited from a law approved on 9 January 1818 "to incorporate the City and Bank of Cairo," which named Bond, Michael Jones (Jesse B. Thomas's half-brother), and seven other men as incorporators. Five days later that group conveyed a trust deed encompassing all of the land surrounding Cairo mentioned in the act to Kane and Henry S. Dodge, who practiced law and real estate in Kaskaskia.[7] The following month Kane was offered a position as judge of the territory's Eastern Circuit, which would have made him the counterpart to Daniel Pope Cook, who had been appointed to the same position on the Western Circuit. Kane, however, declined to serve.[8]

His motives in declining that position are not hard to understand. Such a territorial position was by definition a temporary one, because it was very clear by now that statehood—and its attendant patronage—was within reach. On 7 January 1818 the territorial legislature approved a measure to appoint a census taker in each county. These men were enjoined "to take a list of all citizens, of all ages, sexes and colour . . . particularly noting whether white or black, and also noting particularly free male inhabitants above the age of twenty-one years," and to "take in a list of county and territorial taxes, from each and every person subject to taxation." The enumeration was to commence on 1 April and end by 1 June, and the census takers were to be compensated in amounts ranging from forty to eighty dollars. This measure was amended three days later to extend the enumeration period through 1 December, as "a great increase of population may be expected" during that time, which was another way of expressing their uncertainty as to whether the territory would have the requisite population for statehood.[9] Twelve of the commissioners had been appointed by 19 January, two were appointed in March, one in May, and the final one in June.[10] The benefits of serving in this capacity went beyond monetary considerations. Conducting the enumeration meant visiting every household in the county and thus interacting with every eligible voter. Indeed, five of these commissioners—Conrad Will in Jackson, Hezekiah West in Johnson, Joseph Borough in Madison,

Samuel Omelveny in Pope, and John K. Mangham in Washington—took full advantage of this opportunity to campaign for election to Illinois Territory's constitutional convention that summer. (None of the known candidates who were defeated for delegate were appointed as commissioners.)

The difficulties were many. There was the reality that the census was taking place on the frontier; ascertaining that every person had been enumerated was a substantial challenge. Historian Margaret Cross Norton suggested that the commissioners were hobbled by the requirement that they act as tax assessors, combined with a fear on the part of the citizens they were enumerating that they might also be taking note of those who were subject to militia duty. Some might be reluctant to provide these officers with accurate information.[11] The commissioners also felt pressure to ensure that their figures added up to at least forty thousand per Congress's admonition in the enabling act. To that end, Nathaniel Pope had already argued that meeting that standard at any time during the census would automatically qualify the territory for statehood.[12] It was a matter, in other words, of capturing that magic number at just the right moment. Historian Arthur Clinton Boggess believed that the territorial law passed to enable the census made it possible to count and recount immigrants as they made their way into Illinois and passed through on their way westward. "There is no reasonable doubt," Boggess wrote, "that at the time the census was taken, the territory had fewer than forty thousand inhabitants."[13] More charitably, Norton argued that few immigrants had specific destinations in mind and thus they might well be counted more than once in temporary locations; thus, she believed, "the census enumerator was justified in listing them."[14] One could also add, of course, that these commissioners would have no way of knowing for certain whether a particular household—especially one located only for the moment in one fixed spot—had already been enumerated or not.

Not Grants, But Limitations

When Territorial Secretary Joseph Philips reported on 17 June that the census enumerated the total territorial population as amounting to 34,620—not including numbers for Franklin County, which had not yet been submitted—the anxiety was palpable.[15] Acknowledging the decreasing likelihood that the final tally would reach the 40,000 threshold, the *Intelligencer* nervously alluded to doubts "as to the propriety of electing members of the Convention." Consequently, they solicited the judgment of Nathaniel Pope, who had returned to Kaskaskia from Washington only two days before. He shared with them his view that it would be proper to elect and hold a convention. If subsequently it appeared that the enumeration fell short of the required total, it would nonetheless be appropriate "for the Convention to pass an Ordinance, authorising an election for members of [a] convention after the last returns shall be made. . . . And if we then have 40,000 souls, that such Convention will have the right to frame a Constitution."[16]

Pope was suggesting, in other words, that the convention could resume once they made the numbers fit—a highly questionable assertion, given that the admission enabling act had specifically set the date for the election of delegates as 6–8 July and the beginning of the convention as 3 August.[17] To this argument the *Intelligencer* had a ready reply to the effect that the law passed by Congress enabled (rather than authorized) the people of the territory to devise a constitution. The conditions set by Congress for admission, they argued, "are not *grants*, but limitations upon the power of the people. If the terms are accepted by the people, the affair is at an end. . . . But if we do not conform to the terms proposed, we cannot take upon ourselves a *state government*, but may on our part form a constitution, and offer it to congress with our terms, which if accepted, will be binding on all parties."[18]

Admission, in other words, was considered a given. The territory had not completely abandoned its impulse to bargain with the United States on what it considered equal terms. Such an argument provided a potential foundation for a constitution that would legalize slavery. At all events, the suggestion that the convention might have to reconvene inspired the *Intelligencer* to hope that "the honest vigilance of the Commissioners authorised to take the census will not be suffered to sleep so long as our population is found increasing."[19] It would have been difficult to envision finding the 5,638 souls needed to reach 40,000 in Franklin County (which was reported in the end as having a population of 1,281) and in any supplemental enumerations conducted in any of the other counties.

The Polestar of Every Voter

On 6 July Secretary Philips reported with unmistakable concern that the population totals were still short of the required number. He made reference to "repeated reports of official abuse on the part of some of the commissioners employed in taking our territorial census," some of whom "have neglected to take even the citizens of their respective counties; while others with a zeal unbecoming their situation, have taken some people two or three times, and have placed on their lists the mere passengers through their counties and even the territory. It is believed however that this information is not to be credited, for surely the commissioners are honest men."[20] It has never been proven whether or to what extent the census commissioners padded their totals, although both Solon J. Buck and Clarence Alvord maintained that a comparison of the

1818 census with the federal enumeration of 1820 placed the question beyond doubt.[21] It is clear, however, that the men conducting the survey of 1818 possessed the means, the motive, and the opportunity to accomplish that purpose.

Meanwhile the campaign for election to the upcoming constitutional convention had begun in earnest. In selecting delegates, the *Western Intelligencer* exhorted voters that "party and private feeling should alike be suspended, and the public interest alone should be the polestar of every voter." Those who were elected would be entrusted with devising a constitution "on free and liberal principles"; "[W]e must have men," the *Intelligencer* declared, "who are versed in the science of government; men who have correct opinions of human nature, and who have an extensive acquaintance with the effects which the various forms of government have had upon the happiness of the human family."[22]

There is not an abundance of documentation that helps explain what drove the campaign, but the columns of the *Intelligencer* suggest the broad outlines. Somewhat surprisingly, class was an issue; there were foreshadowings of future conflicts between elites and the hoi polloi, between rural and urban populations, between Chicago and Downstate. The poor, wrote "A Friend to Equal Justice," "bear the burthen [*sic*] of everything—while the *rich* are in possession of everything." "Who has kept in operation that system of taxation," he thundered, "against which you have so much cause to complain; but the wealthy farmers, who have heretofore been our *law makers*?" These wealthy land holders, he argued, "are opposed to some other candidates because *they* are not *large land holders*!" He worried about the prospect of "such ignorant wealthy men" shaping Illinois's first constitution. "[W]e may expect that they will be opposed to suffering one to go to the legislature, or to hold a lucrative office, who is not like themselves, a large land holder. . . . It is time to shake off this *odious badge* of aristocracy."[23]

"An Old Farmer" replied that among his ilk, "I must confess, there are too many who hold knowledge in contempt; yet there are numbers of them, men of information, and still more, that have a large share of common sense. . . . I would not exclude the lawyer, merely because he is a lawyer. . . . Our country is, and will continue to be," he added, "an agricultural one—the farmers will always be, to the other professions, as 99 to 100. . . . [W]hen the farming interest begins to be disregarded, and its voteries [*sic*] held in contempt, that nation is sure to become contemptible itself."[24]

There were moments of tension at times between supporters and opponents of particular candidates. George Churchill of Madison County reported that while canvassing on behalf of Abraham Prickett's candidacy, he was upbraided by "one [Jephthah] Lamkin, a potter" for posting handbills: "I then asked

Lamkin if there was any thing incorrect in the handbills? He said he had not read them but that he tore them up as fast as he saw them." Churchill added that Samuel Whiteside, who later represented Madison County in the General Assembly, subsequently called him "that damn'd rascal that brought the damn'd Yankee [presumably antislavery] handbills here!"[25] Andey Kinney, a candidate from Monroe County, complained to the *Intelligencer* that he had been the victim of a whispering campaign falsely accusing him of "offering to purchase votes" and "that I had once rebelled against my country, and had taken a captain's commission under a French officer. And also, stating that I had been tried by a court of justice, fined in a sum of forty dollars, and never to hold a commission in the territory afterwards." He branded all of these charges as lies and published affidavits to that effect from other prominent men of the territory—a vain effort, as it turned out, as Andey Kinney ultimately lost his bid to represent Monroe County in the convention.[26]

One possible reason for Kinney's defeat was his willingness to take a strong and principled stand on the most burning issue of the campaign: the future of slavery in Illinois. As a non-slaveholder himself, Kinney deemed slavery "an abomination which we ought to guard against in every sense of the word."[27] His victorious opponents, Caldwell Cairns and Enoch Moore, cast votes on the question in the convention that revealed them as at least partly antislavery (although Cairns was himself the owner of two enslaved persons).[28] At first glance, slavery would seem to have been a nonissue, given that the enabling act had reaffirmed the Northwest Ordinance's prohibition of the institution. However, it was also true that Article VI was silent on the question as to whether slavery might subsequently be permitted in any *states* formed from the territory. Indeed, "Candor," an antislavery partisan, considered it "self-evident" that the ordinance was only relevant as a document of governance while Illinois was a territory. It could by no means "compel us to prohibit slavery one moment after we come into a state government. . . . [H]ow would our situation be mended, if we were still to be governed by this ordinance and denied the privileges of other states? . . . The principle was never doubted in forming the constitutions for the states of Ohio and Indiana, that they might either tolerate or prohibit slavery."[29] In any case, over time the passage of laws sanctioning indentured servitude contracts had clouded the issue considerably, and there was reason to suppose that some form of slavery could continue in the new state.

Already Have the Advocates of Slavery Taken the Field

Such uncertainty over slavery's status in the prospective state of Illinois fueled its role in the convention campaign as the "object which most interests the public mind, with regard to the approaching election, for members to the convention," as one observer who called himself "The People" wrote in the *Illinois Intelligencer.* In his view, the slavery issue had produced three types of candidates. One group had "made their sentiments known on that head, and pledged themselves to one or other of the parties to support their favorite measure." A second group deliberately obscured their position to avoid committing themselves: "As to this class of candidates, comment is unnecessary—both sides can see their drift." But he deemed the third class of contenders as "more dangerous, and as little to be trusted, who tell you 'my principles, on this point, are so and so; but should a majority of my constituents tell me to act otherwise, I am their humble servant and obsequious slave; their wills shall be done.'" "[W]e cannot trust those who are so pliable," he continued, "and make so light of their opinions as to barter them for an office."[30]

Daniel Pope Cook recognized the importance of slavery in the convention campaign at a very early point—indeed, even before news of the enabling act's passage had reached Kaskaskia. Writing again as "A Republican" on 1 April, he argued that emigration from the free states of the North and the East had outstripped that of every other region, including the South. "Many are in favor of admitting slavery," Cook argued, "because it is already admitted in some of our sister states." Those who supported toleration of the institution did so out of a conviction that "it will render them less dangerous if they are dispersed all over the nation. . . . But who can reason and deny that they will ultimately become more dangerous than if concentrated to narrow limits[?]" He argued that "where slavery supports freedom in idleness, all the train of vices which idleness produces are visited upon the people; discord and party feeling find their way as well into domestic circles as into the body politic."[31] Later, at the end of July—just a few days before the opening of the convention—Cook emphasized his opposition to slavery under his own name and restated many of the same arguments. "I am opposed to it," he wrote in the *Intelligencer*, "because I conceive the practice repugnant to the principles of humanity, to the policy of our general government, and to the best interests of this territory."[32]

Cook's fellow antislavery partisan "Agis" wrote on 17 June: "Already have the advocates of slavery taken the field; and one may frequently hear them descanting upon the advantages which would attend the admission of slavery, and murmuring because this territory is not permitted to enjoy this *inestimable blessing* as well as some other states and territories." He added sarcastically, "'Were slavery admitted,' say they, 'the territory would be immediately settled; mills, manufactories and bridges, would be erected, and the whole country would wear a new appearance.'"[33]

The significance of the slavery issue in the convention campaign comes into sharper relief when considering the individual relationship of each delegate candidate to the institution. Complete lists of successful and unsuccessful candidates are available for ten of the fifteen counties that were then in existence: Gallatin, Jackson, Johnson, Madison, Monroe, Pope, Randolph, St. Clair, Union, and Washington. For the remaining counties—Bond, Crawford, Edwards, Franklin, and White—only the names of those who were elected are available. A careful reading of extant source materials—indentures, census listings, county histories, and other similar records—documents that the fifty-five men who sought election to the thirty-three convention seats were nearly evenly divided between slaveholders and non-slaveholders—twenty-five and twenty-seven, respectively. Slightly more non-slaveholders (eighteen) than slaveholders (thirteen) were ultimately elected to the convention. (No information is available on the remaining three candidates, two of whom were elected and one of whom was defeated.)[34]

The relatively close divide between slaveholders and non-slaveholders is somewhat surprising, given that African Americans made up only 3 percent of a territorial population of just over forty thousand. Furthermore, surviving census records reveal that slaveholding households accounted for only a little over 5 percent of total territorial households.[35] Slaveholders were generally wealthier individuals whose affluence provided them with greater means and opportunities to pursue public office. This helps to account for the fact that they were represented on both the ballot and in the convention out of all proportion to their numbers among the total population.

Documentation on the candidates' precise positions concerning slavery is limited. It is somewhat easier to identify those who were fundamentally opposed to the institution. William H. Bradsby of Washington County—although himself a slaveholder—had supported the repeal of the territory's indentured servitude statutes the previous December, "actuated by a love of the equal rights of man."[36] As a member of the General Assembly in 1824, Andrew Bankson—also of Washington County—was one of fifteen legislators who signed a letter opposing the introduction of slavery into Illinois "in the name of the injured sons of Africa, whose claim to equal rights with their fellow men will plead their own cause against their usurpers." Brothers-in-law George Cadwell of Madison County and John Messinger of St. Clair County had emigrated from Kentucky to Illinois in 1802 with their families in part because they deemed slavery "distasteful," according to historian R. W. Mills.[37] Messinger and two of the other candidates—William Jones of Madison County and Enoch Moore of Monroe County—signed a petition in 1808 protesting the passage of a law permitting slave indentures, which they deemed "the Establishment of disguised slavery."[38] Levi Compton of Edwards County was reputed to have owned many enslaved persons in Kentucky, but as one who disliked the institution, he set all of them free before settling in Illinois in 1804.[39] The candidate who was the most vehement in his denunciation of slavery was James Lemen Jr., whose entire family had left a church to form their own congregation over the issue. In 1821 Lemen would author an address in which he blasted slaveholding as "a violation of the principles of nature, reason, justice, policy, and scripture."[40] Five of these eight—Bankson, Compton, Lemen, Messinger, and Moore—were elected to the convention.

Direct evidence of those who were avowedly pro-slavery is scanty. Adolphus F. Hubbard of Gallatin County—where the largest numbers of enslaved persons and free people of color were located, although there is no direct evidence that Hubbard was himself a slaveholder—was said to have spoken at length in the convention in favor of legalization: "You knows too . . . that slavery is commanded in the scriptures. . . . But to return to our own nation of folks, negroes can draw water better as white folks and make fires too. That is all, Mr. President, that I has to say on that part of my argument. . . . I think slavery a very necessary thing in a free government, where we is all republicans."[41] George Fisher of Randolph County had argued the previous winter in the territorial legislature against repealing the law on indentures, given that the Illinois Country had benefited from the introduction of enslaved persons and "*their* situation has been much ameliorated thereby."[42] Then there were those who were more ambivalent, such as Joseph Kitchell of Crawford County, who as a member of the Illinois senate in 1829 would give a speech deeming the very presence of African Americans—whether enslaved or free—as "productive of moral and political evil."[43]

Jesse B. Thomas, who was also a slaveholder, had consistently equivocated on the issue over the course of his career. He had been intimately involved with the separation of Illinois from Indiana Territory that had everything to do with perpetuating slavery in the former. As a member of the Indiana territorial assembly in 1805 he had signed a petition to Congress (along with George Fisher, Pierre Menard, and John Rice Jones) that advocated for the introduction of slavery to the territory. The petition expressed regret that slavery had ever taken root in the United States, and Thomas and his colleagues argued that "dispersing them [enslaved persons] through the Western Territories is the only means by which a gradual emancipation can ever be effected."[44]

A First Principle in Politics

And what of Elias Kent Kane? There is no contemporaneous account of his position, but two years later, when running for Congress against Daniel Pope

Cook in the aftermath of the Missouri Compromise and in the midst of a controversy over whether there was a subterranean effort to transform Illinois into a slave state, Kane acknowledged a certain degree of fence straddling. "It is with me a first principle in politics," he declared, "that a representative is bound by the voice, wishes and instructions of his constituents." He recalled that while he ran for the convention unopposed—and "my own opinion, as uniformly expressed, was opposed to slavery"—two other candidates were in contention for the other delegate seat from Randolph County—John McFerron, who also opposed slavery, and George Fisher, who favored its legalization. Kane recounted that he was pressed to state "whether I would obey the voice of my constituents, as expressed by the result of the election between the two gentlemen. . . . What ought to have been my answer! It was as it should be—in the affirmative. The candidate in favor of slavery was elected, and my course of conduct on that subject was thereby fixed."[45]

One can assess these sentiments in a variety of ways. It would be easy to dismiss them as evidence of a go-along-to-get-along mentality. "The People" had already derided candidates of this ilk as their constituents' "humble servant and obsequious slave; their wills shall be done."[46] But on closer inspection Kane's thought process speaks to a tangible degree of caution and uncertainty intermingled with no small amount of ambition. He was, after all, only twenty-four years old and had only been a denizen of Illinois since 1814. He had hitched his wagon to Jesse B. Thomas's political star—that is to say, to the opposition party—and there was no guarantee that this would lead to a lifetime of patronage and public offices. His membership in Randolph County's convention delegation was safe, but the fate of slavery in the future state of Illinois was still very much up in the air. Kane's entire political career could hinge upon his own response to the question.

And in the end he based his decision on what he believed was the popular will. To the extent that anyone raised the issue, Kane could have pointed to the fact that neither McFerron nor Fisher was a slaveholder, and consequently no one could argue that their positions were based on self-interest. As matters turned out, Elias Kent Kane was faithful to his pledge, voting in the convention in unison with Fisher not only on the issue of slavery but on almost every other question as well. In this situation at least, Kane seems to have satisfied himself that his own self-interest and the interests of his constituents could be one and the same.

13

THE GREAT WORK BEFORE US

As June faded into July the voters of Kaskaskia, Shawneetown, and Edwardsville and their brethren among the western frontier's rising settlements began to prepare themselves for the most momentous election in the history of Illinois Territory. The *Illinois Intelligencer* struck an optimistic note in its last issue before the selection of convention delegates began, reporting that upcoming census returns from the counties of Gallatin and Franklin were likely to number in the range of three thousand inhabitants altogether. "From the information we have received, it is probable, that if the commissioners for the several counties will be vigilant, that our numbers will increase to forty thousand by the first of August."[1] As if to underscore the point, they approvingly quoted a news item from New York's *National Advocate* reporting on the arrival of a gentleman from England "whose object is to settle in the Illinois territory; that his family and settlers brought over with him, amount to 51 persons. . . . This is doing business in a great national as well as individual profit; and if gentlemen of fortune and enterprize [*sic*] will emigrate in the same manner, our western states will shortly be the most flourishing part of the world."[2]

The territorial capital marked Independence Day with a public celebration under the leadership of the Kaskaskia Independent Rifle Company. The revels featured the usual toasts from leaders such as John Edgar and Secretary Joseph Philips, and an eloquent patriotic oration delivered by Theodore V. W. Varick. Varick took pains to single out Nathaniel Pope for particular praise. "Our gratitude is unquestionably due to him," he proclaimed, "whose exertions have attained for us the liberal terms under which we are about to enter into the federal union; terms which will give character and greatness to the state of Illinois."[3]

But first there was the matter of selecting delegates to a constitutional convention to synthesize the instruments and structures of state government. Candidates trotted patiently from cabin to cabin in dogged search of sympathetic voices and votes. An aspiring frontier Robert Burns anointing himself as "Felty, Monroe County" sketched a crude tableau of the canvass:

In dreary woods, remote from social walks
I dwell. From year to year, no friendly steps
Approach my cot, save near election days,
When throngs of busy, bustling candidates
Cheer me with their conversation so soft and sweet—
I list' with patience to their charming tales,
Whilst gingerbread and whisky they disperse,
To me, my wife and all the children round.
Some bring a store of little penny books
And trinkets rare for all my infants young.—
My health and crops appear their utmost care,
Fraternal squeezes from their hands I get—
As tho' they lov'd me from their very souls—
Then—"Will you vote for me my dearest friend?
Your laws I'll alter, and lop taxes off:—
'Tis for the public weal I stand the test
And leave my home, sorely against my will:
But knowing that the people's good require
An old substantial hand—I quit my farm
For patriotism's sake, and public good;"
Then fresh embraces close the friendly scene
With protestations firm, of how they love.
But what most rarely does my good wife pleate
Is that the snot nos'd baby gets a buss!!
O that conventions ev'ry day were call'd,
That social converse might forever reign.[4]

The supply of gingerbread, whiskey, trinkets, and snot-nosed babies having largely thinned out, Monday, 6 July 1818 marked the commencement of three days of voting. Eligible voters—white males aged twenty-one or older—gathered to cast their ballots at a single polling station in each county, which meant that many had to travel long distances. Balloting was viva voce; as "Agis" explained in the *Illinois Intelligencer*, "[T]he vote of each elector is placed upon record and proclaimed aloud by the sheriff." The writer expressed some foreboding that this method could potentially create a situation in which "the wealthy and the powerful acquire an alarming influence over our elections" or that an individual voter would hesitate to cast a ballot contrary to that of his neighbors.[5]

Although returns from the election are only available for Gallatin and Madison Counties, they provide us with a rough sense of the degree of electoral participation. Three delegates were to be chosen in both counties; thus, Gallatin County's 1,055 votes were cast by approximately 352 out of 909 potential electors (39 percent) and Madison County's 1,551 were cast by around 517 voters out of 1,012 electors (51 percent). Neither of these elections was particularly close.[6] But the voters had spoken; for better or worse they had chosen 33 men to represent them in Illinois's first constitutional convention. And among the victorious candidates was one Elias Kent Kane, formerly of Whitesboro, New York; New York City; New Haven, Connecticut; Nashville, Tennessee; and now representing Randolph County.

Public interest in the convention that opened in Kaskaskia on Monday, 3 August 1818 was substantial. John Mason Peck reported that when he attempted to stop at Bennett's hotel—the only lodging available in the village—the proprietor expressed serious doubts as to the availability of accommodations, given that every available room was taken. He added, however, that one of the guests was absent that night, which meant that Peck had the option of sharing a bed—"none too wide for two"—with Adolphus F. Hubbard, one of the delegates from Gallatin County. "Mr. H. had seen me in Shawneetown," Peck recalled, "and no sooner was my name announced to him by the landlord than he insisted I should share the hospitality of his bed. Being thus made comfortable, I learned from my room-mate something of the progress made in the construction of the new Government."[7]

A Sociable Group

The men who had been elected to the convention and were now charged with the task of defining and organizing state government were generally reflective of the citizens of the territory. Like the people they represented, the largest number of delegates hailed from the South, including five from Virginia, three from South Carolina, two from Maryland, and one each from North Carolina and Georgia.[8] Seven had been born in mid-Atlantic states: four from Pennsylvania, two from New Jersey, and one from New York.[9] Two were originally from New England—one from Massachusetts and one from Connecticut.[10] And four delegates were native to the West—two from Kentucky and two native-born Illinoisans.[11] Only one, an Irish immigrant, is known to have been of foreign birth.[12] The birthplaces of seven delegates are unknown.[13]

Solon Buck observed that a substantial number of immigrants "had made one or two other moves before coming to Illinois."[14] The delegates' movement westward had been similarly gradual. More than two-thirds of them settled for a time in other areas of the West—Tennessee, Ohio, Indiana, and especially Kentucky—before arriving in Illinois Territory.[15] Members had lived in the territory for an average of twelve years; eighteen had arrived before 1809, and the remaining fifteen had reached Illinois after it had separated from Indiana in that year. Enoch Moore of Monroe County and the Reverend James Lemen Jr. of St. Clair County were both born in Illinois in the 1780s.[16] As the first and second child respectively born to American parents in the Illinois country, they were in effect the residents of longest standing. Joseph Kitchell and John K. Mangham were probably the last to arrive, Kitchell having settled in Palestine in 1817 and Mangham perhaps as late as early 1818.[17]

The delegates represented a multitude of occupations. Among them were farmers, millers, storekeepers, ferry boat operators, lawyers, teachers, surveyors, doctors, preachers, salt manufacturers, innkeepers, flatboaters, authors, carpenters, blacksmiths, mapmakers, coopers, lead mine operators, tanners, and distillers. Several delegates diversified their economic interests. Edward N. Cullom of Crawford County was a land speculator and farmer. After raising a large corn crop in the summer of 1815, Cullom became the first person to send a flatboat down the Wabash River from Illinois Territory to New Orleans; his resulting profit made him a rich man.[18] James Hall Jr. of Jackson County operated a blacksmith shop, a cooperage, a cotton gin, a distillery, and a grist mill.[19] Conrad Will, likewise of Jackson County, had a farm, a general store, a mill, and a tannery, and he was also a talented physician.[20] Jesse B. Thomas established what he claimed was the first fulling mill in Illinois Territory, featuring two wool-carding machines.[21] Will and at least three other delegates—Michael Jones of Gallatin County, Willis Hargrave of White County, and Benjamin Stephenson of Madison County—leased salines in southern Illinois from the federal government for salt production.[22]

Many of the vocations and occupations of the delegates are noteworthy for the substantial degree of sociability they required. By the very nature of their work, millers, merchants, ferry operators, tavernkeepers, lawyers, doctors, and the like interacted on a daily basis with large numbers of people from all walks of life. None of the delegates demonstrates this better than the multiskilled Conrad Will. Good-natured, garrulous, and a talented joke teller, Will was one of the most popular men in Jackson County.[23] If these qualities were profitable to him as the operator of watermills, tanneries, and salines, they proved indispensable in his quest for public office. Alone of all the members of the convention, Will never lost an election, either before or after 1818.

If less successful than Will, the other men at the convention were equally active in seeking public office, both during the territorial period and afterward. Twenty-nine held appointive or elective office in the years before 1818, ranging from justice of the peace to county coroner to member of the territorial legislature. Benjamin Stephenson and Jesse B. Thomas had served as territorial delegates to Congress from Illinois and Indiana respectively. George Fisher and John Messinger had both served in the territorial legislature. Messinger, a surveyor and cartographer who later became professor of mathematics at Rock Spring Seminary, had been one of the members of the Indiana territorial legislature who colluded with Jesse B. Thomas to separate the territory back in 1808.[24] Such positions of trust guaranteed continued prominence in the public eye and access to public largesse. It was a shrewd politician who used his office as a stepping-stone to the convention.

Thirteen of the delegates are documented as having been slaveholders. The three delegates who held the largest number of enslaved persons—Willis Hargrave (fourteen), Michael Jones (twelve), and Benjamin Stephenson (eight)—were, not surprisingly, saline operators. This was also true of Leonard White (two enslaved persons) and Conrad Will (one). Several of these delegates also availed themselves of the territory's indenture law to establish contracts for enslaved labor, including Caldwell Cairns, James Hall Jr., Elias Kent Kane, Benjamin Stephenson, Jesse B. Thomas, and Conrad Will.[25]

A Spirit of Indulgence and Harmony

At the time of the convention, the War of 1812 and related violent confrontations with Native Americans on the frontier were a very recent memory. Under Illinois's territorial code "every free, able bodied white male citizen" between the ages of eighteen and forty-five was required—with some exceptions—to serve in the territorial militia.[26] Consequently, twenty-two—two-thirds—of the delegates had some measure of military experience. Elias Kent Kane had himself briefly served as a sergeant in Captain William Alexander's Company of the Mounted Illinois Militia sometime toward the end of the War of 1812. John Whiteaker of Union County had been an ensign in the Third Regiment of the militia during the war and later was promoted to lieutenant. Some, such as Willis Hargrave and Andrew Bankson, had attained positions of high rank; both had risen to the rank of colonel. Benjamin Stephenson had been adjutant general and colonel of Illinois militia during the war.[27]

There were some distinctive characters among their number. William McFatridge of Johnson County was garrulous and well-liked but given to overindulgence in his later years as a member of the General Assembly. Long afterward William H. Brown remarked diplomatically that McFatridge "drank more liquor than his legislative duties actually required." Once, when the house was adjourned in spite of his fervent opposition, he shouted, "Mr. Speaker—Mr. Speaker,—you may adjourn the House, and be hanged, but old Billy

McFatridge will remain in session until sundown, and look after the interests of his constituents, while you and the rest of you are '*cavorting*' at Capp's grocery [a Vandalia tavern within easy staggering distance of the capitol building], and getting drunk upon the hard earnings of the people!"[28] Adolphus F. Hubbard, in running for governor against Ninian Edwards in 1826, modestly disdained any suggestion that he was "a man of extraordinary talents; nor do I claim to be equal to Julius Caesar or Napoleon Bonaparte, nor yet to be as great a man as my opponent. . . . Nevertheless, I think I can govern you pretty well. I do not think that it will require a very extraordinary smart man to govern you; for to tell you the truth, fellow-citizens, I do not think you will be very hard to govern, no how."[29]

They were a relatively young group. The twenty-four members whose birthdates could be determined averaged thirty-nine years of age at the time of the convention. The oldest member, Isham Harrison of Franklin County, was between fifty-six and fifty-eight years of age and was one of three Revolutionary War veterans at the convention. And the youngest was twenty-four-year-old Elias Kent Kane of Randolph County.[30]

His youth notwithstanding, Kane was undoubtedly the most well-educated member of the convention by virtue of having studied at Yale and having read for the law in New York.[31] Consequently, when the newly elected convention delegates gathered together for the first time on 3 August 1818—in the same building that housed the territorial legislature[32]—it was only natural that they would look for leadership to a man who had risen to the very top of the legal profession in a relatively brief time. Governor Thomas Ford wrote that Kane was the delegate to whom "we are mostly indebted for the peculiar features of the Constitution."[33] Indeed, the young New Yorker's name appears in the journal of the convention more frequently—43 times—than any other delegate. For that matter, Kane made more floor motions than any other delegate—a total of 34 out of the 134 motions recorded and identified with specific delegates (more than 25 percent).[34]

But for now there were other more practical considerations. All 33 members were present at the opening of the assembly, according to the *Intelligencer*. After electing William C. Greenup as convention secretary, their first order of business was to select a president to direct their debates into the most productive channels. [35] Jesse B. Thomas was the natural choice, given his status as a high-ranking territorial official and as a leader of one of the two major local political factions. That he was also Elias Kent Kane's political patron undoubtedly worked to the advantage of his younger colleague's pervasive influence within the convention. Thomas was elected president "without a dissenting voice," the *Illinois Intelligencer* reported. Thanking his colleagues for their support, he remarked: "[I]t is with extreme diffidence, that I enter upon the discharge of the duties of the situation thus assigned me. . . . And whilst I solicit your aid and indulgence on this occasion, suffer me to remark, that a spirit of indulgence and harmony amongst ourselves, is the surest guarantee to a happy termination of the great work before us." Thomas stepped quickly into his new role and immediately immersed the convention in some mundane but important logistics, appointing a committee (of which Kane was a member) to verify delegate credentials and another to devise convention rules and regulations. The following day—4 August—Kane made a motion to appoint yet another committee to examine census returns and certify whether or not the territory met the population standard set forth in the enabling act. The convention agreed, and Kane found himself taking another lead role as a member of this group with Joseph Kitchell and Caldwell Cairns.[36]

Strong Exertions Will Be Made in the Convention

When the delegates met again on 5 August, Elias Kent Kane was chosen to make the report from both of his committees. The working group on credentials, he noted, had verified that all 33 members were eligible to take their seats. Kane then reported that the census committee had concluded that the population of Illinois Territory amounted to 40,258, representing an increase of 5,638 since the territorial secretary's report of 17 June.[37] That result was good enough for Abraham Prickett of Madison County, who moved that, given that Illinois had surpassed the standard set by Congress, it was now "expedient to form a constitution and state government." Somewhat surprisingly, Kane opposed this proposal, moving—unsuccessfully—to postpone it until the following day. His motivations are unclear; possibly he was uncertain of the result of any vote by the convention on the question, given that the territory had just barely reached the necessary population threshold. He may also have been concerned that any debate might raise questions about the possibly illicit means by which census commissioners had arrived at their results. Such concerns proved to be baseless as the convention approved Prickett's resolution.[38]

Now came the most fundamental and important action of the convention as they voted to charge a fifteen-man committee—with one delegate from each county—with the task of devising the initial draft of a constitution.[39] The members of this group were nearly equally divided between slaveholders and non-slaveholders at seven each; the status of the remaining member is unknown. Three of them—Andrew Bankson, Levi Compton, and James Lemen—professed to be antislavery. They and five of their fellow committee members—Caldwell Cairns, William Echols, Thomas Kirkpatrick, Abraham Prickett, and Hezekiah West—ultimately voted to a greater or lesser degree along antislavery lines in the later full convention votes on the subject. The remaining seven—Edward N. Cullom, James Hall Jr., Willis Hargrave, Elias Kent Kane, Samuel Omelveny, Thomas Roberts, and Leonard White—four of whom were slaveholders, voted largely in accordance with pro-slavery interests.[40] That the drafting committee was almost equally divided on the issue reflected the larger composition of the convention, underscoring again the disproportionate influence of slaveholders in the territory.

A letter published in the *Illinois Intelligencer* on the same day emphasized this point. It was signed by thirteen men from the counties of St. Clair, Madison, Monroe, and Washington. Among them was Charles R. Matheny, who (in conjunction with fellow signer William Bradsby) had unsuccessfully advocated for repeal of the territory's indenture law the previous December. Bradsby, of course, had been defeated in his effort to run for convention delegate. Two of the other signers were related to James Lemen Jr., who was on the drafting committee. "We are informed," they declared, "that strong exertions will be made in the Convention to give sanction to that deplorable evil in our state." The authors asserted that antislavery sentiments prevailed in their home counties. Their fear of a pro-slavery constitution impelled them to urge their fellow citizens to oppose that outcome, even to the extent of encouraging them to petition Congress to reject such a document.[41]

The drafting committee spent one week—a surprisingly short period of time—in developing the initial version of the constitution. Historian Janet Cornelius attributed this to two factors: a "desire to beat Missouri to statehood" and the natural inclination of "writers of frontier constitutions in their impatience with the time and effort it would have taken to formulate a flexible, coherent statement of the principles of state government."[42] According to John F. Snyder, Sidney Breese, a legal protégé of Elias Kent Kane's, reported that his mentor actually drafted the document in his law office "some time before the meeting of the convention."[43] There is no direct contemporary evidence to support this secondhand anecdote, but in any case Kane by virtue of his education was uniquely well-equipped to take a leading role in the process. In the meantime, the convention approved its rules of order and—in response to a motion from Kane—authorized the drafting committee to "consider of the expediency of accepting or rejecting the propositions made to this convention by the congress of the United States"; if the former, the committee was directed to draft an ordinance complying with those conditions.[44]

On 7 August Kane presented a pair of curious petitions from some of his Randolph County constituents. One prayed "that this convention shall declare in the constitution to be formed that the moral law is the basis of its structure." The other asked "that this convention may declare the scriptures to be the word of God, and that the constitution is founded upon the same." Both were referred to a select committee, where they languished and died in hopes of a glorious resurrection. A similar petition submitted on 22 August from "William Thompson and others, praying that the moral law shall be taken as the foundation of the constitution, and the scriptures declared to be the word of God, the supreme rule of faith and practice," was tabled until 4 March of the following year.[45]

The work of the convention was briefly and unexpectedly brought to a screeching halt on the morning of 11 August. Andrew Bankson announced "with deep regret" that his fellow Washington County delegate John K. Mangham had died a few hours earlier at 1:00 AM. Funeral arrangements were delegated to a select committee, and members were requested to wear crape on their left arms in Mangham's memory for thirty days. Many of them attended his obsequies at 6:00 PM that same day. Subsequently, upon the recommendation of a special committee, the convention deemed it inexpedient to order an election to fill Mangham's vacancy, given time constraints.[46]

The Vast and Mighty Work Assigned to Them

The convention resumed its deliberations on 12 August. Leonard White of Gallatin County reported that the drafting committee had completed their work, which he handed to convention secretary Greenup for reading aloud to the members.[47] The document was a fascinating synthesis of provisions from several contemporary state charters. Janet Cornelius demonstrated that the committee was influenced by constitutional models from Tennessee (1796), Kentucky (1799), Ohio (1802), and Indiana (1816).[48] A careful comparison of the first draft with those documents makes a strong case that Illinois's immediate neighbors to the east—Indiana and Ohio—provided the lion's share of source material, with substantial contributions from Kentucky and Tennessee and additional ideas drawn from New York's 1777 constitution, the latter reflecting Elias Kent Kane's influence.[49] After a preamble confirming the boundaries outlined in the enabling act—the Mississippi, Ohio, and Wabash Rivers, Lake Michigan, and a line set at 42°30′ north latitude—and Article I outlining the distribution of powers, the draft described a state government structure encompassing the standard executive, legislative, and judicial branches.

Article II established a General Assembly composed of a house of representatives and a senate, drawing largely on the Indiana and Ohio constitutions. All members were to be chosen every two years, and the terms of the first senators were staggered. Minimum ages of twenty-one and twenty-five were set respectively for representatives and senators; they were also required to have lived in their districts for at least a year prior to election. Members of both houses were prohibited from appointment to any other civil office, although they were not restricted from *running* for any other office. Copying from New York (again probably at Kane's behest) and Tennessee, the draft Article II excluded preachers from serving in the legislature to ensure that they would not be diverted from their dedication to God and the care of souls.[50] The convention hastened to add, however, that men of the cloth were also exempted from militia duty, working on roads, and serving on juries. "An Observer" in the *Illinois Intelligencer* remarked acidly that all could surely agree the provision was "humane" when one took into consideration "1st. The vast and mighty work assigned them to perform for men's souls. This work is never done. (*how inhuman to impose on THEM additional labor*?) But—2d. The arduous and servile drudgery of electioneering and preaching politicks on Sundays, &c. 3d. The arduous and servile drudgery of legislation."[51] Later the members decided that although the Lord delivers the righteous from their afflictions, there was no similar obligation upon the state legislature, and consequently the convention deleted both provisions.[52]

The logistics of lawmaking were primarily patterned after Indiana and Ohio. Legislation could be introduced in either chamber, but all revenue bills were to originate in the house. The draft constitution also decreed that the legislature could bar anyone convicted of "bribery, perjury or any infamous crime" from running for a seat in either chamber. The power of impeachment lay with the house of representatives and required a majority vote of all its members. The trial would be conducted by the senate, where a two-thirds vote of all members *present* was necessary for conviction.[53] This was a change from Ohio and Indiana, where conviction was the result of a vote of two-thirds of all members *elected*.

Article II set somewhat more liberal standards for voting eligibility than its predecessors. Like New York, Kentucky, Ohio, and Indiana, Illinois defined electors as white males aged twenty-one and older. However, whereas Illinois required these voters to have been residents six months previous to the election, Ohio and Indiana had set that standard at one year, while Kentucky set it at two years. New York only required six months' residence, but eligible voters in that state were also required to own property with a minimum value of twenty pounds. The draft constitution also provided for a census of all white inhabitants over twenty-one to be conducted every five years beginning in 1825, much to the delight of future genealogists; this was altered almost immediately to encompass all free whites of both genders, with censuses now beginning in 1820.[54]

Following the Indiana and Ohio models, Article II of the draft constitution set specific annual salaries for the governor and secretary of state; it also initially set compensation and travel allowances for members of the General Assembly. However, Article III, section 6 of the draft also decreed that the governor would receive a salary that was not to be increased or decreased during his term. The convention resolved this contradiction on 19 August when Kane and Messinger successfully moved to prohibit the General Assembly from changing those salaries until 1824, although it augmented the secretary of state's salary to $600, reduced the governor's to $1,000, and deleted all references to per diem and mileage for legislators.[55]

Article III describing the executive branch represented a substantial challenge for the drafting committee. The initial statehood movement had been energized, after all, in part by Daniel Pope Cook's ferocious denunciations of executive power.[56] Unfortunately for the convention, the available model state constitutions were inconsistent as to the governor's proper role. In Ohio and Tennessee, the executive played no part whatsoever in the legislative process; there are no references to a veto power. Indiana and Kentucky specified the executive's power to reject legislation passed by their assemblies, but it was substantially mitigated by the legislature's ability to override vetoes by a mere majority—in Indiana, a majority of those present for the vote, and in Kentucky, a majority of all those *elected*. Thus the drafting committee was faced with the dilemma of limiting gubernatorial power while still creating a workable executive branch.

Once again Elias Kent Kane played a crucial role, as Janet Cornelius observed.[57] The constitution of his home state provided "that the governor for the time being, the chancellor, and the judges of the supreme court, or any two of them, together with the governor, shall be, and hereby are, constituted a council to revise all bills about to be passed into laws by the legislature." If a given bill were returned to the legislature, it could then only become law by a vote of two-thirds of both houses. This seemed a suitable compromise, and consequently Kane and his fellow members of the drafting committee copied this provision almost verbatim. The convention as a whole, however, had different ideas at first, voting on 14 August to restore veto power to the governor and retaining the requirement of a two-thirds majority to override. Three days later (on 17 August) they thought better of it and returned once again to the council of revision, calling for only a simple majority to override as in Indiana and Kentucky.[58] This system proved to be problematic over the next thirty years given its fundamental breach in the separation of powers. It served "an advisory purpose," wrote Janet Cornelius, "by calling legislators' attention to technical deficits in laws passed, but the supreme court ruling on the constitutionality of state laws was continually embarrassed by the fact that the justices had already passed on the laws in their role as members of the council of revision." This body ultimately proved ineffective given that its vetoes were easily overturned by a simple majority in the General Assembly.[59]

The drafting committee drew primarily on Ohio, Indiana, and Kentucky to set the governor's qualifications. He was required to be at least thirty years old and a U.S. citizen for ten years (later changed to thirty years). Subsequently the requirement of two years' residence was added.[60] The committee does not seem to have considered drawing on either New York or Tennessee's constitution, which both required property ownership. New York did not specify any age qualification. Its only requirement was that an eligible candidate be "wise and descreet." Perhaps Kane and his cohorts feared setting too high a standard.

The governor's term of office was set at four years—breaking with the other constitutional models setting the term at two or three years—and no governor would be able to serve more than four in any period of eight years.[61] Kentucky had established that limit at seven years, and all of the other states except New York had similar restrictions. In addition to his responsibility for the faithful execution of the laws, the governor was initially given appointive powers limited to the secretary of state, justices of the peace, and filling vacancies during legislative recesses. As in other states, the General Assembly could select judges for both the supreme and inferior courts.[62] Later in August the convention added a section in Article III (on Kane's motion) giving the governor the power to "appoint all officers . . . whose appointments are not otherwise herein provided for." Elias Kent Kane simultaneously moved to enable the General Assembly to appoint biennially "the state treasurer and public printer or printers."[63]

Motives of Favor

The following day (21 August), however, the convention added a section to the constitution's schedules that only served to blur the distinctions between the executive and legislative branches. Section 10 gave the General Assembly the authority to appoint the auditor of public accounts, the attorney general, "and such other officers as may be necessary."[64] Years later Governor Thomas Ford declared that the delegates were moved by "motives of favor to particular persons who were looked to to hold office under the new government." The convention, he explained, had its heart set on Elijah Berry as auditor of public accounts, a position he had held under the territorial government. They believed that the new governor, whom everyone expected to be Shadrach Bond, would not appoint Berry to the office, hence the provision giving the General Assembly this power. The ambiguity of the phrase "and such other officers as may be necessary" was the source of confusion over the following three decades in clearly defining who was an officer of the state. It amounted to a formula for reducing the governor's patronage, and the "constant changing and shifting of powers" between the executive and legislative branches "rendered it impossible for the people to foresee exactly for what purpose either the governor or legislature were elected. . . . It led to innumerable intrigues and corruptions, and for a long time destroyed the harmony between the executive and legislative departments."[65]

The draft constitution initially identified the speaker of the senate as being next in the governor's line of succession. On 18 August Kane, taking an idea suggested by a select committee appointed to consider additional articles or sections, moved that Article III be revised to create the office of lieutenant governor, who would also act as Speaker of the senate and in effect be simultaneously a member of both the executive and legislative branches.[66]

Article IV dealing with the judicial branch was most clearly rooted in the Ohio constitution. It established a supreme court and inferior courts, the former designated to have only appellate jurisdiction save in limited circumstances. It was to consist of a chief justice and three associate judges, but the General Assembly was given the power to increase their numbers. As in Ohio and Tennessee, both the supreme court justices and inferior court judges were to be appointed by a joint ballot of the General Assembly. Whereas Indiana and Ohio had limited judges to terms of seven years, Illinois made them life appointments "during good behaviour."[67]

Article V of the constitution focused upon the state's militias and seems to have been drawn from Indiana's charter. Like the latter, Illinois organized its militias to encompass "all free male able bodied persons, negroes, mulattoes and Indians excepted, resident in the state, between the ages of 18 and 45 years" and "armed, equipped, and trained" as the General Assembly should see fit. It provided for exemptions for conscientious objectors—but only in times of peace—who paid for that privilege. Like Ohio and Indiana, it provided for the election of officers by the men under their command. All officers were to be commissioned by the governor and to hold their commissions on condition of good behavior until they reached age sixty.[68]

The convention had begun—with some fits and starts—to create the semblance of a rough structure of state governance under the steady guidance of Elias Kent Kane. Up to this point any disagreements had been largely low-key, with the possible exception of the convention's discussions concerning the veto power. But in general their work had been noncontroversial; perhaps John K. Mangham's death in the midst of the constitution's birth throes had impressed his fellow delegates with a greater seriousness of purpose. And they would surely need it during the next phase of deliberations, because they were about to face the most daunting issue of all: the life or death of slavery in the future state of Illinois.

14
A LITTLE "PRUDENCE"

Given that the enabling act as passed by Congress had clearly specified that the new state's constitution be "not repugnant" to the Northwest Ordinance, the question of slavery's legality in the future state of Illinois would seem on its face to have been a settled matter. But public discussion of the issue during the convention campaign had amply demonstrated that the debate was far from over, both in the convention and in the public arena. Any resolution was bound to be both complex and elusive.

One profoundly odd contribution to the debate in late July 1818 came from a writer who called himself "A Friend to Enquiry." Characterizing slavery as "fraught with cruelty and injustice," he nevertheless put forth the novel argument that the best way to abolish the institution in Illinois was to first legalize it—one cannot, after all, free people from bondage without enslaving them first. The foundational prejudices of slavery as an institution, he argued, were "deeply rooted," "and consequently would it not be most expedient to devise a system by which those prejudices would be subdued, and which in itself, by remunirating [*sic*] the owner, and preparing the slave, for the right exercise of his liberty, would give to the system appearance of perfect justice and equity?" "[I]t is our duty as men and christians," he concluded, "to do all we can in exterminating the baneful influence of slavery." Legalization, for that matter, could serve as the prerequisite to emancipation not only in Illinois but in other slaveholding states as well. "And would it not be a proud triumph in our posterity, after the business of universal emancipation shall have been effected, in tracing the effect to the cause, to find its origin in the benevolent policy of our territory?"[1]

"A Friend to Enquiry" evoked a scornful response from "Prudence" in the following issue. He dismissed "Enquiry's" proposal as a desperate last resort "of an expiring party, who finding that the naked book of *unconditional slavery*, will not be swallowed by the people, have adroitly enough, gilded it [slavery] over with the form of general humanity." He questioned the basis for introducing enslaved persons to Illinois "to the exclusion of those more beneficial to society." "I could wish the people in general," he warned, "the convention, and the convention's dictator, in particular, to take into view the serious evils arising from admitting among us a host of free negroes; and that with their schemes of humanity they would mix a little PRUDENCE."[2] His own antislavery sentiments, in short, were rooted in an aversion to the simple presence of African Americans—whether free or enslaved—in Illinois.

This exchange represented just one example of the very public and very spirited debate over the future of slavery in Illinois foreshadowing the upcoming deliberations in the convention. The thirty-three men who would soon represent their counties at that assemblage were painfully aware of this reality, fresh as they were from the rigors of the campaign trail. But if the pages of the *Intelligencer* served to expose such territorial divisions in their rawest form, they could also provide a venue for the convention to guide the public debate and to finesse the issue. Thus, in the *Intelligencer*'s issue of 12 August 1818—two days before deliberations on Article VI were to begin—a writer by the name of "Pacificus" sought to find a middle ground. Directly addressing the members of the convention, he advised caution "and to look well to the consequences which may fairly be expected to result from a decision either for or against the point in issue. The question is, *ought slavery* to be permitted to exist in the state whose constitution you are about to frame or not?" Were the question up to him alone, he affirmed, "[*I*]*t ought not to be tolerated*." "[W]hat are we to say," he worried, "with respect to those who not only hold many of their fellow creatures in bondage; but who sturdily maintain . . . the strict correctness of their so doing? Can we say you are wrong, and therefore we . . . will either compel you to abandon your slaves or quit the country? Would not this be exercising the superiority which we posses [*sic*] in a harsh and oppressive manner?"[3]

"Pacificus" suggested a compromise plan "which might gratify the wishes of those who are in favor of slavery, and not materially, if at all, affect the future prosperity of our infant state." It would require the registration of enslaved persons with the county clerk, who would record their vital statistics and assess a heavy bond to ensure that they would never become a public charge. It called for emancipating all enslaved persons brought to Illinois—males at the age of forty and females at age thirty-five. "Pacificus" also advocated that owners give bond ensuring those emancipated would be able to read and "have correct ideas of the general principles of the christian religion," along with any other regulations "as might be deemed advisable." He likewise proposed that all children born to enslaved persons or indentured servants should become free—males at age thirty-two and females at twenty-eight. They would be registered by the age of six months with a bond similar to that of their parents. He envisioned that as of 1 January 1860, "slavery of every kind or character should then and from thenceforth cease." At that time slaveholders would be required to ensure that none of their bondspersons who were infirm or over the age of fifty would ever become a public charge. Finally, "Pacificus" stipulated that enslaved persons be subject to judicial oversight and "liable to a certain penalty in proportion to the character or degree of the offence"—always to be an addition of days, months, or years to term of service. A system for regulating the transfer of enslaved persons would also be implemented.[4]

Compromises of Conflicting Interests

Many of these ideas ultimately found their way into both the constitution and the body of laws passed by the new state legislature governing both enslaved persons and free African Americans (the so-called "black codes") in the years immediately following admission to the Union. But the sentiments expressed by "Pacificus" are fascinating for reasons that go beyond the extent to which his ideas were reflected in Article VI of the constitution. In 1824—in the midst of a fierce election campaign over whether a new constitutional convention should be called to consider the possibility of Illinois becoming an unrepentant slave state—"Pacificus" revealed himself as Henry S. Dodge, Elias Kent Kane's business associate. Dodge admitted as much in a letter published in the *Kaskaskia Republican* on 23 March 1824. He argued that creating a social compact—devising a new state constitution—"always involved compromises of some kind or other of conflicting interests" and given "that there was, at that period, a very large and respectable minority of the people in favor of slavery, even in an unlimited form, at the suggestion and request of a gentleman then high in office, in the territory, I wrote the piece in question."[5]

Who was the "gentleman then high in office"? Kane would seem to be the likeliest candidate given his connection to Dodge, except for the fact that he was not—nor had he ever been—"high in office" in the territory. Another possibility was Jesse B. Thomas, given his status as a territorial judge and his predilection for finding the middle ground. Both Kane and Thomas implicitly understood the connection between the public debate over slavery and the deliberations within the convention. Whatever resolution they determined would have to be palatable to a diversity of voices and opinions. Consequently, both Dodge's link to Kane and the latter's political alliance with Thomas, taken together with the fact that the convention was even then preparing to confront the issue of slavery, strongly suggest that the "Pacificus" letter was a trial balloon written on their behalf to prepare the public for a compromise.

The outlines of that resolution began to emerge on 14 August, when Secretary William Greenup gave the first reading of the draft Article VI prohibiting slavery and indentured servitude except for the punishment of crimes. It decreed that no one beyond an age yet to be determined could "be held to serve any person as servant under pretence [*sic*] of indenture or otherwise, unless such person shall enter into such indenture while in a state of perfect freedom, and on condition of a bona fide consideration, received or to be received for their service." Any future indenture of "any negro or mulatto" executed outside of Illinois "or if made in the state where the term of service exceeds one year" would be deemed invalid "except those given in the case of apprenticeships."[6] The passage was drawn word for word from Article VIII, section 2 of the Ohio constitution, and the resemblance became complete when the convention set the age limits for persons to be held under pretense of indenture at twenty-one for males and eighteen for females. Indiana's language was very similar.

Any potential revisions were halted for the time being that same day when pro-slavery Adolphus Hubbard of Gallatin County moved to postpone further consideration of the passage until the second reading of the full draft constitution. It is significant that on Tuesday, 18 August it was the antislavery Seth Gard of Edwards County who moved not only that reading commence but that it start specifically with consideration of Article VI. In the process the convention made three noteworthy changes. First, they altered "There shall be neither slavery nor involuntary servitude in this state" to "Neither slavery nor involuntary servitude shall *hereafter* be introduced into this state" (emphasis added). Second, they changed the provision forbidding the holding of "any person as servant under pretence [*sic*] of indenture or otherwise" to outlaw holding them "under any indenture *hereafter* made" (emphasis added). Finally, they added a second section prohibiting the indenture of enslaved persons from other states "except within the tract reserved for the saltworks near Shawneetown, nor even at that place for a longer period than one year at one time; nor shall it be allowed there, after the year ______." Any violation of Article VI would "effect the emancipation of such person from his obligation to service."[7]

The addition of "hereafter" in two crucial places underscores the convention's effort to strike the delicate balance advocated by "Pacificus." On the one hand, they were charged with satisfying the conditions set forth by Congress in the enabling act that the constitution be "not repugnant" to the Northwest Ordinance. At the same time, Illinoisans who practiced slavery continued to advocate for their property rights; the territory's separation from Indiana had been, after all, partly the result of an effort to perpetuate slavery in the former and abolish it in the latter.[8] The fact that thirteen of the thirty-three delegates were themselves slaveholders was more important at this point than at any other time during the convention. In the end, the change in wording preserved existing indentures and property rights in spite of Illinois's status as a free state. And the continuation of indentures in the Shawneetown saltworks in particular highlighted the industry's ongoing importance to the region and the significance of enslaved persons as its primary labor supply. Slaveholding stood poised to maintain a foothold in Illinois until some future date when it could be fully legalized.

These changes to Article VI marked the first time that the convention recorded a roll-call vote, in this case by a margin of 17 in favor (including Elias Kent Kane) and 14 against. Still, the *Intelligencer* observed the following day, "The question of *slavery* is not yet decided; a majority however, are said to be opposed to it."[9]

Pro-slavery, Antislavery, and Compromisists

That judgment proved to be premature. On 19 August, Hubbard's fellow delegate from Gallatin County—the very heart of the saltworks industry and therefore the most reliant upon enslaved labor—Leonard White, who had served as the federal government's saline district agent from 1808 to 1811 and who was himself the owner of two enslaved persons, moved to add yet another section to Article VI in which all existing indentures would continue to be valid.[10] The new section, again echoing "Pacificus," also provided for the emancipation of their descendants, although it set the age of manumission at twenty-five. Like the first vote on Article VI the previous day, White's motion passed by a vote of 17–14, with some delegates changing sides. Abraham Prickett of Madison County, who had opposed the proposal and who generally leaned to the antislavery side, moved immediately to reconsider the vote, but the motion was defeated.[11]

That was still not the end of the issue, however. On 20 August Seth Gard moved to delete all of section 2 of Article VI. His proposal was resoundingly defeated 21–10. Joseph Kitchell then moved successfully to set 1825 as the date after which indentures would be prohibited even in the saline district. Perhaps seeking to soothe the feelings of the antislavery contingent, John Messinger of St. Clair County, who in spite of his reputed misgivings about slavery voted consistently with the pro-slavery delegates, moved to lower the age at which children (rather than descendants) of indentured or enslaved persons would become free to twenty-one for males and eighteen for females. Messinger also followed "Pacificus's" suggestion that such children be registered with the county clerk at the age of six months. The convention approved the motion.[12]

In his seminal 1904 work on the history of slavery in Illinois, Norman Dwight Harris described the members of the convention as falling into three categories: those who favored a purely pro-slavery constitution, those who sought to abolish the institution completely, and those he called "compromisists."[13] A careful analysis of the three recorded roll-call votes on Article VI supports his conclusions.

The first slavery vote that passed 17–14 on 18 August approved the draft Article VI prohibiting the future introduction of slavery, invalidating indentures, and allowing for the use of enslaved labor at the Shawneetown saltworks.[14] A "yea" vote on this question amounted to a pro-slavery position, while a "nay" vote marked the delegate as antislavery.

The second slavery vote that passed 17–14 on 19 August approved Leonard White's motion to hold those bound to indentures to the specific performance of those contracts for their duration and emancipated their descendants at age twenty-five.[15] A "yea" vote on this question amounted to a pro-slavery ballot; those voting "nay" were choosing the antislavery position.

The third slavery vote on Seth Gard's motion to strike out section 2 entirely forbidding the hiring of enslaved persons except at the Shawneetown saltworks was defeated by a margin of twenty-one nays to ten yeas on 20 August. In this instance, "yea" votes marked the antislavery position, while "nay" designated those favoring slavery.[16]

Over the course of these three votes, there were four factions that emerged. The largest group was composed of thirteen delegates who were *completely pro-slavery*—those voting yea/yea/nay.[17] The second largest faction was composed of seven delegates who were *completely antislavery*—those voting nay/nay/yea.[18] The two remaining factions included eleven delegates who fit Harris's definition of "compromisists." One of these—the group encompassing six delegates who *leaned antislavery* (the third largest faction) included those voting either yea/nay/yea or nay/nay/nay.[19] The other bloc of "compromisists"—the smallest contingent—was composed of five delegates who *leaned pro-slavery*—they voted either yea/nay/nay or nay/yea/nay.[20]

Overall, then, there were eighteen delegates who were either fully or primarily pro-slavery, outnumbering the thirteen who were either fully or predominantly antislavery.[21] Clearly, "compromisists" held the balance of power in such a way that restrictions on slavery in the constitution were relatively limited and Illinois became a state where slaveholding was at least partially tolerated. This became manifest the following year when the first state legislature (which included ten members of the constitutional convention) passed the state's first "black code" that placed severe restrictions on civil rights of African Americans and made their emigration into the state difficult, if not altogether impossible.

In general, slaveholding delegates voted along pro-slavery lines. Only three of them sided in any way with the antislavery contingent, with two of them (Caldwell Cairns and Thomas Kirkpatrick) among the faction that was partially antislavery. Levi Compton was the only slaveholder who cast all three votes in complete opposition to the institution.

Evaluating the motivations of the ostensibly antislavery delegates who voted pro-slavery is complicated. Joseph Kitchell and John Messinger are cases in point. As evidenced by his 1829 speech in the state senate, Kitchell's opposition to the institution appears to have been rooted in a distinct discomfort with the very presence of African Americans whether enslaved or free. His voting with the fully pro-slavery faction is consistent with this point of view. At first glance Messinger's position eludes easy analysis. A New Englander by birth, he had migrated over the course of his life from Massachusetts to Vermont, where he became a skilled carpenter and a millwright and received training in mathematics, cartography, and surveying. In 1799 he arrived in Kentucky with his father-in-law Matthew Lyon, his brother-in-law George Cadwell, and their families. Here he presumably came into contact with slavery for the first time. Reportedly revolted by that experience, he and Cadwell migrated across the Ohio River three years later.[22]

On at least two occasions in the years before the convention, Messinger publicly expressed his opinion of slavery in petitions sent to Congress. In 1806 his name was affixed to a request that the Illinois Country be separated from Indiana Territory and that Congress lift the Northwest Ordinance's ban on slavery. "However unnecessary this state of servitude may be thought in the eastern part of this territory [i.e., Indiana itself], no man has doubted its importance here, where among whites health and labour are almost incompatible."[23] In the second instance, Messinger signed a petition in 1808 again requesting division of the territory and objecting this time to the toleration of indentures of enslaved persons.[24]

In this context historian Francis Philbrick expressed puzzlement that the delegate from St. Clair County would side completely with the pro-slavery faction in August 1818, especially given that in 1823 he acted as president of an antislavery convention in Belleville seeking to prevent the institution from taking root in Illinois. Philbrick speculated that "it is possible that Messinger was a man whose opinions could be changed by argument."[25] It is also conceivable that his view of slavery resembled Kitchell's—that is to say, it was not so much that he was morally opposed to the institution. Rather, it had everything to do with his uneasiness with the presence of African Americans in Illinois.

Geographical voting patterns by county are likewise intriguing. Delegates in each of seven counties voted as blocs. The Edwards, Johnson, and Union delegations were *completely* antislavery, while Madison, Monroe, and Washington were *predominantly* antislavery. The delegates from Gallatin, Jackson, and Randolph, by contrast, voted *completely* pro-slavery, while their colleagues from Crawford, Franklin, and Pope were divided between *completely* and *predominantly* pro-slavery votes. Those from Bond and St. Clair were evenly divided—that is to say, in each case half of the delegates were *completely* pro-slavery and the other half either *completely* or *predominantly* antislavery. All of the White County representatives were *predominantly* pro-slavery.[26]

It is difficult to draw any conclusions about a possible correspondence between the number of enslaved persons in each county and the net pro-slavery or antislavery position of its representatives at the convention. It is not surprising that the delegates from Gallatin County, with the largest number of enslaved persons in the territory (321), voted consistently as a group along pro-slavery lines. However, St. Clair County, with the second most enslaved persons (88), was equally divided between the two factions, while Madison County, with 77 enslaved persons, leaned to the antislavery position. White (57), and Jackson (53) sided with Gallatin. Full data on the population of enslaved persons in Edwards (*completely* antislavery) and Randolph (*completely* pro-slavery) are no longer extant.[27]

Disappointed Slavocrats

How, in the end, did the convention arrive at a consensus regarding Article VI? In 1840, newspaper editor Hooper Warren, who in 1824 played a leading role in successfully opposing a second constitutional convention that had the potential for transforming Illinois into a fully slave state, claimed that Benjamin Stephenson had told him that "a decided majority of the delegates were in favor of admitting slavery." According to Warren, Stephenson believed that this was prevented as a result of the influence of Ninian Edwards, Nathaniel Pope, and Daniel Pope Cook. "As this fact was known to the disappointed slavocrats," Warren continued, "they conceived the design of trying the question again at a future period." There is no contemporary evidence to support Warren's claim, although Stephenson was a close friend and political ally of the governor.[28] There is something to Warren's assertion that a majority of the delegates favored legalizing slavery, although their endorsement of the institution was intended to skirt Congress's admonition that the constitution be "not repugnant" to the

Northwest Ordinance. But the reality is that ultimately credit for the passage of Article VI in its final form seems to rest largely with Elias Kent Kane and his ally Jesse B. Thomas. They were "determined to prevent fire from breaking out," wrote historian Matthew Hall, hoping to "preserve the possibility of approving slavery in Illinois in the future, but . . . decided they could not submit a constitution openly authorizing slavery. Their strategy seems to have been to achieve as much as they thought possible in the original constitution and to set the stage for a revision of the constitution after statehood."[29]

It is in this context that the convention's disposition of the next section of the constitution—Article VII, which dealt with the amendment process—assumed particular significance. Kane and his colleagues created this provision largely by drawing upon similar sections in the Ohio and Indiana constitutions. The one obvious change appears relatively innocuous. Ohio's charter had directed that the question of calling a constitutional convention be sent to the voters upon a two-thirds vote of the general assembly—that is to say, two-thirds of those present. Illinois's provision clarified that this vote should amount to "two-thirds of the whole number of members elected to" the general assembly. In effect, Illinois was setting a higher bar for revising its constitution. More important was what the Kaskaskia convention left out. Both Ohio and Indiana had specifically decreed that under no circumstances could the constitution be altered so as to allow the introduction of slavery or indentured servitude. In Article VII of the Illinois constitution this provision was absent. The article's precise wording was approved on 15 August—significantly, immediately after the delegates voted to postpone full consideration of Article VI—and it was approved in its final form on 20 August, immediately after the third and last vote on the slavery provisions.[30] Providing for the continuing tolerance of slavery while refusing to definitively rule out its full legalization in the future seems to have been a deliberate choice by the convention.

Having decided to constrain the civil rights of Illinois's African American denizens, the convention declared its dedication to fundamental civil liberties for everyone else in Article VIII—freedom of worship, freedom of assembly and the press, and the right to trial by jury, due process of law, protection against double jeopardy, and the right to *habeas corpus*. Article VIII seems to have been largely drawn again from Ohio's and Indiana's constitutions and to a lesser extent from those of Kentucky and Tennessee. Its section 15 prohibited imprisonment for debt if the debtor first "deliver[ed] up his estate for the benefit of his creditor or creditors." On 20 August, Elias Kent Kane, perhaps thinking of his father's and uncle's bankruptcies, moved successfully to outlaw imprisonment for debt "unless upon refusal to deliver up his estate for the benefit of his creditors . . . or in cases where there is strong presumption of fraud."[31] Section 20 of Article VIII introduced one feature not present in any of the other constitutional models. It provided that tax levies would be by valuation, "so that every person shall pay a tax in proportion to the value of the property, he or she has in his or her possession."[32]

In the end, the effort to determine the status of slavery in the new state of Illinois—both upon admission and in the uncertain future—was first and foremost an attempt to codify the conflicting sentiments of the public at large within the territory. In that endeavor the convention of 1818 largely succeeded. But the delegates—and none more than Kane and Thomas—were also mindful of the audience far to the east in the nation's capital, where a wary Congress stood ready to judge the extent to which Illinois's new constitution was in accord with—or repugnant to—the Northwest Ordinance.

15
FAIT ACCOMPLI

Over the course of its brief existence, the convention of 1818 was an exercise in navigating a variety of troublesome terrains. First, there was a reckoning with political geography that sought a more general distribution of power. This had resulted in the creation of a governing structure that was intended to enable the popular will and constrain executive authority. Second, the convention negotiated a social geography that defined hierarchies based upon racial lines. As with everything in Illinois history, these realities were inextricable from the state's actual geography, which the convention likewise sought to master through the selection and location of a physical, political center—a state capital. And once again Elias Kent Kane provided crucial leadership to the convention in surmounting these challenges.

But first the convention was faced with the task of clearing up a variety of odds and ends. On 15 August they approved an ordinance "without amendment" accepting the federal enabling act's propositions that devoted land to the use of schools, granted all salt springs and reserved 5 percent of all land sales proceeds to the state to fund roads leading to the state and for the encouragement of learning, reserved land for the use of a seminary of learning, and exempted land sales and military bounty lands from taxation for varying periods. The convention also agreed that lands held by non-Illinoisans would never be subject to higher taxation than those held by inhabitants.[1] Their decision to approve the ordinance without changes underscored their recognition that in the wake of compromising Illinois's status as a free state, it would not be advisable to create any further controversy.

Upon completion of the first reading of the draft constitution on 15 August, Joseph Kitchell moved the creation of a five-man committee to consider any additional further articles or sections. The delegates designated Kitchell, Adolphus F. Hubbard, Joseph Borough, George Fisher, and John Messinger—but not, strangely, Elias Kent Kane—to serve in this capacity. All except Borough (who leaned antislavery) were from the completely pro-slavery faction. Later that day Hubbard reported the committee's recommendation that apportionment of legislators be set and elections scheduled as soon as possible. The convention did so three days later and directed that polling take place "on the days prescribed by the laws of the territory of Illinois."[2]

Drafts and Logistics

On 18 August Hubbard reported a schedule of sixteen additional sections. Although the first draft of the schedules has not survived, it is possible to largely reconstruct it by working backward from the final document through changes specified in the convention journal. The document produced by the schedule drafting committee was primarily drawn from the Ohio and Indiana constitutions, with some text traceable to Kentucky and to a lesser extent Tennessee and New York.

Many of the proposed schedules were logistical in nature, dealing with issues such as the transition from territory to state, conditions for handling public monies, county governance, apportionment of members of the General Assembly, administration of oaths of office, the use of the state seal, and the first elections. The subjects of two of the draft schedules are not known, as the convention journal simply refers to them as having been stricken from the document. One of these schedules—section 3—may have been related to the issue of slavery; it was the pro-slavery Leonard White who proposed its deletion on 18 August, and it was the partially antislavery Caldwell Cairns of Monroe County who moved the following day—unsuccessfully—to reconsider that action.[3]

Sections 11–15 of the schedules establishing the office of lieutenant governor were moved to Article III on motion of Elias Kent Kane on 18 August.[4] A separate related and rather curious provision was added to the schedules toward the very end of the convention that any person who had resided in Illinois for two years before his election would be eligible for this office, "anything in the thirteenth section of the third article of this constitution contained to the contrary notwithstanding."[5] Governor Thomas Ford explained that this was specifically to accommodate the highly regarded Pierre Menard, who "was generally looked to to fill the office of lieutenant governor." Under Article III, section 13, those serving in this capacity were required to have been a U.S. citizen for thirty years. Menard had only recently become a naturalized American citizen, and consequently the convention changed the constitution specifically to enable him to serve.[6]

The schedules also included another of the few truly original innovations devised by the convention. On 20 August Caldwell Cairns proposed "[t]hat it shall be the duty of the general assembly to enact such laws as may be necessary and proper to prevent the practice of dueling." A native Pennsylvanian who practiced medicine, Cairns had dwelt in the territory since at least 1800. His long residence meant that his memory extended back to the feud between Dr. James Dunlap and Rice Jones in 1808. Cairns may also have had in mind the political conflict that nearly resulted in an affair of honor between Ninian Edwards and Jesse B. Thomas in 1814. Solon Buck intimated that there may have been a connection between this proposal and another resolution suggested unsuccessfully earlier that same day by Cairns to allow for settling differences through arbitration.[7]

Section 12 expanded on suffrage qualifications to enable all white males twenty-one or older to vote who had resided in the state six months or longer. On 21 August Joseph Borough offered a resolution that would have enabled all such men to vote who were residents at the time of the first election, "provided however, that nothing herein shall be so construed as to extend any further than the first election under the direction of this constitution." The convention rejected the resolution the next day by a vote of 28–3, possibly because they felt that the last clause was ambiguous. Only Borough and his Madison County colleagues Abraham Prickett and Benjamin Stephenson supported the motion. Borough presented a revision to the convention on 24 August that simply decreed that all white males resident at the time of the signing of the constitution would "have a right to a vote at the election to be held on the third Thursday and the two following days of September next." This rewording made it clear that lifting the six months' residency requirement was a one-time occurrence. It was approved by a vote of 18–12.[8]

The Permanent Seat of Government

The issue that occasioned the most discussion and conflict in the convention—after slavery—was the subject of section 15: locating the new state's seat of government. Congress had stayed silent on the question; in fact, of the three earliest states formed from the Northwest Territory, only Indiana's enabling act had addressed it. In that statute, the federal government had granted four sections of land to Indiana for this purpose.[9]

But there was no such directive in Illinois's enabling act. Identifying a state capital had not been an issue during the convention campaign. Solon Buck highlighted an advertisement appearing in the *Intelligencer* of 3 June 1818 that promoted the prospective town of Ripley in Bond County, with its "central and eligible situation in the territory" giving "rise to a strong presumption, that it will at no distant period become the seat of government." One of Ripley's proprietors listed in the prospectus was future delegate Abraham Prickett of Madison County.[10] Nevertheless, the general assumption during the campaign seems to have been that the government would remain at Kaskaskia.

The members of the convention, however, had other ideas. The temptation for personal and political opportunity, contemporary observer William H. Brown affirmed, was too strong to resist. "Kaskaskia was the focus of influence, and, by the least exertion, it would have retained its superiority. Its principal citizens were, however, interested in commanding points north of it, and, should a change be made, it was confidently anticipated that those individual points would be chosen."[11]

The delegates began deliberating the issue on Tuesday, 18 August when Adolphus Hubbard from the five-man committee appointed to consider additional articles presented a report "accompanied with sundry propositions in writing" to donate land for a capital "from the proprietors of Pope's bluff, Hill's ferry, and Covington." Two days later the convention resolved "that it is expedient at this time to remove the seat of government from the town of Kaskaskia."[12] Moved by the speculating spirit, the delegates immediately began a frenzied clamoring for anointment of their own particular choice locations, or at the very least, for their own particular methods of choosing a site.

Seth Gard of Edwards County proposed the appointment of what amounted to a blue-ribbon panel. Its five commissioners would be charged with the responsibility of examining sites on the Kaskaskia River above the baseline (an east-west line roughly along the northern boundary of modern-day Jefferson County) to determine the most suitable location.[13]

Andrew Bankson advocated for the selection of Covington in his own county of Washington. This town was still very much in the planning stages, but notices promoting the location for settlement had been appearing regularly in the pages of the *Intelligencer* since 13 May. Covington, the promoters declared, "is situated near the centre of the territorial population, and is surrounded by a rich beautiful and extensive tract of country; the site is high, dry and healthy, extending one mile on the margin of the Kaskaskia river." A subsequent advertisement dated 18 July 1818 and announcing the public sale of lots pronounced the area "a fertile and healthy neighborhood, scarcely surpassed by any in the territory in point of fertility of soil and pleasantness of situation." Tellingly, the latter notice was signed by James Bankson—Andrew Bankson's father—as well as by the late John K. Mangham and former delegate candidate William Bradsby.[14]

Perhaps alarmed at the prospect of the convention becoming derailed over an unnecessarily divisive issue, Elias Kent Kane offered a motion to keep the capital in Kaskaskia for five years. Leonard White of Gallatin agreed with Kane in retaining Kaskaskia for that duration, but he added a proposal to move the capital thereafter "to Pope's Bluff on the Kaskaskia river," which was near the location of the site that was ultimately chosen—Vandalia in Fayette County.[15] Half of the land tract suggested by White—320 acres of section 15 in what would become Vandalia Township—had been purchased in September 1816 for two dollars an acre by John Messinger, Nathaniel Pope, and Pope's law partner John Scott. Messinger, Pope, and Benjamin Stephenson purchased the remaining 320 acres of section 15 a month after the convention completed its labors. All told, these four speculators purchased 640 acres for a total price of $1,280 (about $22,000 today).[16] Pope, in fact, submitted a least two proposals to the convention through Messinger offering land for the future state capital. Only the second of these proposals, dated 24 August, has survived. It contained a promise from Pope to divide section 15 into lots, with "a handsome public Square for the capitol, at least four acres for a penitentiary, at least one acre for the Governor's house and one block of lots for the Great State College," dividing the remaining lots "equally with the State."[17] The advocacy of this region for the new state capital by Leonard White—another member of Ninian Edwards's territorial clique—illustrated once again the complicated ways in which political, personal, and financial relationships in Illinois were intertwined.[18] John Messinger had at one time made common cause with Edwards's enemy Jesse B. Thomas to work for the division of Indiana Territory in 1809. This had not prevented him, however, from aligning politically with the Edwards faction, nor was he about to refrain from taking advantage of an investment opportunity with Pope and Benjamin Stephenson, connected as they were to the governor through ties of family, friendship, and political interest.

Abraham Prickett, who had touted Ripley in Bond County as a possible state capital during the height of the convention campaign, offered at this point instead a more detailed motion to select Hill's Ferry—"now called Fredonia"—in what is now Clinton County. Elias Kent Kane responded with a motion to retain the capital in Kaskaskia for four years, "after which time, the general assembly shall have power to remove the same."[19]

Like Gard, Adolphus Hubbard proposed the appointment of five commissioners to investigate possible sites. They would be charged with selecting "the most convenient places and report the same to the next session of the general assembly, who may either reject the whole or select some one from among the places reported, for the seat of government for this state."[20]

All of these motions—Gard's, Bankson's, Kane's, White's, Prickett's, and Hubbard's—were summarily voted down by the delegates.[21] Gard moved on

21 August that the capital remain at Kaskaskia until further provided for by the General Assembly, which would be required to ask Congress for preemption rights on "four sections of land on the Kaskaskia river as near as may be, east of the third principal meridian on said river, to be selected by five commissioners." If the petition to Congress failed, the General Assembly would then choose some other site. The motion passed by a vote of 18–13. All those identified as having vested interests or representing others involved in land speculation—Bankson, Messinger, Stephenson, and White—voted in opposition, as did Prickett.[22] Oddly, Hubbard sided with the naysayers in spite of the fact that the proposal was very similar to his motion of the day before. Elias Kent Kane voted in favor of the plan, presumably for the same reason. Gard made a few more wording changes and presented a revised resolution on 24 August. White attempted to alter it drastically to retain the capital in Kaskaskia "until the general assembly shall otherwise provide," but he was voted down by a margin of 16–15.

The situation was at a standstill. Not only were delegates unable to definitively agree on the capital's location, but they had also failed even to reach consensus on whether it should be relocated at all. Consequently, in the absence of a fixed "permanent seat of government" (as Gard's proposal had termed it), a temporary resolution would have to suffice. And to that end Elias Kent Kane stepped forward once again to provide the convention with a sense of direction. White's resolution had declared that the site selected for the capital "shall be the permanent seat of government for this state." Kane advocated for the removal of the word "permanent" and for setting a time limit for the capital to remain at that site: "[W]hich town so laid out shall be the seat of government for this state for the term of twenty years." The convention approved the change by a margin of 25–6, with Prickett, Stephenson, and White among the "nay" votes.[23]

The Work of Fallible Man

It was Elias Kent Kane's final triumph in the convention and, indeed, the final mention of him in the convention journal, for the single surviving copy of that document is missing a few pages at the end. As a result there is no direct record of any actions taken after 24 August. But what remains provides substantial evidence of Kane's influence upon the convention of 1818. He had submitted the most motions of any member present on a variety of issues, ranging from the procedural to voting qualifications to the separation of powers to the establishment of a state capital. His hand was evident in a host of other actions, such as the formulation of the council of revision and—most importantly—the fate of slavery. He stood apart from his fellow delegates as a member not only of the initial drafting committee but also as a member of the enrollments committee charged at the end of the convention with verifying the accuracy of the finished document.[24] In short, no other member had been so extensively involved in every aspect of the constitution's creation from conception to completion, fully justifying Thomas Ford's description of Kane as the "principal member" of the convention.

In the end analysis the first Illinois constitution was neither particularly distinctive nor innovative. Its only genuinely original features were the ban on dueling and the imposition of tax levies by valuation. Indeed, its lack of innovation underscores the extent to which it was devised—deliberately—in haste. In large measure this is a tribute to the skills of Elias Kent Kane and Jesse B. Thomas in guiding the convention to a successful conclusion and successfully treading a thin line with regard to the slavery issue. In the process the convention sought to give Illinois the veneer of a free state while nevertheless tolerating the institution and leaving open the possibility of its transformation to a genuine slave state at some point in the future. It was, to be sure, a calculated risk. They were well aware that Illinois had far less room for maneuvering on the question of slavery than had been the case for any of the other states that had emerged from the Northwest Territory, especially given that there was no guarantee that Congress would accept their word that the territory's population met the standards set forth in the enabling act. Consequently, James Simeone observed, "the convention bent over backward to make the document as uncontroversial and acceptable to Congress as was palatable."[25] They understood that speed was of the essence. It was vitally important that they make statehood a *fait accompli*, which also helps to explain the subsequent quick election of a governor, state legislators, a member of Congress, and two senators. They gambled that Congress would neither notice nor care that the new constitution tolerated slavery. "There shall be neither slavery nor involuntary servitude in the said territory," the Northwest Ordinance had declared. Its status in any states formed from the territory was another matter, and the convention willingly grasped at this straw of ambiguity. In effect, the constitution failed to settle the issue, leaving any final decision to a later date to be determined.

Ultimately, the specifics of the constitution were secondary to the reality of admission that would open up all the opportunities of public office, of private gain at public expense.[26] As "Citizen" remarked a month later in reviewing their work, "At the out set we will premise that we do not either indiscriminately approve or disapprove of the whole constitution. But we consider it to be the work of fallible man, and that it possesses both merits and defects."[27]

What mattered at this point was that the constitution served to transform the very character of the relationship between the federal government and the people of Illinois. Illinois had made a unique transition from a supplicant confronting a far more powerful national government to the lofty status of a state in the Union. Now the toast that had been offered at Kaskaskia's Fourth of July celebration in 1813—"To the Illinois Territory—May she soon rise and join the Federal Confederation"[28]—was finally coming to fruition. It was a heady and energizing feeling.

On 26 August the delegates signed the completed document. Upon adjourning they joined Ninian Edwards, Joseph Philips, Nathaniel Pope, and many of the citizens of Kaskaskia in witnessing a celebratory rifle salute: "20 rounds were fired," reported the *Illinois Intelligencer*, "and one for the new state of Illinois."

> This was truly a proud day for the citizens of Illinois—a day on which hung the prosperity and hopes of thousands yet to follow—a day which will long be remembered & spoken of with enthusiastic pride; as a day connected with the permanent prosperity of our literary, political and religious institutions—as the main pillar in the edifice of our state independence, and justly the basis of our future greatness.[29]

EPILOGUE: THE ROAD TO KASKASKIA

Ninian Edwards sat at leisure in his home at what is now the corner of Fillmore and East Vandalia Streets in Edwardsville. Two weeks after the convention had adjourned and the celebrations had subsided, he was making the case for his elevation to national office by announcing his candidacy for the U.S. Senate. "[I]f I should be elected," he wrote, "my best talents shall be exerted to protect the interest; and to promote the prosperity of our Infant state. . . . My fellow citizens cannot have forgotten with what zeal, I endeavoured to obtain for them the right of preemption—the right of suffrage—compensation for losses—pay for their services etc. etc. etc."[1]

Fittingly, Edwards's rival, Jesse B. Thomas, was one of five other candidates for the same position. No doubt the governor took some satisfaction in his election to the Senate by the General Assembly on the first ballot, while Thomas was compelled to endure three votes before achieving the same result.[2] Nevertheless, in the end there was something for almost everyone. Running without opposition, Thomas's ally Shadrach Bond was elected the first governor. Pierre Menard (who was associated politically with Governor Edwards)[3] triumphed over two other candidates (including convention delegate Edward N. Cullom) to become the first lieutenant governor. Ten men who had served in the convention (and four who had sought election to that body but had been defeated) were elected to the General Assembly.[4]

Left out of the largesse—at least initially—were Elias Kent Kane, Daniel Pope Cook and Nathaniel Pope. Cook, of course, had been one of the first to announce his intention to run for public office by seeking the new state's single congressional seat. In the thick of his campaign in September he alluded to questions that had been raised concerning his commitment to the new constitution. This he found curious given that "I was the first person in the state who urged the propriety of petitioning congress for leave to form a state government."[5] His opponent was Jesse B. Thomas's ally John McLean, who had announced his candidacy a mere two weeks after Cook. A native of

North Carolina born in 1791, McLean and his parents immigrated to Logan County, Kentucky, around 1795, where in 1810 his father was listed as the owner of seven enslaved persons. Like Cook and Kane, McLean began the study of law at an early age. He traveled north and settled in 1815 in Shawneetown, where he was admitted to the bar the following year.[6] He quickly made a name for himself in the profession to the extent that he was offered—and turned down—the position of judge of the Eastern Circuit on the same day that Daniel Pope Cook was appointed as judge of the Western Circuit—the same position that Kane later refused.[7] Like his colleague, McLean probably preferred the prospect of an office under a state government over one that was bound to be a short-term sinecure.

The campaign for the U.S. House underscored the intensity of the struggle between the two factions over the question of slavery. Cook and McLean argued their opposing positions in a series of public debates "in all the principal counties"; with regard to "oratory and interest," contemporary observer Orlando B. Ficklin deemed them superior to the U.S. Senate campaign debates between Abraham Lincoln and Stephen A. Douglas four decades later: "So sincere and defiant was [Cook's] advocacy of liberty for all, slavery for none . . . that his opponents gave him the nick-name of 'that d—d little Yankee.'" In a fitting conclusion to such a closely fought contest, McLean prevailed by only fourteen votes in spite of winning fewer counties (seven) than Cook (eight).[8]

Pope and Kane had announced their candidacies to represent Randolph County in the state house of representatives in the waning days of the convention. Kane evidently withdrew from that contest; Pope remained, but he ultimately finished third in a field of four candidates. Neither Kane, Cook, nor Pope were forgotten, however; the first two were respectively appointed secretary of state and attorney general by the General Assembly, while Pope was elevated to register of the Edwardsville federal land office and subsequently received a commission as Illinois's first federal judge.[9] There was no definitive proof of a deal to distribute offices among the two factions, "but when the unanimity with which the various officers were chosen is considered," wrote historian Charles Manfred Thompson, "one is led to believe that at least a temporary truce had been declared."[10]

Perpetuating the Union

Almost lost in the electoral rush was the reality that Illinois was still not yet a state in the Union. The speedy establishment of a state political infrastructure underscored the confidence of territorial leaders that congressional approval was a mere formality. If that was the case, John McLean was in for something of a rude awakening.

The congressman and the new state constitution arrived in the nation's capital at about the same time. Convention secretary William Greenup had sent the document on 11 September to Speaker of the House Henry Clay, who submitted it to the House of Representatives on 16 November.[11] It was with some embarrassment that three days later Clay publicly expressed his reservations about administering McLean's oath of office, given that Illinois had not yet been formally admitted to the Union, and he deferred to the judgment of the House. George Poindexter of Mississippi argued that the House should determine whether the conditions of the enabling act had been met and whether the form of government was republican. He wondered what the implications would be if McLean were seated and allowed to vote on legislation, only to have admission defeated. William Henry Harrison—former governor of Indiana Territory and now a congressman from Ohio—thought differently, arguing that the House had already taken those points for granted and had by definition seated the gentleman from Illinois. Timothy Pitkin of Connecticut sided with Poindexter, contending that Illinois's status should be decided first, especially with regard to its population. The House voted to delay administering the oath, and the constitution was referred to a select committee composed of Poindexter, Richard Clough Anderson Jr. of Kentucky, and William Hendricks of Indiana.[12]

The trio reported a draft resolution the following day declaring Illinois's admission into the Union. It was read twice, whereupon Anderson proposed it be engrossed for a third reading. First, however, John Canfield Spencer of New York—former member of the House select committee that had drafted the enabling act the previous spring—inquired after documentation that Illinois had met the population threshold. Anderson rather lamely replied that "the committee had no information on that subject before them, beyond what was contained in the preamble to the constitution. . . . [T]he committee had considered that evidence sufficient; and he had, in addition, himself seen, in the newspapers, evidence sufficient to satisfy him of the fact, that the population did amount to forty thousand souls, the number required."[13]

Three days later—Monday, 23 November 1818—the third reading took place, followed by a vigorous debate focusing upon the questions of population and the status of slavery. The first speaker was James Tallmadge of New York, who only three months later would touch off the Missouri Compromise crisis by proposing that slavery be gradually eliminated in that new state. Tallmadge later recalled that in his remarks during the Illinois statehood debate he had "mentioned that our enemies had drawn a picture of our country, as holding in one hand the Declaration of Independence, and the other brandishing a whip over our affrighted slaves."[14] He argued that Congress should accept Illinois's constitution—and therefore admit the state to the Union—only if it were clearly in compliance with Article VI of the Northwest Ordinance. The new constitution, he argued, "embraced a complete recognition of existing slavery . . . particularly in the passage wherein they permit the hiring of slaves, the property of non-residents, for any number of years consecutively."[15] Poindexter intimated in response that Illinois's approach was an acceptable compromise, and he emphasized that the requirement that enslaved persons be registered was "more secure to the freedom of the people of color, that their births, parentage, &c., should be recorded in the new State." Anderson added—and Harrison agreed—that when all was said and done, the people of Illinois were not ultimately bound by the Northwest Ordinance.

For all the intensity of the debate, once the question of Illinois's admission was put before the entire House it passed with ease by a margin of 117–34. Nearly half of the favorable votes were supplied by representatives from the western states—free and slaveholding alike—and the states of the southern Atlantic seaboard, with not a single nay vote among any of them. The Middle Atlantic states cast 45 votes in favor and 15 against, while New England voted 14 in favor and 19 against. Of the eight congressmen who had served with Nathaniel Pope on the two committees that worked on the enabling act the previous spring, only Ezekiel Whitman of Massachusetts—like the plurality of his fellow New Englanders—opposed statehood.[16]

The drama occasioned by Illinois statehood in the House of Representatives did not follow the bill into the Senate. Senators-elect Edwards and Thomas were nowhere to be found when the admission bill reached the upper house on 25 November, was read twice, and then referred to the Committee on Public Lands. That body was largely unchanged from seven months earlier when it had considered the statehood enabling act. Two of its members—Jeremiah Morrow of Ohio and Waller Taylor of Indiana—were from the Old Northwest, and a third—Thomas Hill Williams of Mississippi—represented the most recent state admitted to the Union. They acted with dispatch, reporting a resolution of admission the next day with no changes. It was considered by the Committee of the Whole and reported to the full Senate on Monday 30 November, where it was read a third time and passed on 1 December.[17] And three days later Ninian Edwards was able to scribble a terse note to both the *Illinois Intelligencer* and the Shawneetown *Illinois Emigrant* announcing that President Monroe had approved the measure.[18] By then he was writing in his official capacity as U.S. senator, having just been sworn into office along with his colleagues Thomas and McLean.[19]

Illinois had entered the Union in the face of some substantial challenges. In the wake of the War of 1812, there was no longer any prospect of diverting the settlers' loyalties to foreign powers. Saddled with officials accountable only to the Congress and the president and armed only with a nonvoting territorial delegate, they had fulminated against a "semi-monarchical" regime. Faced with the prospect of an insufficient population for admission, they managed first to lower the standard—from sixty thousand to forty thousand—and then to fabricate the result. Deprived of the full benefits of federally funded infrastructure improvements, they consoled themselves with an extension of the northern boundary and the acquisition of Chicago. Recognizing that explicit tolerance of slavery in their new constitution would violate the Northwest Ordinance, they concealed it under the cloak of "indentures" and consigned abolition to the Great Hereafter.

And so Illinois stood ready to assume its proper place in the Union—socially, politically, economically, and—most important—geographically. With transportation networks reaching out in every direction—to the south and west via the Mississippi, to the south and east by way of the Ohio and the Wabash, and to the northeast through the Great Lakes—the Prairie State was uniquely positioned to exert a significant influence upon the entire American nation. "Its great extent of territory, its unrivalled fertility of soil and capacity for sustaining a dense population, together with its commanding position," wrote Governor Thomas Ford, were destined to bind Illinois firmly to every region of the country through "[a]ssociations in business, in interest, and of friendship. . . . A State thus situated, having such a decided interest in the commerce and in the preservation of the whole confederacy, can never consent to disunion; for the Union cannot be dissolved without a division and disruption of the State itself." Not only would Illinois amplify the larger growth and development of the American nation, but its very presence might also ultimately serve to perpetuate the entire Union.[20]

But attaining statehood was only the beginning of a long process. And the citizens of Illinois fully understood the true historical weight of the moment. At the very end of a remarkable year, the *Intelligencer* observed: "Indeed this is the epoch, which must, in a great degree, fix the destiny of Illinois."[21]

The Shafts of Party Rancor

Most of the members of the convention of 1818 remained active in public life in Illinois long after the state had been admitted to the Union. As a group they were candidates for, served in, or were appointed to over two hundred public offices ranging from members of the General Assembly to justices of the peace to county commissioners. All but three—Andrew Bankson, Isham Harrison, and Jesse B. Thomas—lived out their lives in the Prairie State. Thomas's time in the U.S. Senate was highlighted by his authorship of the Missouri Compromise, which "he regarded as probably the most important act of his life." After leaving the Senate in 1829, he "gave up his slaves and indentured servants, moved to Ohio, and became a Whig and a member of a church opposed to slavery." Tragically, he committed suicide in 1853, despondent, Matthew Hall speculated, over "the death of his wife and other close family members and the impending demise of the Missouri Compromise."[22]

Thomas's mortal political enemy Ninian Edwards left the Senate in 1824 with his reputation tainted as a result of making ill-advised and anonymous attacks on U.S. secretary of the treasury William Crawford. He went on, however, to serve as governor of Illinois from 1826 to 1830. After one last unsuccessful effort at a political comeback in the form of a campaign for Congress in 1832, he devoted himself to performing charity medical work in Belleville, where he died during a cholera outbreak in 1833 after refusing to abandon his stricken neighbors.[23]

Nathaniel Pope remained on the bench as a federal judge until his death in 1850. He developed a reputation as a stern but knowledgeable jurist. Anson Miller, who argued cases before him, remembered that Pope had a uniquely soft spot in his heart for Abraham Lincoln. The judge "would sometimes rebuke him [Lincoln], but in a sort of fatherly way." Others were not so fortunate. On one occasion another lawyer, David J. Baker, ostentatiously petitioned to be allowed to stand near the courtroom stove owing to an illness; Pope, Miller recalled, "with the utmost gravity, and in a deep, gruff voice, replied, 'Mr. Baker, the court don't care a damn where you stand!'"[24]

After serving as the first secretary of state, in 1820 Elias Kent Kane ran against Daniel Pope Cook to represent Illinois in Congress. During that campaign there were persistent rumors of a secret plan to transform Illinois from a free to a slave state. Kane "denied he had been nominated by 'the old slave party,' [and] denounced the 'scheme to introduce slavery' as a combination that had never been thought of."[25] He lost that election, but four years later Kane was elected to the state legislature and soon afterward was selected for elevation to the U.S. Senate, where he became a supporter of Andrew Jackson. Fittingly, he served on the Committee on Public Lands that had been a crucial component of the admission process, and he helped pass a bill providing for the construction of the Illinois and Michigan Canal that connected the Illinois and Mississippi Rivers with the Great Lakes. He died from bilious fever in the middle of his second term in 1835.[26]

After his disappointing loss to John McLean in the contest to represent Illinois in Congress, Daniel Pope Cook resolved to try again. In April 1819 he wrote an open letter announcing his candidacy in the next election for Congress to be held the following August. He had striven, he declared, "to form a correct opinion on every subject involving the interest of the people, and . . . to convince others of its correctness." He acknowledged that his engagement in Illinois's political gauntlet had rendered him vulnerable "to the shafts of party rancor, and disappointed ambition; but believing firmness to be indispensably necessary to constitute a good citizen and safe politician, I have therefore, never shrunk from such assaults."[27]

As if to prove Cook's point, "$29.75" mockingly cast his letter into verse in the columns of the *Illinois Emigrant*:

> The late election bears so recent date,
> I deem it useless to reiterate
> The many promises I made you then:
> Please to accept those promises *again*. . . .
> I'm well aware, in following such a course,
> I unavoidably shall show my ———;
> And undergo, in this exposed condition,
> Some lusty kicks from Rancor and Ambition.
> But having always entertained the notion,
> That *kicking* is essential to promotion,
> I will not deem this sufferance a disaster,
> But call upon my foes to kick me faster.[28]

This time, however, Daniel Pope Cook managed to withstand such attacks on his character, prevailing over John McLean by over six hundred votes and winning ten counties to his opponent's nine. John Quincy Adams later wrote that McLean lost his seat "in consequence of voting on the Slavery side of the Missouri question at the last session."[29] Cook defeated Elias Kent Kane in the following campaign of 1820 and ultimately served until 1827, including a term as chairman of the House Ways and Means Committee. The passage of legislation (in concert with Kane and Jesse B. Thomas in the Senate) to grant land for the building of the Illinois and Michigan Canal was one of his most momentous achievements.[30] He was defeated for reelection in 1826, much to the surprise of many of his supporters. Ninian Edwards wrote Henry Clay soon afterward that Cook "and his friends felt too secure. None of them, with the exception of myself, could be induced to believe there was the least danger." And Cook, constrained by illness, was unable to compete with his opponent, Joseph Duncan, in campaigning directly for votes.[31] Adams believed that Cook's prospects for reelection were harmed by the latter's opposition to proposals by Senator Thomas Hart Benton of Missouri to reduce the price of public lands.[32] Cook had also endangered his political prospects by casting a crucial—perhaps even decisive—vote in Congress for Adams in the disputed presidential election of 1824. Duncan was a strong supporter of Adams's opponent Andrew Jackson. (Illinois had cast two electoral votes for Jackson and one for Adams, although the latter had received the most popular votes.[33]) Cook remained close to the president, and their relationship ended as it had begun with a diplomatic mission, a final long voyage to Cuba to observe and report on political conditions as well as to improve his declining health. He returned to his father's home in Kentucky thereafter, where he died in October 1827, leaving behind his wife Julia—the daughter of Cook's mentor, Ninian Edwards—and a young son. "In his last days," John Mason Peck wrote, "his frame was completely emaciated, his mind calm, until he sunk in death."[34]

* * * * * * * * * * * * * * * * * * *

If in 1818 all roads led to Kaskaskia, only one road leads there now, and it runs through Missouri. In seasons of heavy rains, that thoroughfare is frequently inundated with overflows from the Father of Waters. Such was the case the last time that I set out to visit Kaskaskia in the summer of 2011. With each passing mile the torrents grew deeper until it became plain that it would be foolhardy to venture any further. I stopped and looked eastward, hoping to catch a glimpse of the Church of the Immaculate Conception or perhaps even the shrine housing the Liberty Bell of the West, the only two vestiges left of the original town. But it was all for naught. Kaskaskia remained utterly separated, detached, and more remote than ever before.

Notes

Bibliography

Index

NOTES

Prologue

1. "Garrison Hill Cemetery, Ft. Kaskaskia, IL," https://web.archive.org/web/20120222194253/http://www.randolphcountyillinois.net/sub43.htm; Montague, *A Directory*, 119–23.
2. Reynolds, *Pioneer History of Illinois*, 294.
3. "Kaskaskia Village, Illinois," U.S. Census Bureau, https://data.census.gov/cedsci/table?q=Kaskaskia+village%2C+Illinois.
4. The Kaskaskia River has come to be called the "Okaw" over the years "because of the French way of saying that they were going *aux Kau*, to Kaskaskia." John T. Faris, *The Romance of Forgotten Towns* (New York: Harper & Brothers, 1924), 89.
5. Burnham, "Destruction of Kaskaskia," 98.
6. Gustavas Pape, quoted in ibid., 103.
7. Burnham, "Destruction of Kaskaskia," map following page 102.
8. John H. Burch, quoted in ibid., 106.
9. "Illinois Scrapbook," 290–91; Neely, *Tales and Songs*, 29.
10. *Blue Book of the State of Illinois 1927–1928*, 478.
11. Reynolds, *Pioneer History of Illinois*, 50; Reynolds, *My Own Times*, 17.
12. Howard, *Illinois*, 44.
13. Ibid., 57.
14. John Mason Peck, "The Religion and Morals of Illinois Prior to 1818," in Reynolds, *Pioneer History of Illinois*, 274.
15. Brown, "Early History of Illinois," 83–84.
16. Ibid., 85.
17. Masters, *Spoon River Anthology*, 288.
18. Bode, "Curse of Kaskaskia."

Introduction

1. Nathaniel Pope, "Postscript: State of Illinois; Extract of a letter from the Hon. N. Pope, to the Editors, dated Washington, April 15, 1818," *Western Intelligencer*, 6 May 1818, p. 3, cols. 3–4.

2. Nathaniel Pope, "Extract of a letter from the Hon. Nat Pope, to the Editors, dated Washington, Jan. 27, 1818," *Western Intelligencer*, 11 March 1818, p. 2, col. 4.
3. *Annals of Congress*, 15th Cong., 1st sess., 1677.
4. Buck, *Illinois in 1818*, xxv.
5. Hammond, "Uncontrollable Necessity," 141.
6. Ibid., 139.

1. Twenty Gallons of Whiskey

1. *Western Intelligencer*, 20 November 1817, p. 3, col. 2.
2. "Ordinance of 1787," in Verlie, *Illinois Constitutions*, 3–4, 6–7. Hereafter referred to as "Ordinance of 1787."
3. Perrin, *History of Bourbon, Scott*, 204.
4. *Return of the Whole Number of Persons within the Several Districts of the United States, According to "An Act Providing for the Enumeration of the Inhabitants of the United States"; Passed March the First, One Thousand Seven Hundred and Ninety-One* , 51; *Return of the Whole Number of Persons within the Several Districts of the United States, According to "An Act Providing for the Second Census or Enumeration of the Inhabitants of the United States"; Passed February the Twenty Eighth, One Thousand Eight Hundred*, 2P; Minnesota Population Center, "D050.V11.0.". Hereafter referred to as Minnesota Population Center.
5. Perrin, *History of Bourbon, Scott*, 203.
6. In a letter dated 1 July 1818 promoting his candidacy for the U.S. House of Representatives, Cook noted that the federal Constitution sets a minimum age for serving in that body at twenty-five. "[I]f men who have but just passed the age of 25, are better qualified than men of 45," he wrote, "the public interest is consulted and promoted by their election." Daniel Pope Cook, "To the electors of Illinois," *Illinois Intelligencer* (Kaskaskia, Ill. Territory: Blackwell & Berry), 8 July 1818, p. 2, col. 2. This supports the notion that he was born sometime in early 1793.
7. "Daniel Pope Cook"; Houck, *History of Missouri*, 1:377n.
8. Reynolds, *Pioneer History of Illinois*, 395.
9. Burns, "Daniel P. Cook," 425; Reynolds, *Pioneer History of Illinois*, 396.
10. Ahlstrom, *Religious History*, 433.
11. Singer, *History of the Baptist Church*, 7.
12. Ibid., 20–21.
13. Ibid., 21.
14. Ibid., 21–22, 23–24.
15. Jewett and Allen, *Slavery in the South*, 103.
16. Ibid., 100–101.

17. 1810 U.S. Federal Census (Population Schedule), Scott County, Kentucky, p. 169, John Cook household, and p. 183, Nathaniel Mothershead household; 1820 U.S. Federal Census (Population Schedule), Georgetown, Scott County, Kentucky, p. 335, John Cook household and Nathaniel Mothershead household.
18. Singer, *History of the Baptist Church*, 263–64.
19. "A Republican" [Daniel Pope Cook], "Slavery," *Western Intelligencer*, 1 April 1818, p. 3, col. 2.
20. 1810 U.S. Federal Census (Population Schedule), Scott County, Kentucky, pp. 167–93.
21. Egerton, *Gabriel's Rebellion*, x–xi, 188.
22. Ibid., 164–66.
23. Pease, *Story of Illinois*, 84–85.
24. Edwards, *History of Illinois*, 254. John Pope himself referred to Cook as "a student of mine" in a later letter of recommendation to the U.S. secretary of state. "John Pope to the [Secretary of State]," 30 September 1816, in Carter, *Territorial Papers*, 17:402.
25. Allen, *History of Kentucky*, 371.
26. John and Nathaniel Pope have been frequently and mistakenly referred to as Daniel Pope Cook's uncles. See Angle, "Nathaniel Pope," 143; Cook, *Daniel Pope Cook and John Cook*, 3; Burns, "Daniel P. Cook," 425; Carter, *Territorial Papers*, 17:455n; and Buck, *Illinois in 1818*, 194. Nancy Lee Grau, who studied Cook's genealogy in detail, concluded that they were at best only distantly related: "[A] brother of Daniel Cook's grandfather married a sister of John and Nathaniel Pope's grandfather." Grau, "Other Famous 19th Century Man," 4–5.
27. Reynolds, *Pioneer History of Illinois*, 395–96. William Shannon was "the principal merchant of Ste. Genevieve" (Houck, *History of Missouri*, 3:194).
28. Reynolds, *Pioneer History of Illinois*, 396; Peck, *Sermon*, 9.
29. Douglass, *History of Southeast Missouri*, 1:63.
30. Minnesota Population Center. More detailed information from the 1810 census is extant concerning only 7,267 individuals; of these, 629 (nearly 9 percent) were enslaved persons or indentured servants. Kaskaskia itself was home to 364 souls, 15 of whom were enslaved persons (4 percent). Norton, *Illinois Census Returns: 1810, 1818*, 24:xxx, 1–3.
31. Aron, *American Confluence*, xvii.
32. Ibid., 41–42, 55; Meyer, *Kaskaskia Chronology*, 2–3.
33. "Ordinance of 1787," 8.
34. French land grants were rectangular shaped and located perpendicular to the Mississippi. They had "a relatively short width (normally one or two arpents) [an arpent being roughly equivalent to 192 feet], and a great length stretching into the backlands." Buisseret, *Historic Illinois from the Air*, 34.
35. Ibid., 36.

2. *The Utmost Good Faith*

1. Lee, *Masters of the Middle Waters*, 4.
2. Eby, *"That Disgraceful Affair,"* 41.
3. "Ordinance of 1787," 6.
4. "Treaty with the Wyandot, Etc., 1795," in Kappler, *Indian Affairs*, 2:39–45.
5. Owens, "Jeffersonian Benevolence," 408.
6. Ibid., 417, 419; Lee, *Masters of the Middle Waters*, 9.
7. Thomas Jefferson to William Henry Harrison, 27 February 1803, Jefferson Papers, 1st Series, vol. 9, no. 208, in Esarey, *Messages and Letters*, 1:71.
8. Davis, *Frontier Illinois*, 119.
9. Buck, *Illinois in 1818*, 2–3.
10. Pease, *Story of Illinois*, 70.
11. Illinois, Secretary of State, Illinois State Archives, *Illinois Public Domain Land Tract Sales Database*. Hereafter referred to as *Illinois Public Domain Land Tract Sales Database.*
12. Pease, *Story of Illinois*, 71.
13. "Ordinance of 1787," 3–4; "Act of Congress, February 3, 1809," in Verlie, *Illinois Constitutions*, 13; Davidson and Stuvé, *Complete History of Illinois* , 283.
14. Pease, *Story of Illinois*, 72.
15. Edgar and the Morrisons were among those whose land claims were under investigation.
16. Rees, "Bond-Jones Duel," 273.
17. James Dunlap, "Kaskaskia, August 1803 [sic]," *Western Sun* (Vincennes, [Indiana Territory]: Elihu Stout), 27 August 1808, p. 3, cols. 1–2.
18. Rice Jones, [Letter to editor Elihu Stout dated 3 September 1808], *Western Sun*, 3 September 1808, p. 3, col. 2; Rice Jones, [Letter to the editor], ibid., 10 September 1808, p. 3, col. 3.
19. James Dunlap, [Letter to the editor], *Western Sun*, 1 October 1808, p. 3, col. 2.
20. "Extract of a letter from E. Backus, Esq. to his friend in Vincennes," *Western Sun*, 15 October 1808, p. 4, col. 3; Robert Robinson, "For the Western Sun," ibid., 22 October 1808, p. 3, cols. 2–3.
21. William Morrison, "For the Western Sun," *Western Sun*, 5 November 1808, p. 1, cols. 1–3.
22. "Spectator," "For the Western Sun," *Western Sun*, 29 April 1809, p. 1, col. 2.
23. Alvord, *Illinois Country*, 426–27.
24. Heerman, *Alchemy of Slavery*, 20, 22.
25. Flower, *History of the English Settlement*, 1:199; Harris, *History of Negro Servitude*, 14–15.
26. Gillespie, *Recollections of Early Illinois*, 10–11. Norman Dwight Harris identified this legislator as John Grammer (or Grammar) of Union County (Harris,

History of Negro Servitude, 7n). An unsuccessful candidate for the state constitutional convention in 1818, Grammer later served as a state senator representing Union County in the 3rd, 4th, 7th, and 8th General Assemblies ("Candidates," *Illinois Intelligencer*, 3 June 1818, p. 3, col. 2; *Blue Book of the State of Illinois 1931–1932*, 739–40, 742). In spite of his defense of slavery, he was not himself a slaveholder (Norton, *Illinois Census Returns 1820*, 293).

27. Philbrick, *Pope's Digest 1815, volume II*, 185–95, 247, 364–72.
28. Allison Mileo Gorsuch, "To Indent Oneself: Ownership, Contracts, and Consent in Antebellum Illinois," in Allain, *Legal Understanding of Slavery*, 140.
29. Sutton, "Edward Coles," 37–38.
30. Finkelman, "Slavery and the Northwest Ordinance," 366–67; Pease, Story of Illinois, 68.
31. Flower, *History of the English Settlement*, 199.
32. Daniel Pope Cook to the *Illinois Intelligencer*, 23 July 1818, *Illinois Intelligencer*, 29 July 1818, p. 3, col. 2. Emphasis in original.
33. William Henry Harrison, "Proclamation: Calling a Convention to Petition Congress to Allow Slavery in Indiana Territory," 22 November 1802, in Esarey, *Messages and Letters*, 1:60–61.
34. "Petition of the Vincennes Convention, December 28, 1802," in ibid., 1:62–67.
35. "Petition from Indiana, Slavery, Sept. 19, 1807," in ibid., 1:253–55.
36. "Randolph's Report on Slavery in Indiana, March 2, 1803," in ibid., 1:75–76.
37. "Second Report on Petition of the Vincennes Convention, February 17, 1804," "House Report,—Slavery, February 14, 1806," "Slavery Petition, February 12, 1807," "Senate Report on Slavery in Indiana, November 13, 1807," and "House Report on Slavery in Indiana, November 17, 1807," in ibid., 1:91–93, 187–90, 202–3, 274–76; *House Journal*, 8th Cong., 1st sess., 17 February 1804, 584–85.
38. "In the House of Representatives of the Indiana Territory, February 7th 1805," in Esarey, *Messages and Letters*, 1:173.
39. Lyon was the father-in-law of John Messinger, one of the signers, member of the territorial legislature, and future member of Illinois's first constitutional convention in 1818. When the lower house of the legislature approved another petition for division on 12 October 1808, Messinger sent Lyon a copy of the petition and requested him "to use your utmost exertions to get a division on some terms or other immediately." Harrington, *History of the Messenger Family*, 2:49–50.
40. "Petition to Congress by the People of the Illinois Country," referred 6 April 1808, in Carter, *Territorial Papers*, 7:546–49.
41. *Annals of Congress*, 10th Cong., 1st sess., 2067–68.
42. "Resolutions of the Territorial House of Representatives," 12 October 1808, in Carter, Territorial Papers, 7:601.
43. *Western Sun*, 29 October 1808, p. 3, col. 1.

44. "Veritas," "Interragatories for the Delegate from Indiana to Congress While at Washington," *Western Sun*, 5 November 1808, p. 1, col. 3.
45. *House Journal*, 10th Cong., 2nd sess., 13 December 1808, 385.
46. "No. 261. Division of Indiana into Two Territories," *American State Papers: Miscellaneous*, 1:945–46.
47. *House Journal*, 10th Cong., 2nd sess., 18 January 1809, 477–78; *Senate Journal*, 10th Cong., 2nd sess., 20 January 1809, 329; 24 January 1809, 331; 31 January 1809, 336; 7 February 1809, 340.

3. Ties of Blood

1. Thompson, "Illinois Whigs before 1846," 9.
2. Simeone, *Democracy and Slavery*, 91–92; John Pope to Ninian Edwards, 9 November 1809, in Washburne, *Edwards Papers*, 38.
3. Howard, *Illinois*, 77; Edwards, *History of Illinois*, 22.
4. Ibid., 15; *Howard, Illinois*, 76–77.
5. Bakalis, "Ninian Edwards," 21–22.
6. Edwards, *History of Illinois*, 19.
7. "John Pope to the President," 19 April 1809, in Carter, *Territorial Papers*, 16:24.
8. Bakalis, "Ninian Edwards," 60.
9. Edstrom, "Congress," 4; Bakalis, "Ninian Edwards," 49–50.
10. Ibid., 2.
11. "Ordinance of 1787," 2; Edstrom, "Congress," 1n.
12. "Ordinance of 1787," 3.
13. Simeone, *Democracy and Slavery*, 68.
14. "Acting Governor Pope to the Secretary of State," 11 May 1809, in Carter, *Territorial Papers*, 16:38.
15. "Governor Edwards to James Gilbreath," 28 June 1809, in ibid., 47–48.
16. Friends of the Benjamin Stephenson House, *"Life in Kentucky."* Benjamin Stephenson and his wife named their second daughter Elvira after Edwards's wife, and the Edwardses returned the favor some years later with the birth of their son Benjamin Stephenson Edwards (ibid.).
17. On 24 December 1814 the territorial legislature approved a measure to pay Nathaniel Pope three hundred dollars to revise "the laws of this Territory making an index to the same, and superintending the printing thereof. . . ." Philbrick, *Laws of Illinois Territory 1809–1818*, 178–79.
18. "Governor Edwards to Joseph Philips," 25 September 1816, in Carter, *Territorial Papers*, 17:414.
19. Warrant nos. 5658 "issued in favour of Danl P. Cook Engrossing & Enrolling Clerk to the Legislature at the last session," 30 December 1813, Record Series

105.004, Auditor of Public Accounts, Daybooks, 2 January 1813–30 September 1841, Illinois State Archives, Springfield, Illinois. Hereafter referred to as Record Series 105.004, Auditor of Public Accounts, "Daybooks."

20. Philbrick, *Laws of Illinois Territory 1809–1818*, 87–88, 89–90, 93.
21. Ibid., 91–92.
22. *History of St. Clair County, Illinois*, 209. The 1818 territorial census recorded that Risdon Moore Sr. and Risdon Moore Jr. were the owners of a total of eleven enslaved persons (Norton, *Illinois Census Returns: 1810, 1818*, 160–61). Four of these were emancipated in 1818, 1819, 1826, and 1827, respectively (Illinois, Secretary of State, Illinois State Archives, *Database of Servitude and Emancipation Records [1722–1863]*. Hereafter referred to as *Database of Servitude and Emancipation Records (1722–1863)*.
23. Peck, *Annals of the West*, 706.
24. For a full discussion of this so-called "Jefferson-Lemen Compact," see Edstrom, "A Mighty Contest," 192–215.
25. *Illinois Intelligencer*, 5 August 1818, p. 3, col. 2.
26. Philbrick, *Laws of Illinois Territory 1809–1818*, 140.
27. Daniel Pope Cook to Ninian Edwards, Kaskaskia, 30 November 1814, Ninian Edwards Papers, Chicago History Museum.
28. "Commission of William Mears as U.S. Attorney," 1 August 1813, in Carter, *Territorial Papers*, 16:352; "Executive Register for the Illinois Territory Commencing the 25th Day of April 1809," Carter, *Territorial Papers*, 17:651 (hereafter referred to as "Executive Register"); Thompson, "Illinois Whigs before 1846," 9–10.
29. Peck, *Sermon*, 9; Daniel Pope Cook to Ninian Edwards, 26 September 1820, in Washburne, *Edwards Papers*, 164–65; Illinois, Secretary of State, Illinois State Archives, *Illinois Statewide Marriage Index, 1763–1900*.
30. Philbrick, *Laws of Illinois Territory 1809–1818, 229*; "Executive Register," 654.
31. Philbrick, *Laws of Indiana Territory, 1801–1809*, 144–45. The provisions of the Indiana territorial code pertaining to the auditor of public accounts were retained in the Illinois code. Philbrick, *Laws of Illinois Territory, 1809–1818*, 63.
32. It is not abundantly clear precisely when Cook assumed ownership of the *Intelligencer*. The earliest extant issue bearing the designation "Dan'l P. Cook & Co." is dated 15 May 1816 (vol. 1, no. 4). Counting backward, vol. 1, no. 1 would have fallen on Wednesday, 24 April 1816. However, there is a notice in the issue of 15 May that is dated Saturday, 20 April 1816, so that may be the date of the first issue instead.
33. Putnam, "Life and Services of Joseph Duncan," 113; Miller, "Journalism in Illinois," 150.

34. D. P. Cook, "To the Public," *Western Intelligencer*, 29 May 1816, p. 3, col. 1; "Executive Register," 661, 664.
35. It also enabled Cook to advertise his legal services as well. A notice dated "April 20, 1816" in the earliest extant issue of the *Intelligencer* assured his readers that "[h]is arrangements for editing the W. Intelligencer will not at all interfere with his professional business." He also noted that he maintained his law office and the auditor's office in the same location (*Western Intelligencer*, 15 May 1816, p. 4, col. 3).
36. Daniel Pope Cook to Ninian Edwards, 8 June 1816, in Washburne, *Edwards Papers*, 123–25.
37. Scott, *Newspapers and Periodicals of Illinois*, xxxvii.
38. Carter, *Territorial Papers*, 17:403n.
39. *Illinois Public Domain Land Tract Sales Database.*
40. "John Pope to [the Secretary of State]," 30 September 1816, in Carter, *Territorial Papers*, 17:402.
41. "Benjamin Stephenson and Edward Hempstead to the President," 1 October 1816, in ibid., 404.
42. "Benjamin Stephenson to [the Secretary of State]," 14 October 1816, in ibid., 417.
43. Carter, *Territorial Papers*, 17:417n. John Mason Peck reported in 1827 that when Cook fell ill soon after commencing his law practice in 1815 he "met with kind and hospitable attention in the family of the late Rev. Mr. Randle, for which he always expressed the most lively gratitude" (Peck, *Sermon*, 9).
44. "Benjamin Stephenson to [the Secretary of State]," 14 October 1816, in Carter, *Territorial Papers*, 17:417.
45. Thomas Ford, *A History of Illinois from Its Commencement as a State in 1818 to 1847* (Urbana, Ill.: University of Illinois Press, 1995), 13–14; Newton Bateman and Paul Selby, eds., *Historical Encyclopedia of Illinois* (Chicago: Munsell Publishing Company, 1900), 423.
46. "Governor Edwards to Joseph Philips," 25 September 1816, in Carter, *Territorial Papers*, 17:414.
47. Bakalis, "Ninian Edwards," 174.
48. Russell E. Heacock, "Circular, to the People of the Illinois Territory," *Western Intelligencer*, 29 May 1816, p. 3, cols. 1–2.
49. "Electoral," *Western Intelligencer*, 22 May 1816, p. 3, col. 3.
50. The earliest extant reference to Philips in Illinois is a land sale purchase listing his residence as Kaskaskia and dated 28 September 1816. *Illinois Public Domain Land Tract Sales Database.*
51. "William Lowry to [the Secretary of State]," 19 November 1816, in Carter, *Territorial Papers*, 17:438.

52. Carter, *Territorial Papers*, 16:323n; "Guy Bryan to the Secretary of State," 4 December 1816, in Carter, *Territorial Papers*, 17:444–45.
53. Suppiger, "Amity to Enmity," 208.
54. Five other candidates are recorded as having applied or been recommended as well: Levi Todd of Kaskaskia; Jason Chamberlain of Cape Girardeau, Missouri Territory; and Nelson Nicholas, Francis E. Walker, and Fidelio Sharp, all of Kentucky (Carter, *Territorial Papers*, 17:444n).
55. "Recommendation of Joseph Philips as Secretary," 30 August 1816; "Joseph Philips to the Secretary of State," 31 August 1816; "George W. Campbell to the Secretary of State," 1 September 1816; and "William O. Winston to the Secretary of State," 10 October 1816, in ibid., 382–83, 412–13, 414n–15n. Claiborne later played a role in the admission of Illinois to the Union as a member of the U.S. House select committee on Illinois statehood in the early months of 1818.
56. "Commission of Obadiah Jones as Judge," 7 March 1809; "Commission of Jesse B. Thomas as Judge," 7 March 1809; "Commission of Alexander Stuart as Judge," 7 March 1809; "Commission of Stanley Griswold as Judge," 16 March 1810; and "Commission of William Sprigg as Judge," 29 July 1813, in Carter, *Territorial Papers*, 16:14–16, 83, 350–51; "Commission of Thomas Towles as Judge," 28 October 1815, in Carter, *Territorial Papers*, 17:233.
57. Daniel Pope Cook to John Quincy Adams, 4 August 1817, Adams Manuscript Trust, Boston, and Massachusetts Historical Society, *Microfilms of the Adams Papers Owned by the Adams Manuscript Trust and Deposited in the Massachusetts Historical Society*, reel 438. Hereafter referred to as *Microfilms of the Adams Papers*.
58. "Governor Edwards to the Secretary of State," 19 January 1817, in Carter, *Territorial Papers*, 17:469–70.

4. A Bearer of Despatches

1. "John Pope to [the Secretary of State]," 11 February 1817, in Carter, *Territorial Papers*, 17:480.
2. Daniel Pope Cook to Ninian Edwards, 6 February 1817, in Washburne, *Edwards Papers*, 128. Cook also shared a piece of political intelligence that was soon to have a momentous impact upon his own career: "John Quincy Adams, Mr. [John] Pope writes, is certainly to be sec'y of state." Ibid., 129.
3. Brown, *Memoir*, 29–30.
4. Daniel Pope Cook to John Quincy Adams, 4 August 1817, *Microfilms of the Adams Papers*, reel 438.
5. James Monroe to John Quincy Adams, 6 March 1817, in ibid., reel 436.
6. Daniel Pope Cook to Ninian Edwards, 7 March 1817, Record Series 100.002, Illinois Territory, Executive Records, 17 May 1809–3 December 1818, Illinois

State Archives, Springfield, Illinois. Hereafter referred to as Record Series 100.002, Illinois Territory, Executive Records.

7. *Western Intelligencer*, 7 May 1817, p. 3, col. 4. This notice underscores that Cook's designation as a diplomatic courier was completely unexpected.
8. "Danl.P. Cook," 10 March 1817, U.S. National Archives and Records Administration, *Registers and Indexes for Passport Applications*, reel 1. Hereafter referred to as *Registers and Indexes for Passport Applications*.
9. *New-York Gazette & General Advertiser*, 13 March 1817, p. 2, col. 2. *The Columbian* later corrected this report, noting that Cook was in fact scheduled to "embark from this city in a merchant vessel, and that Mr. Adams will return home in the same manner." *Columbian*, 17 March 1817, p. 2, col. 2.
10. Pawlyn, "Re: The packet ship Queensbury Res. Enq 23007–248"; Albion, *Square-Riggers on Schedule*, 17.
11. *New-York Gazette & General Advertiser*, 15 March 1817, p. 3, col. 1.
12. By the sheerest of coincidences, Elisha Tyson Jr.'s and Daniel Pope Cook's names appear on the same page of passport applications. "Elisha Tyson Jr.," 29 March 1817, *Registers and Indexes for Passport Applications*, reel 1.
13. White, "Advice to a Young Traveler," 83.
14. Ibid., 81, 82n–83n.
15. Albion, *Square-Riggers on Schedule*, 322.
16. Pawlyn, "Re: The packet ship Queensbury Res. Enq 23007–248."
17. *Commercial Advertiser*, 15 March 1817, p. 2, col. 5.
18. *New-York Gazette & General Advertiser*, 7 April 1817, p. 2, col. 1; Broome, "Re: Queensbury Packet."
19. Ibid.; *Royal Cornwall Gazette, Falmouth Packet & Plymouth Journal*, 3 May 1817, p. 2, col. 6.
20. *Diaries of John Quincy Adams*, 3 May 1817, 181.
21. Ibid., 4–5 May 1817, 182–83; *The Times*, 5 May 1817, p. 2, col. 5 and p. 3, cols. 2–3.
22. *Diaries of John Quincy Adams*, 12 May 1818, 348.
23. Coles followed up on his vow to free his human property in a dramatic ceremony on a flatboat on the Ohio River en route to Illinois in 1818. Daniel Pope Cook acted as Coles's attorney in completing the process. Alvord, *Governor Edward Coles*, 43–47.
24. *Diaries of John Quincy Adams*, 1 March 1817, 148; 6 March 1817, 150; 4 April 1817, 165; 11 April 1817, 168; 16 April 1817, 170; 17 April 1817, 171; 21 April 1817, 172; 25 April 1817, 175; 29 April 1817, 177.
25. Edward Coles to William Barry, 25 June 1858, Edward Coles Papers, Chicago History Museum, Chicago, Illinois.
26. *Diaries of John Quincy Adams*, 28 March 1817, 161.
27. Birkbeck, *Notes on a Journey*, 7.

28. Daniel Pope Cook, "Extract of a letter from Daniel Pope Cook, Esqur. late bearer of American dispatches to the Court of St. James, to his brother in this place, dated New-York, August 8, 1817," *Western Intelligencer*, 10 September 1817, p. 3, cols. 1–2.
29. *Diaries of John Quincy Adams*, 5 June 1817, 209; 12–15 June 1817, 212–14; 26 July 1817, 234; *The Times*, 16 June 1817, p. 3, col. 1.
30. Albion, *Square-Riggers on Schedule*, 9–10.
31. *Diaries of John Quincy Adams*, 16–17 June 1817, 214; *Commercial Advertiser*, 6 August 1817, p. 2, col. 2.
32. Fearon, *Sketches of America*, 2–3. Forty guineas was equivalent to 42 pounds sterling, which today would amount to just under $3,200.
33. *Diaries of John Quincy Adams*, 30 June–1 July 1817, 218–19.
34. Ibid., 23 June 1817, 216; Fearon, *Sketches of America*, 3–4.
35. *Diaries of John Quincy Adams*, 21 July 1817, 228. François André Danican Philidor (1726–1795) was an eighteenth-century chess master and the author of *Analyse du Jeu des Echecs (Analysis of Chess)* (1749), "the first genuine book of instruction which gave a reasoned and lucid explanation of the modern game" and a standard work on the subject for more than a century after his death (Golombek, *Chess*, 118–22).
36. George Washington Adams to Daniel Pope Cook, 4 September 1817, *Microfilms of the Adams Papers*, reel 288.
37. *Diaries of John Quincy Adams*, 2 July 1817, 219.
38. Daniel Pope Cook to John Quincy Adams, 4 August 1817, *Microfilms of the Adams Papers*, reel 438. Emphasis in original.
39. *Commercial Advertiser*, 6 August 1817, p. 2, col. 2. Among those whom Adams encountered in New York was Edward Coles, who had himself just arrived from Liverpool (*Diaries of John Quincy Adams*, 6 August 1817, 239).
40. Cook, "Extract of a Letter . . . ," *Western Intelligencer*, 10 September 1817, p. 3, col. 2.
41. Fearon, *Sketches of America*, 13. Fearon later traveled as far west as Shawneetown in Illinois Territory, apparently with some thought of settling with Morris Birkbeck, but that plan never materialized (ibid., 182, 260).
42. *Diaries of John Quincy Adams*, 10 August 1817, 241; 15 August 1817, 243.
43. Daniel Pope Cook to Ninian Edwards, 11 September 1817, in Washburne, *Edwards Papers*, 137.
44. D.P.C. [Daniel Pope Cook], "No. II. To James Monroe President of the United States of America," *National Register*, 20 September 1817, p. 177, col. 2.
45. *Diaries of John Quincy Adams*, 21 September 1817, 256–57.
46. Daniel Pope Cook to John Quincy Adams, 22 September 1817, *Microfilms of the Adams Papers*, reel 439.
47. *Diaries of John Quincy Adams*, 23–25 September 1817, 257–58.

48. Ibid., 7 March 1821, 547.
49. Daniel Pope Cook to Ninian Edwards, Washington, 25 September 1817, in Washburne, *Edwards Papers*, 137.
50. "Americanus" [Daniel Pope Cook], "For the National Intelligencer," *National Intelligencer*, triweekly ed., 25 September 1817, p. 2, col. 5. Emphasis in original.
51. Daniel Pope Cook to Ninian Edwards, 25 September 1817, in Washburne, *Edwards Papers*, 137–38. Cook also admitted his authorship of the "Americanus" letters to Edwards.
52. James Monroe to John Quincy Adams, 27 September 1817, *Microfilms of the Adams Papers*, reel 439. It seems highly doubtful that Cook ever had any realistic prospect of receiving the Alabama appointment. By the time that he first expressed his interest on 22 September, at least six other men had already applied or been recommended for the position. The two men who were ultimately chosen in succession—John Walker and Henry Hitchcock—had the advantage of sponsorship by the formidable secretary of the treasury, William Crawford. Carter, *Territorial Papers*, 18:59, 166, 166–67n, 217, 306.
53. *Diaries of John Quincy Adams*, 27 September 1817, 259.
54. Daniel Pope Cook to Ninian Edwards, 2 October 1817, in Washburne, *Edwards Papers*, 139–40.
55. Daniel Pope Cook to John Quincy Adams, circa 2 October 1817, *Microfilms of the Adams Papers*, reel 440.
56. *Diaries of John Quincy Adams*, 2 October 1817, 260; Cook to Edwards, 2 October 1817, 140.
57. *Diaries of John Quincy Adams*, 4 October 1817, 261.

5. *The Grievances of Territorial Government*

1. Benjamin Stephenson, "Kaskaskia, June 19, 1816. To the Citizens of Illinois Territory," *Western Intelligencer*, 19 June 1816, p. 2, cols. 34.
2. Bakalis, "Ninian Edwards," 217.
3. "Aristides," "To the Voters of Illinois," *Western Intelligencer*, 21 August 1816, p. 3, cols. 12.
4. Buck, *Illinois in 1818*, 215.
5. Bakalis, "Ninian Edwards," 202.
6. *Western Intelligencer*, 20 November 1817, p. 3, col. 2.
7. "Ordinance of 1787," 8.
8. "A Republican" [Daniel Pope Cook], *Western Intelligencer*, 27 November 1817, p. 3, cols. 23.
9. Ibid., p. 3, cols. 34.
10. Ibid., p. 3, col. 4.
11. *Western Intelligencer*, 4 December 1817, p. 2, col. 3.

12. Matheny was also related by marriage to the fiercely antislavery James Lemen Sr., both having married daughters of the antislavery Captain Joseph Ogle. Johnson, *Charles Reynolds Matheny*, 6; Edstrom, "A Mighty Contest," 194–96.
13. Johnson, *Charles Reynolds Matheny*, 8.
14. McGoorty, "Early Irish of Illinois," 63; Reynolds, *Pioneer History of Illinois*, 385n; Reynolds, *My Own Times*, 182; Allen, *Pope County Notes*, 20; "Executive Register," 625.
15. So-called because "there were no arms for the troops and very frequently they used corn stalks in the place of guns." Young, *History of Jessamine County*, 95.
16. *History and Families of Gallatin County Illinois*, 1:142–43; Stevens, "Illinois in the War," 185; "Executive Register," 653, 668; Berry, "Morris Birkbeck," 265.
17. *Western Intelligencer*, 4 December 1817, p. 2, col. 2.
18. *Western Intelligencer*, 11 December 1817, p. 2, col. 4. Emphasis in original.
19. Ibid., p. 3, col. 1.
20. Daniel Pope Cook to John Quincy Adams, 4 December 1817, *Microfilms of the Adams Papers*, reel 441.
21. "A Republican" [Daniel Pope Cook], *Western Intelligencer*, 11 December 1817, p. 3, col. 2.
22. "Illinois Legislature," *Western Intelligencer*, 18 December 1817, p. 2, col. 4.
23. Johnson, *Charles Reynolds Matheny*, 11.
24. "Illinois Legislature," *Western Intelligencer*, 18 December 1817, p. 3, col. 1.
25. *Western Intelligencer*, 1 January 1818, p. 3, col. 2.
26. Philbrick, *Laws of Illinois Territory 1809–1818*, 315–17.
27. *Western Intelligencer*, 11 December 1817, p. 3, col. 1.
28. "Executive Register," 667.
29. *Western Intelligencer*, 8 January 1818, p. 3, col. 4.

6. Truly an Amiable Character

1. Nathaniel Pope to Ninian Edwards, 21 January 1818, Ninian Edwards Papers, Chicago History Museum, Chicago, Illinois.
2. "Kaskaskia, July 4, 1813," *Missouri Gazette*, 31 July 1813, p. 3, cols. 3–4.
3. Banta, *The Ohio*, 14.
4. "Bear Grass," *Encyclopædia Britannica*, accessed 19 June 2014, http://www.britannica.com/EBchecked/topic/57328/bear-grass.
5. Clark, *Conquest of the Illinois*, 30–32.
6. Angle, "Nathaniel Pope," 113–15.
7. John May to B. Tardiveau, Beargrass [Creek, Ky.], 18 February 1783, in Rice Jr., "News from the Ohio Valley," 282.
8. Collins, *History of Kentucky*, 2:355.
9. Angle, "Nathaniel Pope," 115.

10. 1810 U.S. Federal Census (Population Schedule), Jefferson County, Kentucky, p. 11, William Pope household.
11. McAdams, *Some Ancestors*, 223; Angle, "Nathaniel Pope," 114.
12. Angle, "Nathaniel Pope," 114.
13. Ibid., 115.
14. Ibid., 115–16. Angle cited "a receipt dated May 1, 1802, for 'tuition from Mr. Pope'" as evidence of his attendance at Transylvania, but Pope's name does not appear in any list of graduates (ibid., 116).
15. Ibid., 116–17.
16. Ibid., 117.
17. Schultz Jr., *Travels on an Inland Voyage*, 2:67.
18. Angle, "Nathaniel Pope," 120; "Memorial to Congress by Trustees of the Louisiana Academy," 8 April 1808, in Carter, *Territorial Papers*, 14:180.
19. Carter, *Territorial Papers*, 14:173n.
20. Angle, "Nathaniel Pope," 117–18; "Scott, John, (1785–1861)," *Biographical Directory of the United States Congress*, accessed 24 June 2014, http://bioguide.congress.gov/scripts/biodisplay.pl?index=S000176.
21. Angle, "Nathaniel Pope," 121.
22. Ibid., 121, 123–25
23. "Jesse B. Thomas to the Secretary of State," 11 February 1809, in Carter, *Territorial Papers*, 16:11.
24. "John Pope to [the Secretary of State]," 25 February 1809, in ibid., 12.
25. "Richard M. Johnson to the Secretary of State," 10 February 1809, in ibid., 8–9; "Buckner Thruston and Benjamin Howard to the Secretary of State," 11 February 1809, in ibid., 10–11.
26. "Boyle, John, (1774–1835)," *Biographical Directory of the United States Congress*, accessed 30 June 2014, http://bioguide.congress.gov/scripts/biodisplay.pl?index=B000729.
27. "Richard M. Johnson to the Secretary of State," 10 February 1809, in Carter, *Territorial Papers*, 16:9; "Buckner Thruston, John Pope, and Benjamin Howard to the Secretary of State," 11 February 1809, in ibid., 10; "Jesse B. Thomas to the Secretary of State," 11 February 1809, in ibid., 11.
28. "David Holmes to the [Secretary of State]," 10 February 1809, in ibid., 9; "Richard M. Johnson to the Secretary of State," 10 February 1809, in ibid., 8–9; "Buckner Thruston, John Pope, and Benjamin Howard to [the Secretary of State]," 11 February 1809, in ibid., 10; "Buckner Thruston and Benjamin Howard to [the Secretary of State]," 11 February 1809, in ibid., 10–11; Carter, *Territorial Papers*, 16:12n; "John Pope to [the Secretary of State]," 25 February 1809, in ibid., 12; "W.A. Burwell and Thomas Kenan to [the President]," 11 February 1809, in Carter, *Territorial Papers*, 5:697.

29. "Ordinance of 1787," 2–3.
30. "Governor Boyle to [the President]," 6 April 1809, in Carter, *Territorial Papers*, 16:19–20; Henry Clay to James Madison, 10 April 1809; Henry Clay to Robert Smith, 10 April 1809; and Henry Clay to Caesar Augustus Rodney, 10 April 1809, in Hopkins, *Papers of Henry Clay*, 1:408–9.

7. The Snarl of Suspicion

1. Angle, "Nathaniel Pope," 123.
2. Ibid., 123–24.
3. "A Proclamation by Nathaniel Pope Secretary of the Territory and Exercising the Government Thereof," 28 April 1809, Record Series 100.002, Illinois Territory, Executive Records.
4. "Executive Register," 621–24; Angle, "Nathaniel Pope," 126.
5. "Acting Governor Pope to the Secretary of State," 11 May 1809, in Carter, *Territorial Papers*, 16:38.
6. Angle, "Nathaniel Pope," 126.
7. Francis S. Philbrick, "Special Introduction: Pope's Digest and Its Successors," in Philbrick, *Pope's Digest 1815, volume I*, x.
8. John Edgar and Robert and William Morrison to Matthew Lyon, 12 May 1809, rpt. in ibid., xi. Note that this letter was written on the day after Nathaniel Pope composed his own letter to the secretary of state asking for an assessment of the validity of his own oath of office. Two months earlier Matthew Lyon had written to John Edgar: "Secretary Pope I hear a Good Character of. I respect him much for his brother's sake who is a friend of mine." Matthew Lyon to John Edgar, 11 March 1809, in Carter, *Territorial Papers*, 16:17–18.
9. "Executive Register," 623; Angle, "Nathaniel Pope," 125–26.
10. Ibid., 126.
11. "Executive Register," 626.
12. "The Secretary of the Treasury to Secretary Pope," 10 March 1809, in Carter, *Territorial Papers*, 16:16.
13. "Acting Governor Pope to the Secretary of the Treasury," 11 May 1809, in ibid., 38–39.
14. "The Secretary of the Treasury to Secretary Pope," 8 June 1809, in ibid., 41.
15. "Secretary Pope to the Secretary of the Treasury," 4 July 1809, in ibid., 49–50.
16. "The Secretary of the Treasury to Secretary Pope," 29 July 1809, in ibid., 56.
17. "Secretary Pope to the Secretary of the Treasury," 30 September 1809, in ibid., 60.
18. Anson Miller quoted in Tyler, "One of Mr. Lincoln's," 252–53. Dr. Samuel Johnson, the eighteenth-century English writer and lexicographer, said of his friend Richard Bathurst that he "was a man to my very heart's content; he

hated a fool, and he hated a rogue, and he hated a whig—*he was a very good hater*!" Boswell, *Life of Samuel Johnson*, 1:104. Emphasis in original.

19. Usher F. Linder quoted in Meese, "Nathaniel Pope," 20.
20. Philbrick, "Special Introduction," xii.
21. "The Governor and Judges to the Secretary of State," 2 February 1810, in Carter, *Territorial Papers*, 16:71–72.
22. "Shadrach Bond to the Secretary of State," 5 January 1813, in ibid., 284–85.
23. Angle, "Nathaniel Pope," 132–34.
24. Philbrick, "Special Introduction," xix, xxi; warrant nos. 113–16 "issued in favour of Nathaniel Pope for Revising and Superintending the printing of the Revised Code of Illinois Territory," 20 July 1815, Record Series 105.004, Auditor of Public Accounts, "Daybooks."
25. "Electoral," *Western Intelligencer*, 22 May 1816, p. 3, col. 2.
26. Heacock, "Circular," p. 3, col. 2.
27. Nathaniel Pope, "FELLOW CITIZENS OF ILLINOIS TERRITORY," 29 August 1816, p. 1, cols. 1–2, photostat, Paul M. Angle Papers, accession number M1975.0037, M982.0059, 1995.0206, box 12, folder 2 of 7, Chicago History Museum, Chicago, Illinois.
28. "Aristides," "To the Voters of Illinois," p. 3, col. 2.
29. Angle, "Nathaniel Pope," 138; William Russell, "To the Public," 2 September 1816, p. 1, col. 1 and p. 2, col. 2, photostat, Paul M. Angle Papers, box 12, folder 2 of 7.
30. Pope, "FELLOW CITIZENS OF ILLINOIS TERRITORY," p. 1, col. 2 and p. 2, cols. 1–2.
31. *Indiana Register* (Vevay, Indiana), 30 September 1816, rpt. in Tufts University Library, "Illinois 1816 U.S. House of Representatives (Territorial Delegate)," *A New Nation Votes*.
32. "Secretary Pope to the President," 5 September 1816, in Carter, *Territorial Papers*, 17:386.
33. *Western Intelligencer*, 30 October 1816, p. 2, col. 3.
34. "Governor Edwards to [the President]," 2 November 1816, in Carter, *Territorial Papers*, 17:455.
35. *Annals of Congress*, 14th Cong., 2nd sess., 230; Goldman and Young, *United States Congressional Directories*, 77; "The Metropolitan, Aka Brown's Marble Hotel."
36. Lewis, *District of Columbia*, 18–19.
37. Angle, "Nathaniel Pope," 140.
38. Nathaniel Pope to Elias Kent Kane, 6 January 1817, Elias Kent Kane, Papers, Chicago History Museum, Chicago, Illinois.
39. *Annals of Congress*, 14th Cong., 2nd sess., 337–38.
40. *House Journal*, 14th Cong., 2nd sess., 24 January 1817, 275.

41. Nathaniel Pope, "To the Editors, Washington City, Dec. 6, 1816," *Western Intelligencer*, 1 January 1817, p. 3, col. 2.
42. *House Journal*, 14th Cong., 2nd sess., 24 December 1816, 102; 4 January 1817, 137; 14 January 1817, 200; 24 January 1817, 276.
43. Ibid., 30 January 1817, 312; 1 February 1817, 320; 20 February 1817, 428; *Annals of Congress*, 14th Cong., 2nd sess., 1024.
44. *House Journal*, 14th Cong., 1st sess., 30 March 1816, 554–57.
45. *Annals of Congress*, 14th Cong., 2nd sess., 20–21, 254; *Senate Journal*, 14th Cong., 2nd sess., 12 December 1816, 42; *House Journal*, 14th Cong., 2nd sess., 12 December 1816, 62.
46. *Annals of Congress*, 11th Cong., 3rd sess., 859.
47. *Aggregate Amount*, 1:83.
48. *Annals of Congress*, 14th Cong., 1st sess., 1300.
49. U.S. Congress, Senate, 14th Congress, 1st sess., "Report of the Committee to whom was referred the Bill, Entitled 'An Act to Enable the People of the Mississippi Territory, to form a Constitution and State Government and for the Admission of Such State into the Union, on an Equal Footing with the Original States,'" 16 April 1816, Record Group 46, U.S. Senate Territorial Papers, Mississippi Territory, 13th–15th Congress, U.S. National Archives and Records Administration, Washington, D.C.
50. *House Journal*, 14th Cong., 2nd sess., 3 March 1817, 526–27, 545; *Senate Journal*, 14th Cong., 2nd sess., 3 March 1817, 432.
51. An Act to enable the people of the western part of the Mississippi territory to form a constitution and state government, and for the admission of such state into the union, on an equal footing with the original states, *U.S. Statutes at Large*, 3 (1817): 348–49. Hereafter referred to as: An Act to enable the people of the western part of the Mississippi territory.
52. Nathaniel Pope was still in the nation's capital as late as 3 March 1817, when he wrote a letter dated "Hall of Representatives" to Josiah Meigs, commissioner of the U.S. General Land Office. "Delegate Pope to Josiah Meigs," 3 March 1817, in Carter, *Territorial Papers*, 17:488.
53. *Western Intelligencer*, 18 September 1817, p. 3, col. 1.
54. Edstrom, "Congress," 17.
55. *Diaries of John Quincy Adams*, 4 October 1817, 261; *Western Intelligencer*, 20 November 1817, p. 3, col. 2.
56. Nathaniel Pope, "Extract of a letter from the Hon. Nath. Pope, to the Editors, dated Washington City, Dec. 10, 1818 [i.e., 1817]," *Western Intelligencer*, 21 January 1818, p. 3, col. 3.
57. Goldman and Young, *United States Congressional Directories*, 87; *House Journal*, 15th Cong., 1st sess., 8 December 1817, 26.

8. Candour and Good Faith

1. "Ordinance of 1787," 5.
2. Stephenson, "Kaskaskia, June 19, 1816. To the citizens of Illinois Territory," p. 2, col. 3.
3. *House Journal*, 15th Cong., 1st sess., 10 December 1817, 36; ibid., 18 December 1817, 60.
4. Ibid.; Birkbeck, *Letters from Illinois*, 119 [i.e., 109].
5. Nathaniel Pope to Morris Birkbeck, Washington, D.C., 17 December 1817, rpt. in Flower, *History of the English Settlement*, 81–82.
6. *Diaries of John Quincy Adams*, 10–11 December 1817, 284; 17 December 1817, 286; 20–21 December 1817, 287; 16 January 1818, 297; 19 January 1818, 298; 22 January 1818, 301; 28 January 1818, 303; 2 February 1818, 305; 4 February 1818, 305; 12 February 1818, 308–9; 5 March 1818, 316; 11 March 1818, 319; 26 March 1818, 325; 2 April 1818, 329; 13 April 1818, 335; 18 April 1818, 337; and 20 April 1818, 338.
7. Ibid., 21 December 1817, 287.
8. John Quincy Adams to William Gray, 21 December 1817; John Quincy Adams to W. S. Shaw, 21 December 1817; John Quincy Adams to John Kirkland, 21 December 1817; John Quincy Adams to Thomas Welsh, 21 December 1817; John Quincy Adams to Daniel McCormick, 21 December 1817; John Quincy Adams to John Adams, 21 December 1817; and John Quincy Adams to John Trumbull, 21 December 1817, *Microfilms of the Adams Papers*, reel 143; Samuel Willard Crompton, "Gray, William," *American National Biography Online*, accessed 5 April 2013, http://www.anb.org/articles/03/03-00634.html; Irma B. Jaffe, "Trumbull, John," accessed 5 April 2013, ibid., http://www.anb.org/articles/17/17-00873.html. John D. Knowlton, "Shaw, William Smith," ibid., accessed 5 April 2013, http://www.anb.org/articles/20/20-00932.html; "Harvard Presidents Throughout History," *Harvard University Gazette News*, 15 March 2001, https://news.harvard.edu/gazette/story/2001/03/harvard-gazette-harvard-presidents-throughout-history/; Wright and Hanson, *Biographical Sketches*, 183–88; Barrett, *Old Merchants*, 2:251–53.
9. Adams to Kirkland, 21 December 1817.
10. John Quincy Adams to John Adams, 21 December 1817 (letter no. 120), *Microfilms of the Adams Papers*, reel 143. Coincidentally, the only case in which Crittenden had been involved in as the territory's attorney general was the trial of Michael Jones for the murder of Rice Jones. Kirwan, *John J. Crittenden*, 15–16.
11. Pope, "Extract of a letter . . . Dec. 10, 1818," p. 3, col. 4.
12. Nathaniel Pope to Rufus King, Washington, 10 April 1818, Document #52, box 16, folder 4, MS 1660, Rufus King Papers.

13. Louisa Catherine Adams to Charles Francis Adams, 21 December 1817, *Microfilms of the Adams Papers*, reel 441; Louisa Catherine Adams to Charles Francis Adams, 7 January 1818, in ibid., reel 442.
14. *Diaries of John Quincy Adams*, 16 January 1818, 297. Pope is recorded as having been in the House on 19 December 1817 and then not again until 16 January 1818. Based upon the evidence of a letter to Pope from Postmaster General R. J. Meigs Jr. dated 22 December 1817 in response to "your letter of Yesterday," it is clear that Pope was still in Washington, D.C. as of that date. Senator John Crittenden, who was to have joined Pope's excursion, last appears in the records of the *Senate Journal* on 11 December 1817 and then not again until 12 January 1818. *House Journal*, 15th Cong., 1st sess., 19 December 1817, 65; ibid., 16 January 1818, 151; "The Postmaster General to Nathaniel Pope," 22 December 1817, in Carter, *Territorial Papers*, 17:554; *Senate Journal*, 15th Cong., 1st sess., 11 December 1817, 27; 12 January 1818, 81.
15. *Annals of Congress*, 15th Cong., 1st sess., 782.
16. Johnson's purported act was celebrated in an 1824 poem by Dr. Richard Emmons containing the immortal lines, "Rumpsey, Dumpsey, Colonel Johnson killed Tecumseh." *Argus of Western America*, 4 August 1824, p. 2, col. 3, rpt. in Meyer, *Life and Times*, 316. "It was later said that, in gratitude to Emmons, Colonel Johnson procured a clerkship at Washington for him, valued at eight hundred dollars per annum." Ibid., 316n; *Louisville Daily Journal*, 9 September 1831, p. 2, col. 6.
17. Edgar J. McManus. "Johnson, Richard Mentor," *American National Biography Online*, accessed 2 February 2015, http://www.anb.org/articles/03/03-00246.html.
18. Margaret Bayard Smith to Mrs. Kirkpatrick, 1816, rpt. in Hunt, *First Forty Years*, 128–29.
19. Martineau, *Retrospect of Western Travel*, 1:257.
20. "Richard M. Johnson to the Secretary of State," 10 February 1809, in Carter, *Territorial Papers*, 16:8.
21. Ninian Edwards to Richard M. Johnson, 14 March 1812, Record Group 233, U.S. House of Representatives Territorial Papers (12th–15th Congress), Illinois Territory, 1811–1818, box no. N.A. 85 of Territorial Papers 278, 284, 285, U.S. National Archives and Records Administration, Washington, D.C. Johnson successfully navigated a suffrage bill through Congress that was subsequently approved by President Madison. *Annals of Congress*, 218, 238, 239–40, 1278–79, 1321, 1342.
22. Edstrom, "Congress," 20.
23. Nathan Sargent, quoted in *The National Cyclopaedia of American Biography*, 6:6–7; Ray W. Irwin, "Spencer, John Canfield," *Dictionary of American Biography*, 17:449–50.

24. "FEDERAL REPUBLICAN CANDIDATES FOR MEMBERS OF CONGRESS," *Portland Gazette and Maine Advertiser*, 22 October 1816, p. 1, col. 2.
25. *Annals of Congress*, 15th Cong., 2nd sess., 311.
26. Elizabeth Dubrulle, "Whitman, Ezekiel," *American National Biography Online*, accessed 3 February 2015, http://www.anb.org/articles/03/03-00531.html.
27. *Who Was Who in America*, 175; *Republican Banner*, 10 January 1856, p. 3, col. 1.
28. Pope to Edwards, 21 January 1818.
29. H.R. no. 53, A Bill To enable the people of the Illinois Territory to form a constitution and State Government and for the admission of such state into the Union on an equal footing with the original States, 23 January 1818, Record Group 233, U.S. House of Representatives Territorial Papers (12th-15th Congress), Illinois Territory, 1811–1818, box no. N.A. 85 of Territorial Papers 278, 284, 285, U.S. National Archives and Records Administration, Washington, D.C. Hereafter referred to as H.R. no. 53, 23 January 1818.
30. "Ordinance of 1787," 8.
31. Pope, "Extract of a letter . . . Jan. 27, 1818," p. 2, col. 4.
32. H.R. no. 53, 23 January 1818.
33. "In the enabling acts for Missouri and Alabama, the time was further reduced to three months." Buck, *Illinois in 1818*, 222.
34. An Act to enable the people of the Indiana Territory to form a constitution and state government, and for the admission of such state into the Union on an equal footing with the original states, *U.S. Statutes at Large*, 3(1816): 289. Hereafter referred to as An Act to enable the people of the Indiana Territory.
35. H.R. no. 53, 23 January 1818.
36. An Act to enable the people of the western part of the Mississippi territory, 348.
37. H.R. no. 53, 23 January 1818. Indiana had held its election on a single day (An Act to enable the people of the Indiana Territory, 289).
38. H.R. no. 53, 23 January 1818.
39. Nathaniel Pope, "Extract of a letter from the Hon. N. Pope, to the Editors, dated Washington, Jan. 24, 1818," *Western Intelligencer*, 4 March 1818, p. 3, col. 3.
40. "Ordinance of 1787," 8. Interestingly, Nathan Dane, one of the authors of the Northwest Ordinance, wrote in 1787 to Rufus King—who had helped to draft the ordinance—that he (Dane) thought that a population of sixty thousand was in fact too small; "but having divided the whole territory into 3 States, this number appears to me to be less important . . . ." Nathan Dane to Rufus King, 16 July 1787; Steven E. Siry, "King, Rufus," *American National Biography Online*, accessed 7 July 2015, http://www.anb.org/articles/03/03-00262.html.
41. "Memorial of the Legislative Council and House of Representatives of the Indiana Territory, praying the authority of Congress to call a convention for

the purpose of determining on the propriety of admitting the said Territory into the Union as an independent state. . . ," 1 September 1815, Record Group 46, U.S. Senate Territorial Papers, Indiana Territory, 10th–21st Congress, U.S. National Archives and Records Administration, Washington, D.C.

42. U.S. Congress, Senate, 13th Congress, 3rd sess., "Memorial of the Legislature of the Mississippi Territory praying the admission of said territory into the Union, as an independent state," 27 December 1814, U.S. National Archives, *Miscellaneous Letters,* microcopy no. 179, reel 1; "No. 391. Admission of Mississippi into the Union," 29 December 1815, *American State Papers: Miscellaneous,* 2:276.
43. *Western Intelligencer,* 11 December 1817, p. 2, col. 4.
44. On the original manuscript of the Illinois bill the words "& Lead mines" are inserted almost as an afterthought. H.R. no. 53, 23 January 1818.
45. Usher, "Public Schools," 5.
46. "79. A Bill for the More General Diffusion of Knowledge, 18 June 1779," in Boyd, *Papers of Thomas Jefferson,* 2:526–35.
47. "Land Ordinance of 1785," 20 May 1785, in Carter, *Territorial Papers,* 2:15.
48. "Ordinance of 1787," 6.
49. Usher, "Public Schools," 6, 10.
50. *Western Intelligencer,* 27 November 1816, p. 3, col. 1.
51. Usher, "Public Schools," 14, 17.
52. "Memorial to Congress by Trustees of the Louisiana Academy," 8 April 1808, in Carter, *Territorial Papers,* 14:176.
53. Turner, "Significance of the Frontier," 94.
54. Jakle, "Salt on the Ohio Valley Frontier," 689, 692.
55. "The Secretary of the Treasury to Governor Edwards," 30 April 1809, in Carter, *Territorial Papers,* 16:33–34.
56. "A Resolution of the Legislative Assembly," referred 25 January 1813, in ibid., 296–97.
57. "A Bill Concerning Salt Springs," 26 February 1813, in ibid., 300.
58. Philbrick, *Laws of Illinois Territory,* 157.
59. "No. 492. Lead Mines and Salt Springs, Communicated to the Senate February 8, 1826," *American State Papers: Public Lands,* 4:520.
60. Nathaniel Pope to Josiah Meigs, 12 December 1816, "No. 248. Lead Mines and Salines, Communicated to the House of Representatives January 21, 1817," in ibid., 3:243.
61. Thwaites, "Notes on Early Lead Mining," 286.
62. Davis, *Frontier Illinois,* 168.
63. Thwaites, "Notes on Early Lead Mining," 286–87; "Treaty with the Ottawa, Etc., 1816," in Kappler, *Indian Affairs,* 2:132–33; "The Indian Commissioners to the Secretary of War," 9 September 1816, in Carter, *Territorial Papers,* 17:388.

64. Thwaites, "Notes on Early Lead Mining," 288; *History of Jo Daviess County*, 236; Jillson, "Early Mineral Explorations," 47; "No. 492. Lead Mines and Salt Springs," 4:522.
65. H.R. no. 53, Illinois Admission, 4 April 1818, read twice and ordered to be engrossed for to-morrow, Record Group 233, U.S. House of Representatives Territorial Papers, Illinois Territory, 12th–15th Congress, box no. N.A. 85 of Territorial Papers 278, 284, 285, U.S. National Archives and Records Administration, Washington, D.C. Hereafter referred to as H.R. no. 53, 4 April 1818.
66. An Act to enable the people of the western part of the Mississippi territory, 349; An Act to enable the people of the Indiana Territory, 290; An Act to enable the people of the Alabama territory to form a constitution and state government, and for the admission of such state into the Union on an equal footing with the original states, *U.S. Statutes at Large* 3 (1819): 491; An Act to authorize the people of the Missouri territory to form a constitution and state government, and for the admission of such state into the Union on an equal footing with the original states, and to prohibit slavery in certain territories, *U.S. Statutes at Large* 3 (1820): 547.
67. One proposition that was present in the Indiana enabling act but not in the one for Illinois (or Mississippi, for that matter) was a proviso giving the Hoosier State four sections of land "for the purpose of fixing their seat of government thereon" (An Act to enable the people of the Indiana Territory, 290–91). The specific sections would be chosen by the new state legislature. The omission of such a land grant in Illinois's enabling act was destined to provoke a lively discussion in the new state's constitutional convention a few months later.
68. H.R. no. 53, 23 January 1818.
69. *House Journal*, 15th Cong., 1st sess., 23 January 1818, 174, 176–77; Pope, "Extract of a letter from the Hon. N. Pope, to the Editors, dated Washington, Jan. 24, 1818," p. 3, col. 3.
70. Edstrom, "Congress," 27.
71. Bloom, "Peaceful Politics," 211.
72. "Convention," *Illinois Intelligencer*, 24 June 1818, p. 3, col. 2.

9. Nothing Certain Can Be Calculated On

1. Nathaniel Pope to *Western Intelligencer*, 21 February 1818, *Western Intelligencer*, 22 April 1818, p. 2, col. 2.
2. Nathaniel Pope to Elias Kent Kane, 8 March 1818, Washington, D.C., Chicago History Museum, Chicago, Illinois.
3. Pease, *The Frontier State*, 10.
4. "Postal-Route Advertisement," 20 May 1814, in Carter, *Territorial Papers*, 16:428.

5. "A Bill Authorising a Survey of Roads," 9 December 1814, Record Series 100.012, Illinois Territory. Territorial General Assembly: Legislative Records, 14 November 1813–14 January 1817, Illinois State Archives, Springfield, Illinois.
6. Buck, *Illinois in 1818*, 113.
7. Putnam, *Illinois and Michigan Canal*, 1–2.
8. "Emigration," *Eastern Argus*, 22 July 1817, p. 3, col. 2.
9. Edwards, *History of Illinois*, 99.
10. Stephen H. Long to George Graham, 4 March 1817, "No. 474. Canal to Connect the Illinois River with Lake Michigan, Communicated to the House of Representatives, December 28, 1819," *American State Papers: Miscellaneous*, 2:556.
11. "A Republican" [Daniel Pope Cook], "To the People of Illinois," *Western Intelligencer*, 22 April 1818, p. 2, col. 3.
12. *Annals of Congress*, 15th Cong., 1st sess., 430.
13. Larson, *Internal Improvement*, 110–11.
14. Edstrom, "Congress," 31.
15. *Annals of Congress*, 14th Cong., 2nd sess., 361.
16. "Veto Message, March 3, 1817" in Hunt, *Writings of James Madison*, 8:386.
17. James Madison to James Monroe, 29 November 1817, in ibid., 8:397. Emphasis in original.
18. *Annals of Congress*, 15th Cong., 1st sess., 17–18.
19. Ibid., 401, 405.
20. Ibid., 21–24.
21. Ibid., 453, 460.
22. "Internal improvements," *Eastern Argus*, 30 December 1817, p. 2, col. 4.
23. Edstrom, "Congress," 35.
24. Colton, *Life and Times*, 1:428.
25. *Annals of Congress*, 15th Cong., 1st sess., 1126. Despite his central role in the advocacy for internal improvements, Tucker later voted against most of the roads and canals propositions (ibid., 1384–89).
26. Ibid., 1128–30, 1193.
27. Ibid., 1277.
28. Ibid., 1317.
29. Ibid., 1201–2.
30. Ibid., 1140, 1142, 1145.
31. Larson, *Internal Improvement*, 119.
32. *Annals of Congress*, 15th Cong., 1st sess., 1249.
33. Ibid., 1384–89.
34. Larson, *Internal Improvement*, 118.
35. *Annals of Congress*, 15th Cong., 1st sess., 1384–89.
36. Meyer, Life and Times, 163.
37. *Annals of Congress*, 15th Cong., 1st sess., 1383–84.

10. *To Accomplish This Object Effectually*

1. John Quincy Adams, "Weather record, Washington, D.C., January 1818–May 1825," *Microfilms of the Adams Papers*, reel 250.
2. *Annals of Congress*, 15th Cong., 1st sess., 1675–76. Livermore opposed the final admission of Illinois the following November (ibid., 15th Cong., 2nd sess., 311).
3. H.R. no. 53, 4 April 1818; *Annals of Congress*, 15th Cong., 1st sess., 1677.
4. Ford, *History of Illinois*, 9–10.
5. *Annals of Congress*, 15th Cong., 1st sess., 1677.
6. H.R. no. 53, 4 April 1818; *Annals of Congress*, 15th Cong., 1st sess., 1677–78. The reference to one-sixth of the three-fifths fund being diverted to a college or university does not appear in the record of debates in *Annals of Congress* or in the final draft of the House bill; it first appears in the draft approved by the House and presented to the Senate for their consideration. H.R. no. 53, 15th Cong., 1st sess., An act To enable the people of the Illinois territory to form a Constitution and State government and for the admission of such state into the Union on an equal footing with the original states, 1818 April 7, Read and refd to Comte. On Public Lands, Record Group 46, U.S. Senate Territorial Papers, Illinois Territory, 11th–23rd Congress, U.S. National Archives and Records Administration, Washington, D.C. Hereafter referred to as H.R. no. 53, 7 April 1818.
7. H.R. no. 53, 4 April 1818; *Annals of Congress*, 15th Cong., 1st sess., 1678; Pope, "Extract of a letter from the Hon. N. Pope, to the Editors, dated Washington, Jan. 24, 1818," p. 3, col. 3.
8. H.R. no. 53, 4 April 1818; *Annals of Congress*, 15th Cong., 1st sess., 1678, 1681.
9. "Postscript," *Western Intelligencer*, 29 April 1818, p. 3, col. 2–page 3, col. 3.
10. *Senate Journal*, 15th Cong., 1st sess., 26 March 1818, 283. The Senate never took up the issue of a constitutional amendment on internal improvements. The first session of the Senate in the 15th Congress ended on 20 April 1818, and the second session did not commence until 16 November.
11. H.R. no. 53, 7 April 1818; *Annals of Congress*, 15th Cong., 1st sess., 345, 351; "Morrow, Jeremiah, (1771–1852)," *Biographical Directory of the United States Congress*, accessed 29 September 2015, http://bioguide.congress.gov/scripts/biodisplay.pl?index=M001003.
12. Pope to King, 10 April 1818. Emphasis in original,
13. *Illinois Intelligencer*, 17 June 1818, p. 2, col. 2.
14. Pope to King, 10 April 1818. Emphasis in original.
15. *Annals of Congress*, 14th Cong., 2nd sess., 88.
16. Steven E. Siry, "King, Rufus," *Dictionary of American Biography*, 10:398–400.
17. Rufus King to Elbridge Gerry, 4 June 1786, King Papers, New-York Historical

Society, rpt. in "Rufus King to Elbridge Gerry, New York, June 4, 1786," *Proceedings of the Massachusetts Historical Society*: 9–10.

18. Prescott, *Drafting the Federal Constitution*, 370–71.
19. Ernst, Rufus King, 362.
20. *Diaries of John Quincy Adams*, 13 April 1818, 335.
21. *Annals of Congress*, 15th Cong., 1st sess., 363.
22. Pope, "Postscript," p. 3, col. 3.
23. Rufus King, "On the Bill for the Admission of the State of Illinois," [April 1818], box 3, folder 6, MS 350, King Family, Papers.
24. Ibid. As a member of the Senate's select committee recommending the admission of Mississippi the previous December, King had voiced no objections in spite of the fact that that territory based its petition in part upon its own census rather than the federal enumeration of 1810 (*Annals of Congress*, 15th Cong., 1st sess., 10, 20).
25. Jeremiah Morrow quoted in Pope, "Postscript," p. 3, col. 3.
26. Bakalis, "Ninian Edwards," 2.
27. *Annals of Congress*, 15th Cong., 1st sess., 363.
28. *House Journal*, 15th Cong., 1st sess., 14 April 1818, 462–63.
29. *Annals of Congress*, 15th Cong., 1st sess., 1274–78, 1384–89.
30. Goldman and Young, *United States Congressional Directories*, 87.
31. *Diaries of John Quincy Adams*, 11 December 1817, 284. Adams mistakenly referred to him as "G. Robinson."
32. *Annals of Congress*, 15th Cong., 1st sess., 1738; *House Journal*, 15th Cong., 1st sess., 15 April 1818, 466–67; ibid., 18 April 1818, 492.
33. James Monroe to Thomas Jefferson, New York, 19 January 1786, in Hamilton, *Writings of James Monroe*, 1:117–18.
34. Pope, "Postscript," p. 3, cols. 3–4.
35. *Diaries of John Quincy Adams*, 20 April 1818, 338.
36. *Illinois Intelligencer*, 17 June 1818, p. 2, col. 2.

11. A Spirit of Enterprise

1. Pope, "Postscript," p. 3, col. 3.
2. "One of the People," "To the People of Illinois," *Western Intelligencer*, 6 May 1818, p. 2, cols. 3–4. Emphasis in original.
3. "Executive Register," 667.
4. *Western Intelligencer*, 6 May 1818, p. 2, col. 3. Cook resigned his judgeship later that month on 27 May 1818 ("Executive Register," 670). In July Cook explained that he had resigned due to "the delicacy of my health," and he feared that his condition "rendered it probable, that I should fail in the regular discharge of my duties." (Daniel Pope Cook, "To the electors of Illinois," *Illinois Intelligencer*, 8 July 1818, p. 2, col. 2.)

5. *Western Intelligencer*, 6 May 1818, p. 2, col. 3.
6. Pease, *Story of Illinois*, 85.
7. Ford, *History of Illinois*, 11, 47.
8. Reynolds, *Pioneer History of Illinois*, 410.
9. Pease, *Frontier State*, 94.
10. Ford, *History of Illinois*, 10.
11. "Kane, Elias Kent, (1794–1835)," *Biographical Directory of the United States Congress*, accessed 15 April 2005, http://bioguide.congress.gov/scripts/biodisplay.pl?index=K000006; Smith, "Life and Public Services," 190; Wager, "Whitesboro's Golden Age," 90. His father was recorded in the 1790 federal census as living in "Canajoxharrie" (Canajoharie) in Montgomery County forty-five miles to the south of Whitesboro, and in 1792 was listed as a resident of Herkimer County, which had been formed from Montgomery in 1791. 1790 U.S. Federal Census (Population Schedule), Canajoxharrie, Montgomery County, New York, p. 87, Elias Kane household; *Poughkeepsie Journal*, 12 September 1792, p. 3, col. 3.
12. Pease, *Frontier State*, 94.
13. Wager, "Whitesboro's Golden Age," 67.
14. Dennistoun Kane, *Story of John Kane*, 43, 49, 77–78, 83–84.
15. Ibid., 85; Wager, "Whitesboro's Golden Age," 90; Elias Kane to Elias Kent Kane, Albany [New York], 20 September 1814, Elias Kent Kane Papers, Chicago History Museum; Smith, "Life and Public Services," 191. George W. Smith was married to Elias Kent Kane's granddaughter (Snyder, *Adam W. Snyder*, 107n).
16. Davis, *Frontier Illinois*, 160.
17. *Return of the Whole Number of Persons within the Several Districts of the United States . . . One Thousand Seven Hundred and Ninety-One*, 33, 41, 55.
18. White, "Slavery in New York," 4, 5, 8, 15.
19. Dennistoun Kane, *Story of John Kane*, 73, 78; 1800 U.S. Federal Census (Population Schedule), Westfield, Washington County, New York, p. 582, Charles Kane household.
20. 1810 U.S. Federal Census (Population Schedule), *New York Ward 2*, New York, New York, p. 129, Elias Kane household; *Aggregate Amount*, 1:28.
21. 1820 U.S. Federal Census (Population Schedule), Albany, New York, p. 179, Elias Kane household.
22. White, "Slavery in New York," 9.
23. *New-York Evening Post*, 27 May 1802, p. 3, col. 4; 5 June 1802, p. 2, col. 1; 8 June 1802, p. 3, col. 4; 8 July 1802, p. 3, col. 5.
24. James Kane to Alida Van Rensselaer, March 1849, rpt. in Dennistoun Kane, *Story of John Kane*, 100.

25. *Laws of Yale-College*, 8–10, 15.
26. Dexter, *Biographical Sketches*, 6:578.
27. Smith, "Life and Public Services," 190–91; Bateman, *Biographical and Memorial Edition*, 1:312.
28. John Kintzing Kane, quoted in Dennistoun Kane, *Story of John Kane*, 109.
29. John Kintzing Kane to Elias Kent Kane, Yale College, 28 April 1814, Elias Kent Kane Papers.
30. Elias Kane to Elias Kent Kane, Albany [New York], 20 September 1814; Sarah Kane Morris quoted in Dennistoun Kane, *Story of John Kane*, 109. Britain's Orders in Council and Napoleon's Berlin and Milan decrees authorized economic blockades that disrupted transatlantic shipping during the Napoleonic Wars. Congress responded with the Embargo Act of 1807, closing U.S. ports to most foreign trade. "Embargo Act," *Encyclopædia Britannica*, accessed 10 February 2022, https://www.britannica.com/topic/Embargo-Act.
31. John Kintzing Kane to Elias Kent Kane, Yale College, 28 April 1814.
32. In April 1814 the *Carthage Gazette* published a notice dated 31 March that the local post office had three letters waiting for Kane that would be sent to the dead letter office if not claimed before 1 July. "A List of Letters remaining in the Post Office at Carthage (Ten.) on the 31st of March, 1814, which, if not taken out before the 1st of July next, will be sent to the General Post-Office as dead letters," *Carthage Gazette*, 9 April 1814, p. 3, col. 4, and 23 April 1814, p. 3, cols. 3–4.
33. *Nashville Whig*, 20 July 1813, p. 3, col. 4.
34. *"State of Tennessee, Supreme Court of Errors and Appeals in the fourth Circuit, July Term 1812*, William L. Bledsoe & others, vs. Oliver Kane and Ann Eliza, his wife, and Harriett Clark, heirs of John Clark, dec'd.," *The Democratic Clarion & Tennessee Gazette*, 11 August 1812, p. 5, col. 2.
35. Elias Kane to Elias Kent Kane, Albany [New York], 20 September 1814. If Kane was writing to announce his wedding plans on 4 August, then he must have been living in Kaskaskia for some time—enough time to meet and propose to his fiancée, at any rate.
36. Norton, *Illinois Census Returns: 1810, 1818*, 4; Greene and Alvord, *Governors' Letter-Books*, 1n.
37. Smith, "Life and Public Services," 192. There is no documentation in the Illinois State Archives that Kane ever emancipated any of his enslaved persons. *Database of Servitude and Emancipation Records (1722–1863)*, accessed 6 June 2003.
38. Ibid.
39. 1820 U.S. Federal Census (Population Schedule), Kaskaskia Township, Randolph County, Illinois, p. 256, Elias Kent Kane household; 1830 U.S. Federal Census (Population Schedule), Randolph County, Illinois, p. 144, Elias Kent

Kane household; 1840 U.S. Federal Census (Population Schedule), Randolph County, Illinois, p. 235, Felicité P. Kane household.

40. Snyder, *Adam W. Snyder*, 62.
41. "Vindex," "E.K. Kane," *Kaskaskia Republican*, 20 July 1824, p. 2, col. 4. Emphasis in original.
42. Reynolds, *My Own Times*, 134.
43. Samuel Morrison, Indianapolis, Indiana, 4 September 1884, quoted in Reynolds, *Pioneer History of Illinois*, 402n.
44. Ford, *History of Illinois*, 15.
45. Snyder, "Forgotten Statesmen of Illinois: Hon. Jesse Burgess Thomas," 514; 1850 U.S. Federal Census (Population schedule), Knox County, Ohio, Mount Vernon, Ward 1, dwelling 326, Jesse B. Thomas household.
46. Esarey, *Messages and Letters*, 1:152n.
47. Jesse B. Thomas to William Henry Harrison, 11 August 1810, SC1531, Letters and papers of Jesse B. Thomas, Manuscripts Division, Abraham Lincoln Presidential Library, Springfield, Illinois. Hereafter referred to as Letters and papers of Jesse B. Thomas.
48. Hall, *Dividing the Union*, 37–38.
49. *Western Sun*, 29 October 1808, p. 3, col. 1. Michael Jones of Kaskaskia is sometimes confused with another prominent politician of the same name from Shawneetown who was Jesse B. Thomas's half-brother. Jones of Shawneetown served with his sibling in the constitutional convention of 1818. Relf, "The Two Michael Joneses," 148–49.
50. "Veritas," "Interragatories for the Delegate from Indiana to Congress while at Washington," *Western Sun*, 5 November 1808, p. 1, col. 3.
51. Rice Jones to Jesse B. Thomas, 17 November 1808, Letters and papers of Jesse B. Thomas. Emphasis in original. Jones also reported that Dr. George Fisher indicated the "Veritas" letter had been written the day before Jesse B. Thomas had left for Washington, D.C., which, Jones speculated, made it "still more probable that Randolph is the author" (ibid.). To some extent this is supported by the possibility that Thomas Randolph had some personal reasons for his attacks on the territorial delegate. The previous July Governor William Henry Harrison had written President Thomas Jefferson that "I have some expectation that Mr Thos. Randolph from Virga [Virginia] whom I have appointed to succeed Mr [Benjamin] Parke as Atty. General will also succeed him as Deligate [*sic*] & I am certain that nothing will prevent it but the short time he has been in the Territory" (William Henry Harrison to Thomas Jefferson, 16 July 1808, in Esarey, *Messages and Letters*, 1:297).
52. "Richard M. Johnson to the Secretary of State," 10 February 1809, in Carter, *Territorial Papers*, 16:8; "David Holmes to the Secretary of State," 10 February

1809, in ibid., 9; "John Pope to [the Secretary of State]," 25 February 1809, in ibid., 12.

53. Suppiger, "Amity to Enmity," 201, 204, 206–7.
54. Ninian Edwards to Jesse B. Thomas, 28 June 1814, Letters and papers of Jesse B. Thomas. Emphasis in original.
55. Francis S. Philbrick, "Introduction," in Philbrick, *Laws of Illinois Territory*, xlix–li; "An Act establishing a supreme Court for Illinois Territory," in ibid., 136–41; Edwards, *History of Illinois*, 86–92. The territorial legislature petitioned Congress in December 1814 to declare that they possessed the power to make such changes. Congress subsequently passed a law that for all intents and purposes had largely the same effect of adding to the territorial judges' responsibilities. "Memorial to Congress by the Legislative Assembly," Carter, *Territorial Papers*, 17:51–53; An Act regulating and defining the duties of the United States' Judges for the territory of Illinois, *U.S. Statutes at Large* 3 (1815): 237–39.
56. Elias Kent Kane to the editor of the *Illinois Herald*, 3 August 1814, Letters and papers of Jesse B. Thomas.
57. Elias Kane to Elias Kent Kane, Albany [New York], 25 April 1815, Elias Kent Kane Papers.

12. The Right to Frame a Constitution

1. John Kintzing Kane to Elias Kent Kane, 27 January 1820, rpt. in Smith, "Life and Public Services," 193.
2. Elias Kane to Elias Kent Kane, 10 January 1825, rpt. in ibid., 194.
3. John Kintzing Kane to Elias Kent Kane, 27 January 1820, 192.
4. Reynolds, *Pioneer History of Illinois*, 410; Crossley, *Courts and Lawyers*, 1:206.
5. Smith, "Life and Public Services," 203.
6. Nathaniel Pope to Elias Kent Kane, 6 January 1817.
7. *Laws passed by the General Assembly of the Illinois Territory, at Their Sixth Session, held at Kaskaskia 1817–18*, 46–50, 72–82; Philbrick, *Laws of Illinois Territory*, 278, 362; Lansden, *History*, 34; Buck, *Illinois in 1818*, 304.
8. "Executive Register," 668.
9. *Laws passed by the General Assembly of the Illinois Territory, at Their Sixth Session, held at Kaskaskia 1817–18*, 42–45.
10. "Executive Register," 666–68, 670–71.
11. Norton, *Illinois Census Returns: 1810, 1818*, xvi.
12. *Illinois Intelligencer*, 17 June 1818, p. 2, col. 2.
13. Boggess, *Settlement of Illinois*, 117.
14. Norton, *Illinois Census Returns: 1810, 1818*, xv.
15. Joseph Philips, *Illinois Intelligencer*, 17 June 1818, p. 2, cols. 2–3.
16. *Illinois Intelligencer*, 17 June 1818, p. 2, col. 2.

17. An Act to enable the people of the Illinois territory to form a constitution and state government, and for the admission of such state into the Union on an equal footing with the original states, *U.S. Statutes at Large* 3 (1817): 429.
18. "Convention," *Illinois Intelligencer*, 24 June 1818, p. 3, col. 2.
19. *Illinois Intelligencer*, 17 June 1818, p. 2, col. 2.
20. Joseph Philips to Messrs. Blackwell & Berry, *Illinois Intelligencer*, 15 July 1818, p. 3, col. 2.
21. Buck, *Illinois in 1818*, 240; Alvord, *Illinois Country*, 462n.
22. "Convention for Illinois," *Western Intelligencer*, 11 March 1818, p. 2, col. 3.
23. "A Friend to Equal Justice," "An Oppressive System of Taxation," *Illinois Intelligencer*, 3 June 1818, p. 3, cols. 2–3. Emphasis in original.
24. "An Old Farmer," *Illinois Intelligencer*, 17 June 1818, p. 3, col. 2.
25. Diary of George Churchill, 8 July 1818, SC 290, George Churchill Papers, 1816–1871, Manuscripts Division, Abraham Lincoln Presidential Library, Springfield, Illinois. Jephthah Lampkin originally emigrated from Kentucky in 1813 to Edwardsville, where "for five or six years [he] carried on a potter's shop, which stood on Main Street." *History of Madison County, Illinois*, 336.
26. Andey Kinney, "Look at Truth," *Illinois Intelligencer*, 10 June 1818, p. 3, cols. 3–4.
27. Ibid., p. 3, col. 4.
28. *Database of Servitude and Emancipation Records (1722–1863)*; *Combined History of Randolph, Monroe and Perry Counties, Illinois*, 132; Norton, *Illinois Census Returns: 1810, 1818*, 143.
29. "Candor," "For the Intelligencer," *Western Intelligencer*, 6 May 1818, p. 2, col. 4.
30. "The People," *Illinois Intelligencer*, 27 May 1818, p. 3, col. 1.
31. "A Republican" [Daniel Pope Cook], "Slavery," *Western Intelligencer*, 1 April 1818, p. 3, cols. 1–3.
32. Daniel Pope Cook to the *Illinois Intelligencer*, 23 July 1818, *Illinois Intelligencer*, 29 July 1818, p. 3, col. 1.
33. "Agis," "No. 1. To the People of Illinois," *Illinois Intelligencer*, 17 June 1818, p. 2, col. 3. Emphasis in original. "Agis" was George Churchill, a professional printer from Vermont who had arrived in Illinois in 1817 and purchased a farm in Madison County. On 5 June 1818 he recorded in his diary that he had sent "the 3 nos. of Agis to Blackwell & Berry to be put in the P[ost]O[ffice]" (Diary of George Churchill, 5 June 1818). Over the years he was active in the columns of both the *Missouri Gazette*—where he advocated for the admission of Missouri as a free state—and the *Edwardsville Spectator*, where he actively campaigned in 1822–24 against calling a second constitutional convention that had the potential for legalizing slavery in Illinois. He later served in the General Assembly as both a representative and a senator. "Letter of George Churchill," 66–67.

34. 1820 U.S. Federal Census (Population Schedule), Edwards County, Illinois, p. 61, Seth Gard household; Gallatin County, Illinois, p. 47, Thomas Sloo household; Johnson County, Illinois, p. 79, John Copland household; Madison County, Illinois, p. 146, William Jones household; 1830 U.S. Federal Census (Population Schedule), Livingston County, Kentucky, p. 15, Hamlet Ferguson household; *Biographical Review of Johnson, Massac, Pope and Hardin Counties, Illinois*, 353–54; "Candidates," *Illinois Intelligencer*, 3 June 1818, p. 3, col. 2; *Combined History of Edwards, Lawrence and Wabash Counties, Illinois*, 298; Dunne, *Illinois*, 4:38; "The Election," *Illinois Emigrant*, 8 July 1818, p. 3, col. 1; "Illinois 1818 Constitutional Convention, Madison County," Tufts University Library, accessed 22 March 2016, https://elections.lib.tufts.edu/catalog/08612p59g; *Illinois Intelligencer*, 27 May 1818, p. 3, col. 1; 17 June 1818, p. 2, col. 2; 24 June 1818, p. 3, col. 2; and 1 July 1818, p. 3, col. 3; *Database of Servitude and Emancipation Records (1722–1863)*; Norton, *Illinois Census Returns: 1810, 1818*, 14, 57, 63, 72, 80, 82, 84, 91, 93, 95, 98, 101, 103, 106, 113, 115, 117, 127, 130, 136, 139, 143–46, 150, 161, 168, 177, 178, 181, 186, 190, 196, 202; Norton, *Illinois Census Returns 1820*, 237–38, 261, 293, 298; Pease, *County Archives*, 410; *Western Intelligencer*, 13 May 1818, p. 3, col. 1. The elected delegates will be discussed in chapter 13. The defeated candidates were: William Boon (Jackson—slaveholder), William H. Bradsby (Washington—slaveholder), John Bradshaw (Union—slaveholder), George Cadwell (Madison—non-slaveholder), John Copland (Johnson—slaveholder), Thomas Cox (Union—slaveholder), Matthew Duncan (Jackson—slaveholder), William Ellis (Gallatin—slaveholder), G. B. Field (Pope—non-slaveholder), John Grammar (or Grammer) (Union—non-slaveholder), R. E. Hancock (or Heacock) (Jackson—non-slaveholder), Jephthah Hardin (Gallatin—slaveholder), Samuel Hayes (Gallatin—non-slaveholder), William Jones (Madison—non-slaveholder), Andey Kinney (Monroe—non-slaveholder), John McFerron (Randolph—non-slaveholder), Joseph Meacham (Madison—unknown), William Mears (St. Clair—slaveholder), Joseph Palmer (Union—non-slaveholder), John Robinson (Gallatin—slaveholder), Thomas Sloo (Gallatin—slaveholder), and Joseph M. Street (Gallatin—slaveholder).

Here are the summary totals of convention delegate candidates in relation to their status as slaveholders or non-slaveholders:

Slaveholder status	*Defeated candidates*	*Elected candidates*	*Total*
Non-slaveholder	9	18	27
Slaveholder	12	13	25
No information available	1	2	3
Total	22	33	55

35. The total African American population of Illinois Territory amounted to 1,095 individuals—317 free persons of color and 778 enslaved persons. All told, there were 265 slaveholding households out of a total of 4,926 households in the territory. Norton, *Illinois Census Returns: 1810, 1818*, 55–210. The census schedules that have not survived include all of Edwards County and most of Randolph County; consequently, the total numbers of enslaved persons and slaveholding households for those counties are unavailable. Parts of the St. Clair County schedules were destroyed by fire. Ibid., xxxi.
36. Ibid., 190; "Illinois Legislature," *Western Intelligencer*, 18 December 1817, p. 2, col. 4.
37. Mills, "Dr. George Cadwell," 113, 119–20.
38. "Petition to Congress by the People of the Illinois Country," in Carter, *Territorial Papers*, 7:545–50.
39. *Combined History of Edwards, Lawrence and Wabash Counties, Illinois*, 298.
40. James Lemen Jr., "A Circular Address. Written by Rev. James Lemen, Jr., September 1821," rpt. in Lemen, *History*, 128.
41. Adolphus F. Hubbard quoted in "A Voter," "For the *Spectator*," *Edwardsville Spectator*, 29 January 1822, p. 3, col. 3.
42. "Illinois Legislature," *Western Intelligencer*, 18 December 1817, p. 3, col. 1. Emphasis in original.
43. *Illinois Senate Journal*, 1828–1829, 182, rpt. in Harris, *History of Negro Servitude*, 233.
44. "Legislative Petition of Dec. 18, 1805," in Dunn, "Slavery Petitions and Papers," 476–83.
45. Elias Kent Kane, "To the People of Illinois," *Edwardsville Spectator*, 25 July 1820, p. 1, col. 1.
46. "The People," *Illinois Intelligencer*, 27 May 1818, p. 3, col. 1.

13. The Great Work Before Us

1. *Illinois Intelligencer*, 1 July 1818, p. 3, col. 3.
2. "Emigration," *Illinois Intelligencer*, 1 July 1818, p. 3, col. 2.
3. "4th of July," *Illinois Intelligencer*, 8 July 1818, p. 3, col. 1; "ANNIVERSARY ORATION, *Delivered in this place on the 4th of July, 1818*, by Theo. V. W. Varick, esquire," ibid., 15 July 1818, p. 2, col. 2.
4. "Felty," "Candidates," *Illinois Intelligencer*, 1 July 1818, p. 4, col. 3.
5. "Agis," "To the People of Illinois, No. III," *Illinois Intelligencer*, 1 July 1818, p. 1, col. 4 and p. 2, col. 1. Three days before the publication of this letter, George Churchill ("Agis") attended a meeting in Edwardsville where he queried the Madison County convention delegate candidates on their views "on the subjects of slavery and of election viva voce." "Mr. [Abraham] Prickett returned a satisfactory answer; but Messrs. [Benjamin] Stephenson and [Joseph] Borough

were not in favor of election by ballot." On election day (6 July) Prickett assured Churchill "that he would use his influence [in the convention] in favor of election by ballot." Churchill recorded that he voted for Prickett, Dr. George Cadwell, and Joseph Meacham (Diary of George Churchill, 27 June and 6 July 1818).

6. Norton, *Centennial History*, 1:146; "The Election," *Illinois Emigrant*, 8 July 1818, p. 3, col. 1; Norton, *Illinois Census Returns: 1810, 1818*, 102, 137; "Illinois 1818 Constitutional Convention, Madison County," Tufts University Library, https://elections.lib.tufts.edu/catalog/08612p59g.
7. Babcock, *Forty Years*, 97–98.
8. Virginia: Isham Harrison, Levi Compton, George Fisher, James Hall Jr., and Jesse B. Thomas. Maryland: Hezekiah West and Thomas Roberts. North Carolina: Andrew Bankson. South Carolina: Hamlet Ferguson, Willis Hargrave, and Thomas Kirkpatrick. Georgia: Abraham Prickett. Carpenter, "Illinois Constitutional Convention of 1818," 336, 343; *Jackson County, Illinois Formation and Settlement*, 109; Johnson County Historical and Genealogical Society, *Johnson County, Illinois History & Families*, 276; Malone, *Group of Family Trees*, 1; "Families of Gillespie Bankston & Cook in Dubuque County 1835 to 1878?" vertical file, Carnegie-Stout Public Library, Dubuque, Iowa; Allen, *Pope County Notes*, 75; *History and Families of Gallatin County Illinois*, 142; Kirkpatrick, *Kirkpatrick Genealogy*, 23; *Portrait and Biographical Record of Madison County, Illinois*, 164; File W10089, "Harrison, Isham," U.S. National Archives and Records Service, *Revolutionary War Pension and Bounty-Land-Warrant Application Files*, reel 1204; Ferguson, "He Acted Well His Part," 272; 1850 U.S. Federal Census (Population schedule), Knox County, Ohio, Mount Vernon, Ward 1, dwelling 326, Jesse B. Thomas household.
9. Pennsylvania: Caldwell Cairns, William McFatridge, Benjamin Stephenson, and Conrad Will. New York: Elias Kent Kane. New Jersey: Seth Gard and Joseph Kitchell. "Dr. Caldwell Cairns," *Find A Grave*, accessed 23 January 2021, https://www.findagrave.com/memorial/131050129/caldwell-cairns; Reynolds, *Pioneer History of Illinois*, 360; Snyder, "Forgotten Statesmen of Illinois: Hon. Conrad Will," 351; *Edwardsville Spectator*, 12 October 1822, p. 3, col. 5; Johnson County Historical and Genealogical Society, 276; Chamberlin, "Elias Kent Kane," 162–63; Perrin, *History of Crawford*, 58; Gibson, "Seth Gard"; Kestenbaum, "Cemeteries and Memorial Sites."
10. Massachusetts: John Messinger. Connecticut: Samuel G. Morse. "An Old Settler Dead," *Belleville Advocate*, 17 September 1846, p. 2, col. 2; 1850 U.S. Federal Census (Population schedule), Warren County, Illinois, dwelling 372, Samuel G. Morse household.
11. Kentucky: Adolphus F. Hubbard and Michael Jones. Illinois: James Lemen Jr. and Enoch Moore. Suppiger, "Jesse Burgess Thomas," 27n; Lemen, *History*,

55; "Adolphus Frederick Hubbard," *Find a Grave*, accessed January 23, 2021, https://www.findagrave.com/memorial/214124771/adolphus-frederick-hubbard; Carpenter, "Illinois Constitutional Convention," 335.

12. Ireland: Samuel Omelveny. McGoorty, "Early Irish of Illinois," 63; Holcomb, *South Carolina Naturalizations*, 160.
13. Unknown birthplaces: Joseph Borough, Edward N. Cullom, William Echols, John K. Mangham, William McHenry, Leonard White, and John Whiteaker.
14. Buck, *Illinois in 1818*, 95.
15. Carpenter, "Illinois Constitutional Convention," 332; "William Biggs to the Secretary of the Treasury," 31 October 1810, in Carter, *Territorial Papers*, 16:136; *Census of Indiana Territory for 1807*, 27, 34, 39, 43; Ferguson, "He Acted Well His Part," 273; Perrin, *History of Crawford*, 130–31; Relf, "Two Michael Joneses," 148; *Sangamo Journal*, 29 September 1832, p. 2, col. 6; Snyder, "Forgotten Statesmen of Illinois: Hon. Jesse Burgess Thomas," 514–15; Suppiger, "Jesse Burgess Thomas," 2–3.
16. Carpenter, "Illinois Constitutional Convention," 333, 335.
17. Perrin, *History of Crawford*, 131; William H. Bradsby to Ninian Edwards, 6 March 1818, Record Series 100.002, Illinois Territory, Executive Records.
18. Perrin, *History of Crawford*, 32.
19. *Jackson County, Illinois Formation and Settlement*, 110. The James Hall Jr. who served as a member of the convention has been confused on occasion with the writer and editor James Hall (1793–1868) (e.g., Carpenter, "Illinois Constitutional Convention," 337–38). R. C. Buley pointed out that the latter could not have been a member of the convention given that he did not arrive in Illinois until 1820. Buley, *Old Northwest*, 1:86n.
20. Dunne, *Illinois*, 4:33; Snyder, "Forgotten Statesmen of Illinois: Hon. Conrad Will," 356.
21. "Carding and fulling" [advertisement], *Illinois Intelligencer*, 3 June 1818, p. 3, col. 4.
22. "Michael Jones and Shadrach Bond to Josiah Meigs," 11 January 1816, and "Thomas Sloo to Josiah Meigs," 18 March 1815, in Carter, *Territorial Papers*, 17:115, 153; *History and Families of Gallatin County Illinois*, 143.
23. Snyder, "Forgotten Statesmen of Illinois: Hon. Conrad Will," 353–54.
24. Reynolds, *Pioneer History of Illinois*, 331.
25. The other slaveholders were Levi Compton, Hamlet Ferguson (who owned nine enslaved persons in Livingston County, Kentucky), Isham Harrison, and Thomas Kirkpatrick. 1830 U.S. Federal Census (Population Schedule), Livingston County, Kentucky, p. 15, Hamlet Ferguson household; *Combined History of Edwards, Lawrence and Wabash Counties, Illinois*, 298; *Database of Servitude and Emancipation Records (1722–1863)*; Norton, *Illinois Census*

Returns: 1810, 1818, 80, 95, 106, 130, 143, 168, 202; Norton, *Illinois Census Returns 1820*, 238; Pease, *County Archives*, 410; Snyder, "Forgotten Statesmen of Illinois: Hon. Conrad Will," 357. The non-slaveholders were Andrew Bankson, Joseph Borough, Edward N. Cullom, William Echols, George Fisher, Seth Gard, Joseph Kitchell, James Lemen Jr., John K. Mangham, William McFatridge, William McHenry, John Messinger, Enoch Moore, Samuel G. Morse, Samuel Omelveny, Thomas Roberts, Hezekiah West, and John Whiteaker. No documentation has been discovered indicating whether Adolphus F. Hubbard and Abraham Prickett were slaveholders or not. Norton, *Illinois Census Returns: 1810, 1818*, 14, 57, 63, 72, 82, 113, 115, 136, 143–44, 150, 161, 177, 186, 190, 196; 1820 U.S. Federal Census (Population Schedule), Edwards County, Illinois, p. 61, Seth Gard household.

26. Philbrick, *Laws of Indiana Territory*, 399. Illinois Territory had retained Indiana's laws governing the militia.
27. The other delegates with military experience were Joseph Borough, Edward N. Cullom, William Echols, Hamlet Ferguson, George Fisher, Seth Gard, Isham Harrison, Thomas Kirkpatrick, Joseph Kitchell, William McFatridge, William McHenry, Enoch Moore, Samuel G. Morse, Abraham Prickett, Thomas Roberts, Hezekiah West, and Leonard White. Whiteaker may also have been a political ally of Ninian Edwards; both lived in Logan County, Kentucky before moving to Illinois, and Whiteaker apparently named his son after the governor in 1810. "The Acting Secretary of War to Leonard White," 7 June 1817, in Carter, *Territorial Papers*, 17:512; Dunne, *Illinois*, 4:40; Carpenter, "Illinois Constitutional Convention," 331, 334–35; *Edwardsville Spectator*, 8 January 1822, p. 3, col. 3; "Executive Register," 622, 630, 633, 634, 636, 637, 638, 639, 641, 646, 648, 649, 652, 653, 654, 657, 660, 665, 668, 669, 671; Stevens, 72, 172–73, 175–77, 180, 182–83, 185, 189–90, 193, 195; Gwathmey, *Historical Register*, 354; *History of Marion and Clinton Counties, Illinois*, 120; *History and Families of Gallatin County Illinois*, 142; Grau, *William McHenry*, 44, 51; Mrs. Carl W. McGhee, *Pension Abstracts*, 32; File W10089, "Harrison, Isham," U.S. National Archives and Records Service, Revolutionary War Pension and Bounty-Land-Warrant Application Files, reel 1204; Gibson, "Seth Gard"; Ausmus, "William Michael 'Billy' McFatridge"; J. M. Moore, *Reminiscences of the Moore Family* (Oakland, Calif.: Evening Tribune and Job Printing House, 1882), rpt. in Moore, "Biography of Enoch Moore"; "Cullom, Edward N.," "Echols, William," and "Kane, Elias K.," *Index to Compiled Service Records*; Whiteaker family Bible records (photocopy), vertical file, Abraham Lincoln Presidential Library, Springfield, Illinois.
28. Brown, *Historical Sketch*, 19n.
29. Adolphus F. Hubbard, quoted in Ford, *History of Illinois*, 38.

30. File W10089, "Harrison, Isham," U.S. National Archives and Records Service, *Revolutionary War Pension and Bounty-Land-Warrant Application Files*, reel 1204; Chamberlin, "Elias Kent Kane," 162.
31. The only other delegate with a comparable education was Conrad Will; it was said that he had "studied medicine in one of the Philadelphia medical colleges and received from it the doctor's degree." Snyder, "Forgotten Statesmen of Illinois: Hon. Conrad Will," 351.
32. The building was the property of Dr. George Fisher, the other delegate representing Randolph County. He later received forty-eight dollars in rent for its use as the site of the convention. Warrant no. 874, "George Fisher for house rent during the sitting of Convention," 26 April 1819, Record Series 105.004, Auditor of Public Accounts, "Daybooks."
33. Ford, *History of Illinois*, 10.
34. Joseph Kitchell of Crawford County was second after Kane in the number of motions made (twenty-two), followed by John Messinger of St. Clair County (twelve).
35. "The Illinois Constitutional Convention of 1818: Journal of the Convention," 356. Hereafter referred to as "Journal of the Convention."
36. "Convention," *Illinois Intelligencer*, 5 August 1818, p. 3, col. 1.
37. "Journal of the Convention," 358–59. Interestingly, the *Intelligencer* reported in its issue of the same date: "Since the above was in type [i.e., the newspaper's story on Kane's motion to appoint a committee on the census], we have been informed by the committee appointed to examine the returns . . . that the actual population returned, (with the addition which has been made since the 1st of June) amounts to 40,156." "Convention," *Illinois Intelligencer*, 5 August 1818, p. 3, col. 1. This issue of the *Intelligencer* was being prepared for publication sometime after adjournment on 4 August but before the final census report was discussed on the morning of the fifth. Presumably the committee calculated the corrected total of 40,258 during that same time. The *Intelligencer* reported the new number in its following issue ("Illinois Convention," *Illinois Intelligencer*, 12 August 1818, p. 3, col. 1).
38. "Journal of the Convention," 359.
39. The members of the committee were Leonard White of Gallatin, Elias Kent Kane of Randolph, Abraham Prickett of Madison, James Lemen Jr. of St. Clair, Caldwell Cairns of Monroe, Edward N. Cullom of Crawford, Willis Hargrave of White, Levi Compton of Edwards, Thomas Roberts of Franklin, Thomas Kirkpatrick of Bond, Andrew Bankson of Washington, James Hall Jr. of Jackson, Hezekiah West of Johnson, William Echols of Union, and Samuel Omelveny of Pope. Ibid., 359–60.
40. Ibid., 401, 407, 411–12. The non-slaveholders were Bankson, Cullom, Echols, Lemen, Omelveny, Roberts, and West. The slaveholders were Cairns, Compton,

Hall, Hargrave, Kane, Kirkpatrick, and White. Prickett's status as either a slaveholder or a non-slaveholder is unknown.

41. *Illinois Intelligencer*, 5 August 1818, p. 3, col. 2. The relatives of James Lemen Jr. who signed the letter were his father, James Lemen Sr., and his uncle, Jacob Ogle.
42. Cornelius, *Constitution Making in Illinois*, 10–11.
43. Snyder, "Forgotten Statesmen of Illinois: Hon. Conrad Will," 360n.
44. "Journal of the Convention," 360, 365.
45. Ibid., 365, 418.
46. Ibid., 366, 388–89; *Illinois Intelligencer*, 12 August 1818, p. 3, cols. 1–2.
47. "Journal of the Convention," 368.
48. Cornelius, *Constitution Making in Illinois*, 11.
49. All references to these state constitutions are taken from Wallis, *NBER/Maryland State Constitutions Project*.
50. "Journal of the Convention," 369–74, 386–87, 404–5.
51. "An Observer," *Illinois Intelligencer*, 12 August 1818, p. 3, col. 2. Emphasis in original.
52. "Journal of the Convention," 404.
53. Ibid., 371–74, 388.
54. Ibid., 373, 388–89, 397.
55. Ibid., 371–72, 375, 396–97, 405–6, 422. Samuel Morse of Bond County moved to reconsider the final vote dealing with salaries on 21 August, which Messinger supported and Kane opposed. The motion failed by a vote of 16–15. Abraham Prickett succeeded in convincing the convention to reconsider on 24 August by a vote of 16–14. The convention's subsequent vote to decrease the salary was by a margin of 17–14. Ibid., 415–16, 422.
56. "A Republican" [Daniel Pope Cook], *Western Intelligencer*, 27 November 1817, p. 3, col. 3.
57. Cornelius, *Constitution Making in Illinois*, 13.
58. "Journal of the Convention," 376–77, 390–91, 398.
59. Cornelius, *Constitution Making in Illinois*, 35.
60. "Journal of the Convention," 375, 389, 404.
61. Ibid., 404.
62. Ibid., 375–79.
63. Ibid., 413–14.
64. Ibid., 415, 417.
65. Ford, *History of Illinois*, 11–13. Berry had also been one of Daniel Pope Cook's successors as publisher of the *Western Intelligencer*.
66. "Journal of the Convention," 402.
67. Ibid., 377–78, 391.
68. Ibid., 379, 392.

14. A Little "PRUDENCE"

1. "A Friend to Enquiry," *Illinois Intelligencer*, 22 July 1818, p. 2, cols. 2, 4.
2. "Prudence," *Illinois Intelligencer*, 29 July 1818, p. 2, col. 4. Emphasis in original. It is possible that the "convention's dictator" is a reference to Kane, who was reputed to have composed the first draft of the constitution even before the convention began.
3. "Pacificus" [Henry S. Dodge], "*To the honorable members of the convention of the Illinois Territory*," *Illinois Intelligencer*, 12 August 1818, p. 2, col. 1. Emphasis in original.
4. Ibid., p. 2, cols. 2–3.
5. Henry S. Dodge, *Kaskaskia Republican*, 23 March 1824, p. 3, col. 3. Dodge was not himself a slaveholder (1820 U.S. Federal Census [Population Schedule], Kaskaskia Township, Randolph County, Illinois, p. 94).
6. "Journal of the Convention," 380.
7. Ibid., 392, 400–401.
8. Hall, *Dividing the Union*, 100.
9. "Illinois convention," *Illinois Intelligencer*, 19 August 1818, p. 3, col. 2. Emphasis in original.
10. Smith, "Salines of Southern Illinois," 249; Norton, *Illinois Census Returns: 1810, 1818*, 95.
11. "Journal of the Convention," 406–7.
12. Ibid., 411–12.
13. Harris, *History of Negro Servitude*, 21. Remarkably, Harris arrived at his conclusions before the only extant copy of the convention journal was located in 1905.
14. "Journal of the Convention," 400–401.
15. Ibid., 406–7.
16. Ibid., 411.
17. Completely pro-slavery delegates: Samuel G. Morse (Bond County), Joseph Kitchell (Crawford County), Isham Harrison (Franklin County), Adolphus F. Hubbard (Gallatin County), Michael Jones (Gallatin County), Leonard White (Gallatin County), James Hall Jr. (Jackson County), Conrad Will (Jackson County), Benjamin Stephenson (Madison County), Samuel Omelveny (Pope County), George Fisher (Randolph County), Elias Kent Kane (Randolph County), and John Messinger (St. Clair County).
18. Completely antislavery delegates: Levi Compton (Edwards County), Seth Gard (Edwards County), William McFatridge (Johnson County), Hezekiah West (Johnson County), James Lemen Jr. (St. Clair County), William Echols (Union County), and John Whiteaker (Union County).
19. Delegates leaning antislavery: Thomas Kirkpatrick (Bond County), Joseph Borough (Madison County), Abraham Prickett (Madison County), Caldwell

Cairns (Monroe County), Enoch Moore (Monroe County), and Andrew Bankson (Washington County).

20. Delegates leaning pro-slavery: Edward N. Cullom (Crawford County), Thomas Roberts (Franklin County), Hamlet Ferguson (Pope County), Willis Hargrave (White County), and William McHenry (White County).
21. It bears mentioning that as president of the convention, Jesse B. Thomas refrained from casting a vote on all but two of the sixteen recorded roll-call votes, neither of them dealing with Article VI. Given that he was the mentor of Elias Kent Kane, who seems to have been the prime mover in the evolution of the slavery provision, and taking into account Thomas's status as a slaveholder, it seems likely, as Matthew W. Hall observed, that Thomas supported the compromise. He can be considered, in other words, as standing with the pro-slavery contingent (Hall, *Dividing the Union*, 103).
22. Reynolds, *Pioneer History of Illinois*, 330–31; Mills, "Dr. George Cadwell," 112–13.
23. "Memorial of Randolph and St. Clair Counties Jan. 17–1806," in Dunn, "Slavery Petitions and Papers," 498–502. Interestingly, one of the other signers was James Lemen; possibly this was Messinger's future fellow convention delegate James Lemen Jr., but since he left off any designation as either "Junior" or "Senior" it may well have been the elder Lemen. In any case both were equally and profoundly opposed to slavery.
24. "Petition to Congress by the People of the Illinois Country," in Carter, *Territorial Papers*, 7:545–50.
25. Philbrick, *Laws of Indiana Territory*, cclin; *Edwardsville Spectator*, 12 April 1823, p. 3, col. 1.
26. Here are the precise numbers for each county:

Fully antislavery delegations (voting antislavery on all three votes):

Edwards: 2 fully antislavery delegates
Johnson: 2 fully antislavery delegates
Union: 2 fully antislavery delegates

Delegations leaning toward antislavery

Madison: 2 delegates leaning antislavery, 1 delegate fully pro-slavery
Monroe: 2 delegates leaning antislavery
Washington: 1 delegate leaning antislavery

Fully pro-slavery delegations (voting pro-slavery on all three votes):

Gallatin: 3 fully pro-slavery delegates
Jackson: 2 fully pro-slavery delegates
Randolph: 2 fully pro-slavery delegates

Fully or leaning pro-slavery delegations:

Crawford: 1 fully pro-slavery delegate and 1 delegate leaning pro-slavery
Franklin: 1 fully pro-slavery delegate and 1 delegate leaning pro-slavery

Pope: 1 fully pro-slavery delegate and 1 delegate leaning pro-slavery
White: 2 delegates leaning pro-slavery

Mixed pro-slavery and antislavery delegations:

Bond: 1 fully pro-slavery delegate and 1 delegate leaning antislavery
St. Clair: 1 fully pro-slavery delegate and 1 delegate fully antislavery

27. The enslaved populations of the other counties in 1818 in descending order: Monroe (41), Union (39), Washington (31), Johnson (24), Crawford (20), Bond and Franklin (15 each), and Randolph (2). Norton, *Illinois Census Returns: 1810, 1818*, 61, 77, 83, 102, 110, 116, 137, 144, 155, 170, 182, 192–93, 210. The returns for Pope County only list that its population included "64 Blacks"; no distinction was made between those who were free and those who were enslaved (ibid., 153).
28. H.W. [Hooper Warren], "A Voice from the Past," *Genius of Liberty*, 19 December 1840, p. 1, col. 3. In a diary entry dated 11 August 1818, George Churchill recorded a rumor he had heard from Dr. George Cadwell's son Bache that Ninian Edwards had "sold his slaves, turned opponent to slavery, and influenced 5 or 6 members of the Convention to turn also" (Diary of George Churchill, 11 August 1818). Aside from the direct evidence within the convention, the story was demonstrably false, for Edwards, who held four enslaved persons at the time, added two more by the time of the 1820 federal census (Norton, *Illinois Census Returns: 1810, 1818*, 130; 1820 U.S. Federal Census [Population Schedule], Six Mile Prairie, Madison County, Illinois, page 17, Ninian Edwards household).
29. Hall, *Dividing the Union*, 99.
30. "Journal of the Convention," 380, 392, 412.
31. Ibid., 380–83, 402, 412. Kane's father had written to him of his financial troubles at some length in 1814: "To fall from the proud standing I held in society as a merchant to irretrievable bankruptcy, has so overcome and disheartened me that I shall never attempt to rise in that line again, even if I should get clear of my debts, which I see no present prospect of." Elias Kane to Elias Kent Kane, Albany [New York], 20 September 1814.
32. "Journal of the Convention," 383.

15. *Fait Accompli*

1. "Journal of the Convention," 384–86, 393.
2. Ibid., 393–94, 400.
3. Ibid., 402–3.
4. Ibid., 402.
5. "Constitution of 1818," in Verlie, *Illinois Constitutions*, 46. There does not seem to be any reference to this section of the schedule in the "Journal of the Convention." It seems likely that it was inserted in the part of the convention described in the missing pages of the journal—i.e., later on 24 or on 25 or 26 August.

6. Ford, *History of Illinois*, 11–12.
7. "Journal of the Convention," 412, 414; Buck, *Illinois in 1818*, 286.
8. "Journal of the Convention," 416, 418–19, 420–21.
9. An Act to enable the people of the Indiana Territory, 290–91.
10. Buck, *Illinois in 1818*, 287; "Ripley," *Illinois Intelligencer*, 3 June 1818, p. 4, col. 1.
11. Brown, "Early History of Illinois," 89.
12. "Journal of the Convention," 402–3, 407.
13. Ibid., 407–8.
14. Ibid., 408; "Covington," *Western Intelligencer*, 13 May 1818, p. 3, col. 3; "Town of Covington," *Illinois Intelligencer*, 29 July 1818, p. 3, col. 4.
15. "Journal of the Convention," 408.
16. *Illinois Public Domain Land Tract Sales Database.*
17. Nathaniel Pope, "Proposal to fix the seat of government of the state of Illinois on Pope's Bluff, 24 August 1818," box 1, folder 1810–1818, John Messinger Papers, 1797–1878, Manuscripts Division, Abraham Lincoln Presidential Library, Springfield, Illinois.
18. Buck, *Illinois in 1818*, 291–92.
19. "Journal of the Convention," 408.
20. Ibid., 408–9.
21. Ibid., 409.
22. Ibid., 416–17.
23. Ibid., 423–24. The 1st General Assembly sent a petition requesting this land donation to Congress, where it was introduced by Illinois's first representative John McLean on 7 December 1818. As one of the state's first U.S. senators, Jesse B. Thomas introduced a bill to this effect on 25 February 1819. The Senate approved the bill on 1 March and sent it to the House of Representatives, which concurred on the following day. It was signed into law by President Monroe on 3 March. *House Journal*, 15th Cong., 2nd sess., 7 December 1818, 67; *Senate Journal*, 15th Cong., 2nd sess., 25 February 1819, 306; 1 March 1819, 323; 2 March 1819, 337; 3 March 1819, 356.
24. "Journal of the Convention," 415. Kane's associate Henry S. Dodge—"Pacificus"—was designated to assist William Greenup, secretary of the convention, "in enrolling the different articles of the constitution," for which he was later paid a total of fifty dollars. Ibid.; warrant no. 863, "Henry L. Dodge, for enrolling the Constitution," 14 April 1819, Record Series 105.004, Auditor of Public Accounts, "Daybooks."
25. Simeone, *Democracy and Slavery*, 61.
26. Already the delegates were benefiting personally from the statehood process; they were paid an average of $127.87 for their work during the convention. "The members of the Convention," warrant nos. 467–69, 471–72, 475, 528–31,

15 March 1819; warrant nos. 547, 553–56, 570, 601, 613, 628–31, 639, 650, 652–53, 660–62, 669–71, 696, 718–19, 1 April 1819; warrant no. 816, 8 April 1819; warrant nos. 840–41, 10 April 1819; warrant nos. 865–66, 872–73, 24 April 1819; warrant no. 889, 30 April 1819; warrant nos. 891–95, 7 May 1819; warrant nos. 920–22, 12 July 1819; warrant no. 933, 17 August 1819; warrant no. 1018, 11 October 1819; warrant no. 1030, 28 October 1819, Record Series 105.004, Auditor of Public Accounts, "Daybooks."

27. "Citizen," "A review of the constitution of Illinois: no. I," *Illinois Intelligencer*, 30 September 1818, p. 3, col. 1.
28. "Kaskaskia, July 4, 1813," *Missouri Gazette*, p. 3, col. 4.
29. *Illinois Intelligencer*, 2 September 1818, p. 2, col. 3.

Epilogue

1. Ninian Edwards, Edwardsville, Illinois, 10 September 1818, SC 447, Ninian Edwards, Letters, 1812–1833, Manuscripts Division, Abraham Lincoln Presidential Library, Springfield, Illinois.
2. "Election Returns," *Illinois Emigrant*, 17 October 1818, p. 2, col. 2.
3. Thompson, "Illinois Whigs before 1846," 10.
4. *Blue Book of the State of Illinois 1931–1932*, 738.
5. Daniel Pope Cook, "To the people of Illinois," *Illinois Intelligencer*, 2 September 1818, p. 3, col. 3.
6. *Western Intelligencer*, 20 May 1818, p. 2, col. 3; Burnham, "Forgotten Statesmen of Illinois: Hon. John McLean," 191–92; 1810 U.S. Federal Census (Population Schedule), Logan County, Kentucky, p. 171, Ephram McLean household. There are no indications that John McLean was himself a slaveholder during his residence in Illinois (1820 U.S. Federal Census [Population Schedule], Gallatin County, Illinois, p. 55, John McLean household; 1830 U.S. Federal Census [Population Schedule], Gallatin County, Illinois, p. 262, John McLean household).
7. "Executive Register," 667–68.
8. Orlando B. Ficklin quoted in Moses, *Illinois, Historical and Statistical*, 1:294–95; *Illinois Intelligencer*, 23 September 1818, p. 3, col. 1; "Election Returns," *Illinois Emigrant*, 17 October 1818, p. 2, col. 2.
9. *Illinois Intelligencer*, 19 August 1818, p. 3, col. 3; "Candidates," *Illinois Intelligencer*, 26 August 1818, p. 3, col. 2; *Illinois Intelligencer*, 9 December 1818, p. 3, col. 2; Angle, "Nathaniel Pope," 150–51.
10. Thompson, 11–12.
11. "William C. Greenup to Henry Clay," 11 September 1818, in Carter, *Territorial Papers*, 17:602; *Annals of Congress*, 15th Cong., 2nd sess., 290–91.
12. Ibid., 296.
13. Ibid., 297–98.

14. *Speech of the Honorable James Tallmadge, Jr.*, 14.
15. *Annals of Congress*, 15th Cong., 2nd sess., 305–7.
16. Ibid., 308–11.
17. Ibid., 23, 26, and 31–32.
18. "Illinois," *Illinois Intelligencer*, 30 December 1818, p. 3, col. 1; Ninian Edwards, "Copy of a Letter to the Editors, dated Washington, Dec. 4, 1818," *Illinois Emigrant*, 26 December 1818, p. 1, col. 1.
19. *Senate Journal*, 15th Cong., 2nd sess., 4 December 1818, 52; *Annals of Congress*, 15th Cong., 2nd sess., 342.
20. Ford, *History of Illinois*, 9–10.
21. "Illinois," *Illinois Intelligencer*, 30 December 1818, p. 3, col. 1.
22. Hall, *Dividing the Union*, 192, 215–16, 217.
23. Pease, *Illinois Election Returns 1818–1848*, 74; Howard, *Illinois Governors*, 25–28.
24. Anson Miller quoted in Tyler, "One of Mr. Lincoln's," 253–54.
25. Harris, *History of Negro Servitude*, 29; Elias Kent Kane, "To the People of Illinois," *Edwardsville Spectator*, 25 July 1820, p. 1, cols. 1–3.
26. Smith, "Life and Public Services," 197, 202.
27. Daniel Pope Cook, "To the Electors of illinois," *Illinois Intelligencer*, 14 April 1819, p. 3, col. 3.
28. "$29.75," "To the Editors of the Illinois Emigrant," *Illinois Emigrant*, 8 May 1819, p. 3, col. 1.
29. Pease, *Illinois Election Returns 1818–1848*, 1–2; Diaries of John Quincy Adams, 2 May 1820, 326.
30. Burns, "Daniel P. Cook," 438–39.
31. Ninian Edwards to Henry Clay, 21 September 1826, in Washburne, *Edwards Papers*, 260–61.
32. *Diaries of John Quincy Adams*, 27 November 1826, 127.
33. Burns, "Daniel P. Cook," 436–37; Pease, *Illinois Election Returns 1818–1848*, 30–35.
34. "COOK, Daniel Pope, (1794–1827)," *Biographical Directory of the United States Congress*, accessed 22 April 2016, http://bioguide.congress.gov/scripts/biodisplay.pl?index=C000716; Kentucky Reporter, 24 October 1827, p. 3, col. 2; "The Late Daniel P. Cook, of Illinois," *New-York Evening Post*, 17 June 1828, p. 2, cols. 1–3; Peck, *A Sermon*, 11.

BIBLIOGRAPHY

"79. A Bill for the More General Diffusion of Knowledge, 18 June 1779." In *The Papers of Thomas Jefferson*, vol. 2, 1777–18 June 1779, edited by Julian P. Boyd, 526–35. Princeton, NJ: Princeton University Press, 1950. Rpt. In U.S. National Archives. *Founders Online*. Accessed 30 June 2015, http://founders.archives.gov/documents/Jefferson/01-02-02-0132-0004-0079.

Adams Manuscript Trust, Boston, and Massachusetts Historical Society. *Microfilms of the Adams Papers Owned by the Adams Manuscript Trust and Deposited in the Massachusetts Historical Society*. Boston: Massachusetts Historical Society, 1954.

"Adolphus Frederick Hubbard." *Find a Grave*. Accessed 23 January 2021, https://www.findagrave.com/memorial/214124771/adolphus-frederick-hubbard.

Aggregate Amount of Each Description of Persons within the United States of America, and the Territories Thereof, Agreeably to Actual Enumeration Made According to Law, in the Year 1810. 2 vols. Washington: n.p., 1811.

Ahlstrom, Sydney E. *A Religious History of the American People*. 2nd ed. New Haven, Conn.: Yale University Press, 2004.

Albion, Robert Greenhalgh. *Square-Riggers on Schedule: The New York Sailing Packets to England, France, and the Cotton Ports*. N.p.: Archon Books, 1965.

Allen, John W. *Pope County Notes*. Carbondale: Southern Illinois University, 1949.

Allen, William B. *A History of Kentucky*. Louisville, Ky.: Bradley & Gilbert, 1872.

Alvord, Clarence Walworth. *The Illinois Country 1673–1818*. Chicago: A. C. McClurg & Co., 1922.

———, ed. *Governor Edward Coles*. Collections of the Illinois State Historical Library, vol. 15. Springfield, Ill.: Trustees of the Illinois State Historical Library, 1920.

American National Biography Online. New York: Oxford University Press, 2000. http://www.anb.org.

American State Papers. Washington, D.C.: Gales and Seaton, 1834.

Angle, Paul M. "Nathaniel Pope, 1784–1850: A Memoir." *Illinois State Historical Society Transactions* 43 (1936): 111–81.

———. Papers. Chicago History Museum, Chicago, Illinois.

Annals of Congress, 10th Cong., 1st sess.

———. 11th Cong., 3rd sess.

———. 14th Cong., 2nd sess.

———. 15th Cong., 1st sess.

———. 15th Cong., 2nd sess.

Argus of Western America. Frankfort, Ky.: Amos Kendall & Co. Newspaper.

Aron, Stephen. *American Confluence: The Missouri Border from Borderland to Border State*. Bloomington: Indiana University Press, 2006.

Ausmus, S. "William Michael 'Billy' McFatridge." *Illinois Trails History and Genealogy*. Accessed 3 January 2005, https://web.archive.org/web/20071011170818/http://www.iltrails.org/mcfatridge_biography.htm.

Babcock, Rufus, ed. *Forty Years of Pioneer Life: Memoir of John Mason Peck D.D.* Philadelphia: American Baptist Publication Society, 1864.

Bakalis, Michael J. "Ninian Edwards and Territorial Politics in Illinois: 1775–1818." PhD diss., Northwestern University, 1966.

Banta, R. E. *The Ohio*. Rivers of America. New York: Rinehart & Company, 1949.

Barrett, Walter. *The Old Merchants of New York City*. 3 vols. New York: M. Doolady, 1870.

Bateman, Newton. *Biographical and Memorial Edition of the Historical Encyclopedia of Illinois*. Chicago: Munsell Publishing Company, 1915.

Bateman, Newton, and Paul Selby, eds. *Historical Encyclopedia of Illinois*. Chicago: Munsell Publishing Company, 1900.

The Belleville Advocate. Belleville, Ill.: Boyd & Clark. Newspaper.

Berry, Daniel. "Morris Birkbeck and His Friends." *Transactions of the Illinois State Historical Society* 9 (1904): 259–73.

Biles, Roger. *Illinois: A History of the Land and Its People*. DeKalb: Northern Illinois University Press, 2005.

Biographical Directory of the United States Congress, 1774–Present. http://bioguide.congress.gov.

The Biographical Review of Johnson, Massac, Pope and Hardin Counties, Illinois. Chicago: Biographical Publishing Co., 1893.

Birkbeck, Morris. *Letters from Illinois*. 2nd ed. London: Printed [by T. Miller] for Taylor and Hessey, 1818.

———. *Notes on a Journey in America: From the Coast of Virginia to the Territory of Illinois*. 2nd ed. London: Severn & Co., 1818.

Bloom, Jo Tice. "Peaceful Politics: The Delegates from Illinois Territory, 1809–1818." *The Old Northwest* 6, no. 3 (Fall 1980): 203–15.

Blue Book of the State of Illinois 1927–1928. Springfield, Ill.: Louis L. Emmerson, Secretary of State, 1927.

Blue Book of the State of Illinois 1931–1932. Springfield, Ill.: Journal Printing Co., 1931.

Bode, Gus. "The Curse of Kaskaskia." *Daily Egyptian* (Carbondale: Southern Illinois University), 30 October 2002. Accessed 6 January 2005, http://dailyegyptian.com/31515/archives/the-curse-of-kaskaskia.

Boggess, Arthur Clinton. *The Settlement of Illinois 1778–1830*. Chicago Historical Society's Collection, vol. 5. Chicago: Chicago Historical Society, 1908.

Boswell, James. *The Life of Samuel Johnson, LL.D Including A Journal of a Tour to the Hebrides*. 2 vols. Boston: Carter, Hendee and Co., 1832.

Broome, Angela, Librarian Archivist, Courtney Library, Royal Institution of Cornwall. "Re: Queensbury Packet" (e-mail communication). 26 October 2007.

Brown, William H. "Early History of Illinois." *Early Illinois*. Fergus Historical Series, no. 14. Chicago: Fergus Printing Company, 1881.

———. *An Historical Sketch of the Early Movement in Illinois for the Legalization of Slavery: Read at the Annual Meeting of the Chicago Historical Society, Dec. 5th, 1864*. Chicago: Fergus Print. Co., 1876.

———. *Memoir of the Late Hon. Daniel Pope Cook: Read before the Chicago Historical Society, June 9, 1857*. Chicago: Scripps, Bross & Spears, 1857.

Buck, Solon Justus. *Illinois in 1818*. Springfield, Ill.: The Illinois Centennial Commission, 1917.

Buisseret, David. *Historic Illinois from the Air*. Chicago: University of Chicago Press, 1990.

Buley, R. Carlyle. *The Old Northwest: Pioneer Period, 1815–1840*. 2 vols. Indianapolis: Indiana Historical Society, 1950.

Burnham, J. H. "Destruction of Kaskaskia by the Mississippi River." *Transactions of the Illinois State Historical Society* 20 (1914): 94–112.

———. "Forgotten Statesmen of Illinois: Hon. John McLean." *Transactions of the Illinois State Historical Society*, no. 8 (1903): 190–201.

Burns, Josephine E. "Daniel P. Cook." *Journal of the Illinois State Historical Society* 6, no. 3 (October 1913): 425–44.

Carpenter, Richard V. "The Illinois Constitutional Convention of 1818: Introduction." *Journal of the Illinois State Historical Society* 6, no. 3 (October 1913): 327–54.

Carter, Clarence Edwin, comp. and ed. *The Territorial Papers of the United States*. Vol. 2: *The Territory Northwest of the River Ohio, 1787–1803*. Washington, D.C.; GPO, 1934.

———. *The Territorial Papers of the United States*. Vol. 5: *The Territory of Mississippi, 1798–1817*. Washington, D.C.: GPO, 1937.

———. *The Territorial Papers of the United States*. Vol. 7: *The Territory of Indiana, 1800–1810*. Washington, D.C.: GPO, 1939.

———. *The Territorial Papers of the United States*. Vol. 14: *The Territory of Louisiana-Missouri 1806–1814*. Washington, D.C.: GPO, 1949.

———. *The Territorial Papers of the United States*. Vol. 16: *The Territory of Illinois, 1809–1814*. Washington, D.C.: GPO, 1948.

———. *The Territorial Papers of the United States*. Vol. 17: *The Territory of Illinois, 1814–1818*. Washington, D.C.: GPO, 1950.

———. *The Territorial Papers of the United States*. Vol. 18: *The Territory of Alabama, 1817–1819*. Washington, D.C.: GPO, 1952.

Carthage Gazette. Carthage, Tenn.: Published by William Moore for X. J. Gaines. Newspaper.

Census of Indiana Territory for 1807. Indianapolis: Indiana Historical Society, 1980.

Chamberlin, Henry Barrett. "Elias Kent Kane." *Transactions of the Illinois State Historical Society* 13 (1908): 162–70.

Churchill, George. Papers, 1816–1871. SC 290. Manuscripts Division, Abraham Lincoln Presidential Library, Springfield, Illinois.

Clark, George Rogers. *The Conquest of the Illinois*. Carbondale: Southern Illinois University Press, 2001.

Coles, Edward. Papers. Chicago History Museum, Chicago, Illinois.

Collins, Lewis. *History of Kentucky*. 2 vols. Covington, Ky.: Collins & Co., 1874.

Colton, Calvin. *The Life and Times of Henry Clay*. 2nd ed. 2 vols. New York: A. S. Barnes & Co., 1846.

The Columbian. New York: H. Levine. Newspaper.

Combined History of Edwards, Lawrence and Wabash Counties, Illinois. Philadelphia: J. L. McDonough & Co., 1883.

Combined History of Randolph, Monroe and Perry Counties, Illinois. Philadelphia: J. L. McDonough & Co., 1883.

Commercial Advertiser. New York: Lewis & Hall. Newspaper.

Cook, C. B. *Daniel Pope Cook and John Cook*. N.p.: n.p., 1971.

Cornelius, Janet. *Constitution Making in Illinois, 1818–1970*. Urbana: Published for the Institute of Government and Public Affairs by the University of Illinois Press, 1972.

Crossley, Frederic B. *Courts and Lawyers of Illinois*. 4 vols. Chicago: The American Historical Society, 1916.

Louisville Daily Journal. Louisville, Ky.: Prentice & Buxton. Newspaper.

Dane, Nathan, to Rufus King. 16 July 1787. Original manuscript in the Wisconsin Historical Society Archives (SC 1423). Rpt. in Wisconsin Historical Society. "Turning Points in Wisconsin History." Accessed 1 July 2015, http://content.wisconsinhistory.org/cdm/ref/collection/tp/id/39613.

"Daniel Pope Cook." *Cook and Related Families Database from the Files of Samuel J. Cook*, Milan, Missouri. Accessed 15 June 2005, http://sjcook.com/genealogy/TNG/getperson.php?personID=I3350&tree=Complete&PHP (site discontinued).

Davidson, Alexander, and Bernard Stuvé. *A Complete History of Illinois From 1673 to 1873: Embracing the Physical Features of the Country, Its Early Explorations, Aboriginal Inhabitants. . . .* Springfield: Illinois Journal Company, 1874.

Davis, James E. *Frontier Illinois*. Bloomington: Indiana University Press, 1998.

The Democratic Clarion & Tennessee Gazette. Nashville, Tenn.: Thomas G. Bradford. Newspaper.

Dexter, Franklin Bowditch. *Biographical Sketches of the Graduates of Yale College with Annals of the College History*. New Haven, CT: Yale University Press, 1912.

The Diaries of John Quincy Adams: A Digital Collection. Boston: Massachusetts Historical Society, 2012. Accessed 11 June 2012, https://www.masshist.org/jqadiaries/php/.

Dictionary of American Biography. 22 vols. New York: Charles Scribner's Sons, 1928.

Douglass, Robert Sidney. *History of Southeast Missouri: A Narrative Account of Its Historical Progress, Its People and Its Principal Interests*. 2 vols. Chicago: Lewis Publishing Company, 1912.

Dunn, Jacob Piatt. "Slavery Petitions and Papers." *Indiana Historical Society Publications* 2, no. 12 (1894): 444–529.

Dunne, Edward F. *Illinois: The Heart of the Nation*. 5 vols. Chicago: The Lewis Publishing Company, 1933.

Eastern Argus. Portland, Mass.: Francis Douglas. Newspaper.

Eby, Cecil. *"That Disgraceful Affair," The Black Hawk War*. 1st ed. New York: W. W. Norton & Company, 1973.

Edstrom, James A. "'A Mighty Contest': The Jefferson-Lemen Compact Reevaluated." *Journal of the Illinois State Historical Society* 97, no. 3 (Autumn 2004): 192–215.

———. "Congress and the Illinois Statehood Movement." MA thesis, University of Illinois at Urbana-Champaign, 1990.

Edwards, Ninian. Letters, 1812–1833. SC 447. Manuscripts Division, Abraham Lincoln Presidential Library, Springfield, Illinois.

———. Papers. Chicago History Museum, Chicago, Illinois.

Edwards, Ninian W. *History of Illinois, from 1778 to 1833; and Life and Times of Ninian Edwards*. Springfield: Illinois State Journal Company, 1870.

Edwardsville Spectator. Edwardsville, Ill.: Hooper Warren. Newspaper.

Egerton, Douglas R. *Gabriel's Rebellion: The Virginia Slave Conspiracies of 1800 and 1802*. Chapel Hill: The University of North Carolina Press, 1993.

Encyclopædia Britannica. Chicago: Encyclopædia Britannica, Inc., 2020. https://www.britannica.com/.

Ernst, Robert. *Rufus King: American Federalist*. Chapel Hill: The University of North Carolina Press, 1968.

Esarey, Logan, ed. *Messages and Letters of William Henry Harrison*. Indiana Historical Collections. 2 vols. New York: Arno Press, 1975.

"Families of Gillespie Bankston & Cook in Dubuque County 1835 to 1878?" Vertical file, Carnegie-Stout Public Library, Dubuque, Iowa.

Faris, John T. *The Romance of Forgotten Towns*. New York: Harper & Brothers, 1924.

Fearon, Henry Bradshaw. *Sketches of America: A Narrative of a Journey of Five Thousand Miles through the Eastern and Western States of America*. London: Printed for Longman, Hurst, Rees, Orme, and Brown, 1818.

Ferguson, Gillum. "'He Acted Well His Part': Hamlet Ferguson and Southern Illinois." *Journal of Illinois History* 6 (Winter 2003): 271–96.

Finkelman, Paul. "Slavery and the Northwest Ordinance: A Study in Ambiguity." *Journal of the Early Republic* 6, no. 4 (Winter 1986): 343–70.

Flower, George. *History of the English Settlement in Edwards County Illinois, Founded in 1817 and 1818, by Morris Birkbeck and George Flower*. Chicago Historical Society's collections, vol. 1. Chicago: Fergus Printing Company, 1882.

Ford, Thomas. *A History of Illinois from Its Commencement as a State in 1818 to 1847*. Urbana: University of Illinois Press, 1995.

Friends of the Benjamin Stephenson House. "*Life in Kentucky and Association with Ninian Edwards.*" *The 1820 Colonel Benjamin Stephenson House. Edwardsville, Ill.* Friends of the Benjamin Stephenson House, 2007. Accessed 6 January 2012, https://web.archive.org/web/20180912083306/http://www.stephensonhouse.org/BenInKy.asp.

"Garrison Hill Cemetery, Ft. Kaskaskia, IL." Randolph County Illinois ". . . Where Illinois Began. . . ." Randolph County, Ill.: n.p., 2000. Accessed 13 January 2005, https://web.archive.org/web/20120222194253/http://www.randolphcountyillinois.net/sub43.htm.

Genius of Liberty. Lowell, Ill.: H. Warren & Z. Eastman. Newspaper.

Gibson, Meredith Dale (Compton). "Seth Gard: Delegate to the Kaskaskia Convention and Signer of the 1818 Illinois State Constitution." *Illinois Trails History and Genealogy*. 11 September 2001. Accessed 5 April 2016, https://web.archive.org/web/20071011170747/http://www.iltrails.org/levi_compton_bio.htm#SETH.

Gillespie, Joseph. *Recollections of Early Illinois and Her Noted Men, Read before the Chicago Historical Society, March 16th, 1880*. Chicago: Fergus Printing Company, 1880.

Golombek, Harry. *Chess: A History*. New York: G. P. Putnam's Sons, 1976.

Goldman, Perry M., and James S. Young, eds. *The United States Congressional Directories 1789–1840*. New York: Columbia University Press, 1973.

Gorsuch, Allison Mileo. "To Indent Oneself: Ownership, Contracts, and Consent in Antebellum Illinois." In *The Legal Understanding of Slavery: From the Historical to the Contemporary*, edited by Jean Allain, 135–51. Oxford: Oxford University Press, 2012.

Grau, Nancy Lee. "The Other Famous 19th Century Man from Illinois: Daniel Pope Cook; New Data on Old Information—and Misinformation." Paper read at Illinois History Symposium, Decatur, Illinois, 2008.

———. *William McHenry: Soldier, Statesman, Frontiersman*. Huntley, Ill.: Nancy Lee Grau, 1987.

Greene, Evarts Boutell, and Clarence Walworth Alvord. *The Governors' Letter-Books 1818–1834*. Collections of the Illinois State Historical Library, vol. 4. Springfield: Trustees of the Illinois State Historical Library, 1909.

Gwathmey, John H. *Historical Register of Virginians in the Revolution*. Richmond, Va.: The Dietz Press, 1938.

Hall, Matthew W. *Dividing the Union: Jesse Burgess Thomas and the Making of the Missouri Compromise*. Carbondale: Southern Illinois University Press, 2015.

Hamilton, Stanislaus Murray, ed. *The Writings of James Monroe*. 7 vols. New York: G. P. Putnam's Sons, 1898–1903.

Hammond, John Craig. "'Uncontrollable Necessity': The Local Politics, Geopolitics, and Sectional Politics of Slavery Expansion." In *Contesting Slavery: The Politics of Bondage and Freedom in the New American Nation*, edited by John Craig Hammond and Matthew Mason, 138–60. Charlottesville: University of Virginia Press, 2011.

Harrington, Estelle Messenger. *A History of the Messenger Family: Genealogy of the Ancestry and Descendants of John Messenger and His Wife Anne Lyon Messenger and Allied Families of Col. Matthew Lyon and Capt. James Piggott*. 2 vols. St. Louis, Mo.: Mound City Press, 1934–1948.

Harris, Norman Dwight. *The History of Negro Servitude in Illinois, and of the Slavery Agitation in That State 1719–1864*. Chicago: A. C. McClurg & Co., 1904.

"Harvard Presidents throughout History." *Harvard University Gazette News*. Cambridge, Mass.: President and Fellows of Harvard College, 2002. 15 March 2001. Accessed 5 April 2013, https://news.harvard.edu/gazette/story/2001/03/harvard-gazette-harvard-presidents-throughout-history/.

Heerman, M. Scott. *The Alchemy of Slavery: Human Bondage and Emancipation in the Illinois Country, 1730–1865*. Philadelphia: University of Pennsylvania Press, 2018.

History and Families of Gallatin County Illinois. Vol. 1: *1988*. Paducah, Ky.: Turner Pub. Co., 1988.

The History of Jo Daviess County Illinois Containing a History of the County—Its Cities, Towns, Etc. Chicago: H. F. Kett & Co., 1878.

History of Madison County, Illinois. Edwardsville, Ill.: W.R. Brink & Co., 1882.

History of Marion and Clinton Counties, Illinois. Philadelphia: Brink, McDonough & Co., 1881.

History of St. Clair County, Illinois. Philadelphia: Brink, McDonough & Co., 1881.

Holcomb, Brent H., comp. *South Carolina Naturalizations, 1783–1850*. Baltimore: Reprinted for Clearfield Company, Inc. by Genealogical Publishing Co., 1997.

Hopkins, James F., ed. *The Papers of Henry Clay*. Ashland ed. 8 vols. Lexington: University of Kentucky Press, 1959.

Houck, Louis. *A History of Missouri from the Earliest Explorations and Settlements until the Admission of the State into the Union*. 3 vols. Chicago: R. R. Donnelley & Sons Company, 1908.

House Journal. 8th Cong., 1st sess., 17 October 1803–27 March 1804.

———. 10th Cong., 2nd sess., 7 November 1808–3 March 1809.

———. 14th Cong., 1st sess., 4 December 1815–30 April 1816.

———. 14th Cong., 2nd sess., 2 December 1816–3 March 1817.

———. 15th Cong., 1st sess., 1 December 1817–20 April 1818.

———. 15th Cong., 2nd sess., 16 November 1818–3 March 1819.

Howard, Robert P. *Illinois: A History of the Prairie State*. Grand Rapids, Mich.: William B. Eerdmans Publishing Company, 1972.

———. *The Illinois Governors: Mostly Good and Competent*. Revised and updated by Taylor Pensoneau and Peggy Boyer Long. Springfield, Ill.: Center Publications/Illinois Issues, 1999.

Hunt, Gaillard, ed. *The First Forty Years of Washington Society, Portrayed by the Family Letters of Mrs. Samuel Harrison Smith* (Margaret Bayard) from the Collection of Her Grandson J. Henley Smith. New York: Charles Scribner's Sons, 1906.

———. *The Writings of James Madison*. New York: G. P. Putnam's Sons, 1908.

"The Illinois Constitutional Convention of 1818: Journal of the Convention." *Journal of the Illinois State Historical Society* 6, no. 3 (October 1913): 355–424.

Illinois Emigrant. Shawneetown, Ill.: Eddy & Kimmel. Newspaper.

The Illinois Intelligencer. Kaskaskia, Ill. Territory: Blackwell & Berry. Newspaper.

"Illinois Scrapbook: The Legend of the Kaskaskia Curse." *Journal of the Illinois State Historical Society* 59, no. 3 (Autumn 1966): 289–90.

Illinois. Secretary of State. Illinois State Archives. *Database of Servitude and Emancipation Records* (1722–1863). Accessed 22 March 2016, http://cyberdriveillinois.com/departments/archives/databases/servant.html.

———. *Illinois Public Domain Land Tract Sales Database*. Accessed 22 April 2016, http://www.ilsos.gov/isa/landsrch.jsp.

———. *Illinois Statewide Marriage Index, 1763–1900*. Accessed 2 July 2016, http://cyberdriveillinois.com/departments/archives/databases/marriage.html.

———. Record Series 100.002. Illinois Territory. Executive Records, 17 May 1809–3 December 1818. Springfield, Illinois.

———. Record Series 100.012. Illinois Territory. Territorial General Assembly: Legislative Records, 14 November 1813–14 January 1817. Springfield, Illinois.

———. Record Series 105.004. Auditor of Public Accounts. Daybooks, 2 January 1813–30 September 1841. Springfield, Illinois.

Index to Compiled Service Records of Volunteer Soldiers Who Served during the War of 1812. Washington, D.C.: National Archives, National Archives and Records Service, 1965.

Jackson County, Illinois Formation and Settlement. Murphysboro, Ill.: Jackson County Historical Society, 1983.

Jakle, John A. "Salt on the Ohio Valley Frontier, 1770–1820." *Annals of the Association of American Geographers* 59, no. 4 (December 1969): 687–709.

Jewett, Clayton E., and John O. Allen. *Slavery in the South: A State-by-State History*. Westport, Conn.: Greenwood Press, 2004.

Jillson, Willard Rouse. "Early Mineral Explorations in the Mississippi Valley (1540–1840)." *Transactions of the Illinois State Historical Society* 31 (1924): 41–57.

Johnson County Historical and Genealogical Society. *Johnson County, Illinois History & Families*. Paducah, Ky.: Turner Pub. Co., 1990.

Johnson, T. Walter. *Charles Reynolds Matheny 1786–1839: An Illinois Pioneer*. N.p.: Privately printed, 1941.

Kane, Elias Kent. Papers. Chicago History Museum, Chicago, Illinois.

Kane, Elizabeth Dennistoun. *Story of John Kane of Dutchess County, New York*. N.p.: Printed by the J. B. Lippincott Company for private distribution, 1921.

Kappler, Charles Joseph, ed. *Indian Affairs: Laws and Treaties*. 2 vols. Washington, D.C.: Government Printing Office, 1904.

Kaskaskia Republican. Kaskaskia, Ill.: William Orr. Newspaper.

Kentucky Reporter. Lexington, Ky.: Thomas Smith. Newspaper.

Kestenbaum, Lawrence. "Cemeteries and Memorial Sites of Politicians in Wabash County." *The Political Graveyard*. Ann Arbor, Mich.: The Political Graveyard, 1996–2019. Accessed 5 April 2016, http://politicalgraveyard.com/geo/IL/WB-buried.html.

King Family. Papers, 1754–1908. MS 350. New-York Historical Society, New York, N.Y.

King, Rufus. Papers, 1766–1899. MS 1660. New-York Historical Society, New York, N.Y.

Kirkpatrick, Melvin E., ed. *A Kirkpatrick Genealogy: Being an Account of the Descendants of the Family of James Kirkpatrick of South Carolina ca. 1715–1786*. Bloomington, Minn.: Melvin E. Kirkpatrick, 1985.

Kirwan, Albert D. *John J. Crittenden: The Struggle for the Union*. N.p.: University of Kentucky Press, 1962.

Lansden, John McMurry. *A History of the City of Cairo*. Chicago: R. R. Donnelly & Sons, 1910.

Larson, John Lauritz. *Internal Improvement: National Public Works and the Promise of Popular Government in the Early United States*. Chapel Hill: University of North Carolina Press, 2001.

The Laws of Yale-College in New-Haven, in Connecticut: Enacted by the President and Fellows. New Haven, CT: Printed by Walter and Steele, 1811.

Laws Passed by the General Assembly of the Illinois Territory, at Their Sixth Session, Held at Kaskaskia 1817–18. Kaskaskia, Ill. Terr.: Berry & Blackwell, 1818; rpt. n.p.: Phillips Bros., State Printers, 1898.

Lee, Jacob F. *Masters of the Middle Waters: Indian Nations and Colonial Ambitions along the Mississippi.* Cambridge, Mass.: The Belknap Press of Harvard University Press, 2019.

Lemen, Frank B. *History of the Lemen Family of Illinois, Virginia, and Elsewhere.* Collinsville, Ill.: n.p., 1898.

"Letter of George Churchill of Madison County, Ill., to Mr. Swift Eldred, Warren, Connecticut." *Journal of the Illinois State Historical Society* 11, no. 1 (April 1918): 64–67.

Lewis, David L. *District of Columbia: A Bicentennial History.* New York: W. W. Norton & Company, Inc., 1976.

Malone, Daisy Roberts. *A Group of Family Trees of the Early Settlers of Corinth Township, Williamson County, Illinois and Allied Families.* N.p.: n.p., 1939.

Martineau, Harriet. *Retrospect of Western Travel.* 2 vols. London: Saunders and Otley, 1838.

Masters, Edgar Lee. *Spoon River Anthology: An Annotated Edition.* Urbana: University of Illinois Press, 1992.

McAdams, Pope, ed. *Some Ancestors of Eugene Perrot McAdams and Mary Elizabeth Pope McAdams of Hawesville, Kentucky.* Shively, Ky.: Mimeographed by Lockard Letter Shop, 1936.

McGhee, Mrs. Carl W. *Pension Abstracts of Maryland Soldiers of the Revolution, War of 1812 & Indian Wars Who Settled in Kentucky.* Washington, D.C.: Mrs. Carl W. McGhee, n.d.

McGoorty, John P. "The Early Irish of Illinois." *Transactions of the Illinois State Historical Society* 34 (1927): 54–64.

Meese, William A. "Nathaniel Pope." *Journal of the Illinois State Historical Society* 3, no. 4 (January 1911): 7–21.

Messinger, John. Papers, 1797–1878. Manuscripts Division, Abraham Lincoln Presidential Library, Springfield, Illinois.

"The Metropolitan, Aka Brown's Marble Hotel." *Streets of Washington: A Collection of Stories and Images of Historic Places in Washington, D.C.* N.p.: n.p., 10 December 2009. Accessed 26 April 2013, http://www.streetsofwashington.com/2009/12/metropolitan-aka-browns-marble-hotel.html.

Meyer, Herb. *A Kaskaskia Chronology.* 3rd ed. Carbondale, Ill.: American Kestrel Books, 1996.

Meyer, Leland Winfield. *The Life and Times of Colonel Richard M. Johnson of Kentucky.* New York: Columbia University Press, 1932.

Miller, Carl R. "Journalism in Illinois before the Thirties." *Journal of the Illinois State Historical Society* 11, no. 2 (July 1918): 149–56.

Mills, R.W. "Dr. George Cadwell." *Transactions of the Illinois State Historical Society* 10 (1905): 112–21.

Minnesota Population Center. "D050.V11.0." *National Historical Geographic Information System: Version 11.0* (Minneapolis: University of Minnesota, 2016), accessed 24 April 2017, http://doi.org/10.18128/D050.V11.0.

Missouri Gazette. St. Louis, Louisiana Territory: Joseph Charless. Newspaper.

Montague, E. J. *A Directory, Business Mirror, and Historical Sketches of Randolph County*. Alton, Ill.: Courier Steam Book and Job Printing House, 1859.

Moore, F. Warren. "The Biography of Enoch Moore, 1818 Delegate from Monroe County." *Illinois Trails History and Genealogy*. Accessed 3 January 2005, https://web.archive.org/web/20071011170704/http://www.iltrails.org/enoch_moore_bio.htm.

Moses, John. *Illinois, Historical and Statistical*. 2 vols. Chicago: Fergus Printing Company, 1889.

The Nashville Whig. Nashville, Tenn.: M. & J. Norvell. Newspaper.

The National Cyclopaedia of American Biography. 76 vols. New York: James T. White & Company, 1892–1971.

National Intelligencer. Triweekly ed. Washington, D.C.: Gales & Seaton. Newspaper.

The National Register. Washington City: Joel K. Mead. Newspaper.

Neely, Charles. *Tales and Songs of Southern Illinois*. Carbondale: Southern Illinois University Press, 1998.

New-York Evening Post. New York: Michael Burnham & Co. Newspaper.

New-York Gazette & General Advertiser. New York: Lang, Turner & Co. Newspaper.

Norton, Margaret Cross, ed. *Illinois Census Returns: 1810, 1818*. Collections of the Illinois State Historical Library, vol. 24. Springfield: Illinois State Historical Library, 1935.

———. *Illinois Census Returns 1820*. Collections of the Illinois State Historical Library, vol. 26. Springfield: Illinois State Historical Library, 1934.

Norton, W. T., ed. and comp. *Centennial History of Madison County, Illinois and Its People*. 2 vols. Chicago: The Lewis Publishing Company, 1912.

Owens, Robert M. "Jeffersonian Benevolence on the Ground: The Indian Land Cession Treaties of William Henry Harrison." *Journal of the Early Republic* 22, no. 3 (Autumn 2002): 405–35.

Pawlyn, Tony, Bartlett Library, NMMC Discovery Quay, Falmouth, Cornwall, United Kingdom. "Re: The packet ship Queensbury Res. Enq 23007–248 (e-mail communication). 3 November 2007.

Pease, Theodore Calvin. *The County Archives of the State of Illinois*. Collections of the Illinois State Historical Library, vol. 12. Springfield: Trustees of the Illinois State Historical Library, 1915.

———. *The Frontier State 1818–1848.* Centennial History of Illinois, vol. 2. Chicago: A. C. McClurg & Co., 1919.

———, ed. *Illinois Election Returns.* Collections of the Illinois State Historical Library, vol. 18. Springfield: Illinois State Historical Library, 1923.

———. *The Story of Illinois.* 3rd ed. Chicago: University of Chicago Press, 1965.

Peck, John Mason. *Annals of the West: Embracing a Concise Account of Principal Events, Which Have Occurred in the Western States and Territories, from the Discovery of the Mississippi Valley to the Year Eighteen Hundred and Fifty.* 2nd ed., rev. and enl. St. Louis: James R. Albach, 1851.

———. *A Sermon, Preached at Edwardsville, Illinois, December 25, 1827: In Reference to the Death of Daniel P. Cook.* Edwardsville, Ill.: R. K. Fleming, 1828.

Perrin, William Henry, ed. *History of Bourbon, Scott, Harrison and Nicholas Counties, Kentucky.* Cincinnati: Art Guild Reprints, Inc., 1968.

———. *History of Crawford and Clark Counties, Illinois.* Chicago: O. L. Baskin & Co., 1883.

Peters, Richard, ed. *The Public Statutes at Large of the United States of America . . .* Vol. 3. Boston: Charles C. Little and James Brown, 1846. https://memory.loc.gov/ammem/amlaw/lwsl.htm.

Philbrick, Francis S., ed. *The Laws of Illinois Territory 1809–1818.* Collections of the Illinois State Historical Library, vol. 25. Springfield: Illinois State Historical Library, 1950.

———. *The Laws of Indiana Territory, 1801–1809.* Collections of the Illinois State Historical Library, vol. 21. Springfield: Trustees of the Illinois State Historical Library, 1930.

———. *Pope's Digest 1815, volume I.* Collections of the Illinois State Historical Library, vol. 28. Springfield: Trustees of the Illinois State Historical Library, 1938.

———. *Pope's Digest 1815, volume II.* Collections of the Illinois State Historical Library, vol. 30. Springfield: Trustees of the Illinois State Historical Library, 1940.

Pope, Nathaniel. Nathaniel Pope to Elias Kent Kane, 8 March 1818, Washington, D.C. Chicago History Museum, Chicago, Illinois.

The Portland Gazette and Maine Advertiser. Portland, Mass.: A. & J. Shirley. Newspaper.

Portrait and Biographical Record of Madison County, Illinois. Chicago: Biographical Publishing Company, 1894.

The Poughkeepsie Journal. Poughkeepsie, Dutchess County, N.Y.: Nicholas Power. Newspaper.

Prescott, Arthur Taylor. *Drafting the Federal Constitution: A Rearrangement of Madison's Notes. . . .* N.p.: Louisiana State University Press, 1941.

Putnam, Elizabeth Duncan. "The Life and Services of Joseph Duncan, Governor of Illinois, 1834 1838." *Transactions of the Illinois State Historical Society* 26 (1919): 107–87.

Putnam, James William. *The Illinois and Michigan Canal: A Study in Economic History*. Chicago Historical Society's Collection, vol. 10. Chicago: University of Chicago Press, 1918.

Rees, James D. "The Bond-Jones Duel and the Shooting of Rice Jones by Dr. James Dunlap: What Really Happened in Kaskaskia, Indiana Territory on 8 August and 7 December 1808?" *Journal of the Illinois State Historical Society* 97, no. 4 (Winter 2004): 272–85.

Relf, Frances H. "The Two Michael Joneses." *Journal of the Illinois State Historical Society* 9, no. 2 (1916): 146–51.

Republican Banner. Nashville, Tenn.: W. F. Bang & Co. Newspaper.

Return of the Whole Number of Persons within the Several Districts of the United States, According to "An Act Providing for the Enumeration of the Inhabitants of the United States"; Passed March the First, One Thousand Seven Hundred and Ninety-One. Philadelphia: n.p., 1793.

Return of the Whole Number of Persons within the Several Districts of the United States, According to "An Act Providing for the Second Census or Enumeration of the Inhabitants of the United States"; Passed February the Twenty Eighth, One Thousand Eight Hundred. N.p.: Printed by Order of the House of Representatives, 1801.

Reynolds, John. *My Own Times: Embracing Also the History of My Life*. Chicago: Chicago Historical Society, 1879.

———. *Pioneer History of Illinois, Containing the Discovery, in 1673, and the History of the Country to the Year Eighteen Hundred and Eighteen, When the State Government Was Organized*. 2nd ed. Chicago: Fergus Printing Company, 1887.

Rice, Howard C., Jr. "News from the Ohio Valley as Reported by Barthélemi Tardiveau in 1783." *Bulletin of the Historical and Philosophical Society of Ohio* 16, no. 4 (October 1958): 266–92.

Royal Cornwall Gazette, Falmouth Packet & Plymouth Journal. Truro, Cornwall: P. Nettleton Jr. Newspaper.

"Rufus King to Elbridge Gerry, New York, June 4, 1786." *Proceedings of the Massachusetts Historical Society* (1866–1867): 9–12.

Sangamo Journal. Springfield, Ill.: S. & J. Francis. Newspaper.

Schultz, Christian, Jr. *Travels on an Inland Voyage through the States of New-York, Pennsylvania, Virginia, Ohio, Kentucky and Tennessee, and through the Territories of Indiana, Louisiana, Mississippi and New-Orleans performed in the Years 1807 and 1808*. 2 vols. New York: Isaac Riley, 1810.

Scott, Franklin William. *Newspapers and Periodicals of Illinois 1814–1879*. Springfield: Trustees of the Illinois State Historical Library, 1910.

Senate Journal. 10th Cong., 2nd sess., 7 November 1808–3 March 1809.

———. 14th Cong., 2nd sess., 2 December 1816–3 March 1817.

———. 15th Cong., 1st sess., 1 December 1817–20 April 1818.

———. 15th Cong., 2nd sess., 16 November 1818–3 March 1819.

Simeone, James. *Democracy and Slavery in Frontier Illinois: The Bottomland Republic*. DeKalb: Northern Illinois University Press, 2000.

Singer, J. W. *A History of the Baptist Church at the Stamping Ground, Ky., 1795–: Revised and Enlarged from the Edition of 1952 in honor of the 175th Anniversary of the Founding of the Church*. N.p.: n.p., 1970.

Smith, George W. "Life and Public Services of Elias Kent Kane." In *Proceedings of the Illinois State Bar Association at Its Eighteenth Annual Meeting*, 189–203. Springfield: Illinois State Register Book Publishing House, 1895.

———. "The Salines of Southern Illinois." *Transactions of the Illinois State Historical Society* 9 (1904): 245–58.

Snyder, John F. *Adam W. Snyder and His Period in Illinois History 1817–1842*. Springfield, Ill.: H. W. Rokker Co., 1903.

———. "Forgotten Statesmen of Illinois: Hon. Conrad Will." *Transactions of the Illinois State Historical Society* 10 (1905): 351–77.

———. "Forgotten Statesmen of Illinois: Hon. Jesse Burgess Thomas." *Transactions of the Illinois State Historical Society* 9 (1904): 514–23.

Speech of the Honorable James Tallmadge, Jr. of Duchess County, New-York, in the House of Representatives of the United States, on Slavery. New York: Printed by E. Conrad, 1819.

Stevens, Frank E. "Illinois in the War of 1812–1814." *Transactions of the Illinois State Historical Society* 9 (1904): 62–197.

Suppiger, Joseph E. "Amity to Enmity: Ninian Edwards and Jesse B. Thomas." *Journal of the Illinois State Historical Society* 67, no. 2 (April 1974): 200–11.

———. "Jesse Burgess Thomas: Illinois' Pro-Slavery Advocate." PhD diss., University of Tennessee, 1970.

Sutton, Robert M. "Edward Coles and the Constitutional Crisis in Illinois, 1822–1824." *Illinois Historical Journal* 82, no. 1 (Spring 1989): 33–46.

Thomas, Jesse B. Letters and Papers of Jesse B. Thomas. SC1531. Manuscripts Division, Abraham Lincoln Presidential Library, Springfield, Illinois.

Thompson, Charles Manfred. "The Illinois Whigs before 1846." *University of Illinois Studies in the Social Sciences* 4, no. 1 (March 1915): 1–165.

Thwaites, Reuben Gold. "Notes on Early Lead Mining in the Fever (or Galena) River Region." *Collections of the State Historical Society of Wisconsin* 13 (1895): 271–92.

The Times. London, England: R. Nutkins. Newspaper.

Tufts University. Library. *A New Nation Votes: American Election Returns 1787–1825*. Lampi Collection of American Electoral Returns, 1787–1825. Worcester, Mass.:

American Antiquarian Society, 2007. Accessed 7 July 2014, http://elections.lib.tufts.edu/.

Turner, Frederick Jackson. "The Significance of the Frontier in American History." *Proceedings of the State Historical Society of Wisconsin* 41 (1893): 79–112.

Tyler, Moses Coit. "One of Mr. Lincoln's Old Friends." *Journal of the Illinois State Historical Society* 28, no. 4 (January 1936): 247–57.

U.S. Federal Census, 1790.

———. 1800.

———. 1810.

———. 1820.

———. 1830.

———. 1840.

———. 1850.

U.S. Census Bureau. *data.census.gov*. Washington, D.C.: Bureau of the Census, 2020. Accessed 5 November 2020, https://data.census.gov.

U.S. National Archives. *Miscellaneous Letters of the Department of State: Roll 1, Calendars to Miscellaneous Letters, 1789–1825*. National Archives microfilm publications; microcopy no. 179, reel 1. Washington, D.C.: National Archives, 1964.

U.S. National Archives and Records Administration. Record Group 46. U.S. Senate. Territorial Papers. Illinois Territory, 11th–23rd Congress. Center for Legislative Research, National Archives, Washington, D.C.

———. Record Group 46. U.S. Senate Territorial Papers. Indiana Territory, 10th–21st Congress. Center for Legislative Research, National Archives, Washington, D.C.

———. Record Group 46. U.S. Senate Territorial Papers. Mississippi Territory, 13th–15th Congress. Center for Legislative Research, National Archives, Washington, D.C.

———. Record Group 233. U.S. House of Representatives. Territorial Papers, 12th–15th Congress. Illinois Territory, 1811–1818. Center for Legislative Research, National Archives, Washington, D.C.

———. *Registers and Indexes for Passport Applications*. Washington, D.C.: National Archives, 1984.

U.S. National Archives and Records Service. *Revolutionary War Pension and Bounty-Land-Warrant Application Files*. Washington, D.C.: NARS, 1969.

Usher, Alexandra. "Public Schools and the Original Federal Land Grant Program." Washington, D.C: Center on Education Policy, 2011. Accessed 24 June 2015, https://web.archive.org/web/20170508200652/https://www.cep-dc.org/cfcontent_file.cfm?Attachment=Usher%5FPaper%5FFederalLandGrants%5F041311%2Epdf.

Verlie, Emil Joseph, ed. *Illinois Constitutions*. Collections of the Illinois State Historical Library, vol. 13. Springfield: Illinois State Historical Library, 1919.

Wager, D. E. "Whitesboro's Golden Age." In *Transactions of the Oneida Historical Society, at Utica, 1881–1884*, 65–144. Utica, N.Y.: Printed for the Society, Ellis H. Roberts & Co., Publishers, 1885.

Wallis, John Joseph. *The NBER/Maryland State Constitutions Project.* College Park: Economics Department, University of Maryland, 2006. Accessed 22 October 2013, http://www.stateconstitutions.umd.edu/.

Washburne, E. B., ed. *The Edwards Papers.* Chicago Historical Society's collection, vol. 3. Chicago: Fergus Printing Company, 1884.

The Western Intelligencer. Kaskaskia, Illinois Territory: Dan'l P. Cook & Co.; Blackwell & Berry. Newspaper.

The Western Sun. Vincennes, [Indiana Territory]: Elihu Stout. Newspaper.

White, Frank F., Jr., ed. "Advice to a Young Traveler Touring the British Isles, 1817." *Historian* 23, no. 1 (November 1960): 79–97.

White, Shane. "Slavery in New York State in the Early Republic." *Australasian Journal of American Studies* 14, no. 2 (December 1995): 1–29.

Whiteaker Family Bible Records (photocopy). Vertical file, Abraham Lincoln Presidential Library, Springfield, Illinois.

Who Was Who in America: Historical Volume, 1607–1896. Rev. ed. Chicago: Marquis Who's Who, 1967.

Wright, Conrad Edick, and Edward W. Hanson. *Biographical Sketches of Those Who Attended Harvard College in the Classes of 1772–1774.* Sibley's Harvard Graduates, vol. 18. Boston: Massachusetts Historical Society; distributed by Northeastern University Press, 1999.

Young, Bennett H. *A History of Jessamine County, Kentucky from Its Earliest Settlement to 1898.* Louisville, Ky.: Courier-Journal Job Printing Company, 1898.

INDEX

Italicized numbers indicate figures

JAMES A. EDSTROM has worked in libraries and archives around the state of Illinois since 1984 and is currently a professor of library services and history at William Rainey Harper College in Palatine, Illinois, where he teaches courses in state and American history. Edstrom has written for publications such as *Illinois Heritage*, *Illinois History*, *Illinois Historical Journal*, *Journal of the Illinois State Historical Society*, and *Illinois History Teacher* on the early statehood period and on Illinois newspaper history. He produced the online video series *Illinois History: An Overview* for use in secondary and college classrooms. A native of Hoffman Estates, Illinois, he currently makes his home with his four teenagers in Wheeling, Illinois, which means that if Nathaniel Pope had been unable to relocate the state's northern boundary, he would have spent most of his life in Wisconsin. This is his first book.